Introducing Latinx Theologies

INTRODUCING LATINX THEOLOGIES

Revised Edition

EDWIN DAVID APONTE

MIGUEL A. DE LA TORRE

ORBIS BOOKS

Maryknoll, New York 10545

ORBIS BOOKS
Maryknoll, New York 10545

Founded in 1970, Orbis Books endeavors to publish works that enlighten the mind, nourish the spirit, and challenge the conscience. The publishing arm of the Maryknoll Fathers and Brothers, Orbis seeks to explore the global dimensions of the Christian faith and mission, to invite dialogue with diverse cultures and religious traditions, and to serve the cause of reconciliation and peace. The books published reflect the views of their authors and do not represent the official position of the Maryknoll Society. To learn more about Orbis Books, please visit our website at www.orbisbooks.com.

Manufactured in the United States of America

Library of Congress Cataloging-in-Publication Data

Names: Aponte, Edwin David, author. | De La Torre, Miguel A., author.
Title: Introducing Latinx theologies / Edwin David Aponte, Miguel A. De La Torre.
Other titles: Introducing Latino/a theologies.
Description: Revised edition. | Maryknoll, NY : Orbis Books, 2020. | Originally published: Introducing Latino/a theologies. Maryknoll, N.Y. : Orbis Books, c2001. | Includes bibliographical references and index. |
Summary: "The fundamental principles and perspectives with which Latinx communities from different faith traditions do theology are articulated" — Provided by publisher.
Identifiers: LCCN 2019048209 (print) | LCCN 2019048210 (ebook) | ISBN 9781626983724 (paperback) | ISBN 9781608338368 (ebook)
Subjects: LCSH: Hispanic American theology.
Classification: LCC BT83.575 .D4 2020 (print) | LCC BT83.575 (ebook) | DDC 230.089/68073—dc23
LC record available at https://lccn.loc.gov/2019048209
LC ebook record available at https://lccn.loc.gov/2019048210

To our children

David, Victoria, and Vincent

May they always remember their roots

Contents

Preface to the 2020 Edition

As authors who also are teachers, scholars, administrators, and activists we are profoundly grateful for the reception of the first edition of our small book and that so many people in multiple contexts not only engaged but also found it useful in many ways. Moreover, we deeply appreciate the many kind suggestions, helpful critiques (friendly and otherwise), and challenges to stretch our thinking in response to that first attempt of those younger scholars whom we were in 2001. This revised edition provides the opportunity for us to respond to many of those reactions, questions, suggestions, and criticisms, as well as engage with the enlarged discourse on Latinx theologies and religious studies. Moreover, we hope to incorporate our developed thinking now seasoned by the years in between, by new insights obtained through teaching, research, struggles, occasional opposition, celebrations, disappointments, deceits, and experiences of grace, hope, and hopelessness. And so we want to thank our editor Jill Brennan O'Brien, production coordinator Maria Angelini, and the entire team at Orbis Books for the great gift to produce this enhanced edition.

From the very start of the project when we were both still doctoral students at Temple University, we wanted this introduction to Latinx-Hispanic/Latino-Latina/o-Latin@-Latinoa theologies to be not only a description but also a living example of *teología en/de conjunto*, that is, a living and practical illustration of theology done through the joys and struggles of genuine encounter, collaboration, partnership, and community.[1] As we wrote then,

---

[1] A discussion on the positive and negative issues related to the ever-evolving pan-ethnic umbrella labels of Latinx, Hispanic, Latina/o, Hispanic/Latino, Latin@, and related terms appears in chapter 1.

This book is a collaborative product. It is about collaborative theology that emerges from communities of Latinas/os. In a true sense it was written together by two persons of different backgrounds, learning to work together, and growing in their relationship with one another as scholars and *hermanos* (brothers), that is, growing in community together. Likewise, Hispanic theology is at its heart a communal endeavor.[2]

Despite all the things that have happened in society, culture, and in our own lives during the in-between times, and the different ways we have changed our minds individually and jointly and hopefully have grown, one of the things that has remained constant over the years is our shared commitment to that goal of a joint endeavor, which is our desire and hope for this revised edition.

Community/*comunidad* was and still is very important to us, and all the more so because of the intervening life experiences that have taught us much over the years that affects our still-developing sense of *comunidad*. And part of that development is the need for us to share some thoughts, perhaps too ambitious or perhaps misplaced hopes, the reality of disappointments, and the power of the mythology of community/*comunidad* among scholars of religion and theology.

In one of the poems in the 1891 collection *Versos sencillos* (*Simple Verses*), the great Cuban philosopher, political activist, and poet José Martí gave an astute observation on life that is still relevant today as it speaks to the challenges for anyone who seeks to remain committed to community and integrity within the many spheres of daily living, *lo cotidiano*:

Cultivo una rosa blanca,
En Julio como en Enero,
Para el amigo sincero
Que me da su mano franca.
Y para el cruel que me arranca
El corazón con que vivo,
Cardo ni oruga cultivo:
Cultivo la rosa blanca.

I cultivate a white rose,
In July as in January,

---

[2] Miguel A. De La Torre and Edwin David Aponte, *Introducing Latino/a Theologies* (Maryknoll, NY: Orbis Books, 2001), xi.

For the sincere friend
Who gives me his hand frankly.
And for the cruel person who wrenches from me
The heart I need to live
Neither thistle nor nettle do I grow:
I cultivate a white rose.[3]

Comunidad, which of course is the Spanish word for "community," is the great motto and stated goal of many in Latinx contexts, whether we are engaged in theological studies, religious studies, or some other undertaking in life. *Comunidad* is employed in a particular way that strongly asserts that while dominant Eurocentric models of academic and scholarly participation most often are based on individualism, many Latinx scholars of religious and theological studies seek to be more mutual and supportive in common cause, working with each other in selfless acts of promoting and helping others in the community for the betterment of the entire community. And the perceived community is not solely a comparatively small community of scholars, but it is asserted that our work as scholars of theology and religion is connected organically to the vast and growing grassroots communities of Latinx peoples across the country. However, upon deeper reflection it must be stated that those of us who are Latinx who engage in the academic study of religion and theology far too often make the error of unquestionably accepting the tenet of *comunidad* and thereby essentializing what it means to be a Latinx. Sadly, despite recurring claims to collaborative work and community, at times we have been guilty of uncritically appropriating the reality of *comunidad* existing among the people in all their diversity—the poor and disenfranchised of the barrios, small towns, cities, and suburbs—upon the relational interplay of comparatively privileged Latinx intellectuals. To be sure, because of the intersectional realities of our multifaceted identities, there are limits to the privilege of any Latinx experience since our class identities and professional roles as intellectuals do not prevent us from being marginalized in other ways, whether by race, ethnicity, gender, or sexual orientation. Nevertheless, after years of writing and singing the praises of *comunidad* as a reality among Latinx academics, we need to acknowledge that sometimes our talk about *comunidad* is a romanticization and that, more often than we care to admit, the reality can be less-than-communal relationships, sometimes masking gossip, backstabbing, and petty jealousies. Yes—the

---

[3] José Martí, "XXXIX," from *Versos sencillos* (1891) in *Obras Completas de José Martí, 26 Volúmenes* (La Habana: Centro de Estudios Martinanos, 2001), 16:117 (authors' translation).

old adage is just as true among Latinx scholars of religion and theology as the rest of the academy, namely, "The academic battles are so fierce because the stakes are so low."

We both have witnessed heartbreaking outcomes for colleagues who lived under the dark shadows of allegations—sadly to be reported with glee within small circles by those same Latinx academics who with crocodile tears later publicly mourn their demise and disappearance. When that happens, such actions turn *comunidad* into a fairy tale among Latinx scholars of religion and theology. At times when we mention a particular Latinx intellectual whom we respect and admire to fellow members of our so-called *comunidad*—scholars who are well published and have helped younger, nontenured scholars get their first works in print or find employment—we are shocked by all the gossip that we hear in response. We are baffled as to how unfounded accusations are repeated as fact. Moreover, we are confounded by how those of us who are supposed to be research experts would rather revel in titillating chatter instead of methodically seeking out, as we are trained to do, what is most likely a boring truth. Intellectual-political intrigues grow, rivalries emerge, turf battles are fought, and alleged scores are created that take on impulses to be settled. Such machinations are compounded by the sad fact that, over the years, while some European American whites loudly proclaimed their progressive credentials as allies through their supposed commitment to justice and solidarity with communities of color, they nonetheless also were the very ones who placed duplicitous knives in our backs. We discovered unhappily that some of the fingerprints on the protruding handles were from those of our so-called *comunidad*.

And before we think this phenomenon of inconsistency is limited to just Latinx theology and religion scholars, it should be noted that some African Americans, Asian Americans, Native People, feminists, and those of the queer community also talk of the comradeship of their identity community as at times experienced as being a false construction, where disunity and contention are more common. In other articles and books Miguel has written about the image of "crabs in a bucket" pulling each other down instead of helping each other out—but as a colleague reminded him, when crabs are in their natural habitat, among the rocks upon which the waves crash, they pull each other up to safety. Like those proverbial crabs, colonialism and white supremacy may have placed Latinx in the limiting white bucket of academic hyperindividualism that is not our natural habitat, pulling each other down through backstabbing rivalry. How do we return to true collegiality and commit ourselves to the life-giving communal inclinations to fight against being placed in buckets of subjugation, or helping each other out when we are?

Although we can detect the various oppressive structures perpetrated against us, the insidious nature of the power at work is that sometimes we can remain oblivious of our complicity with oppression. Being placed in the white bucket by colonialism, class oppression, marginalization, and resurgent white supremacy risks the danger of our replicating oppressive structures or even creating new ones where the faces or ethnicities of new oppressors are the same as those who remain disenfranchised and persecuted. The temptation is for those so marginalized to shape themselves in the image of the dominant culture of oppression, learning to mimic the attitudes, beliefs, behaviors, and actions. Such colonized minds reinforce the marginalized lack of self-worth, which often leads to self-loathing.

Educator Paulo Freire noted that everyone in some part of their being seeks to be a "subject" who is able to act, know, and transform their environment and be directly involved in re-creating, so that by accruing "knowledge of reality through common reflection and action, they discover themselves as its permanent re-creators."[4] Thus, members of marginalized communities who are objects acted upon, rather than subjects who do the acting, have an escape route but also more new ways of understanding their own realities. While habitually alienated and acted upon, some marginalized communities desire a sort of acceptance or at the very least recognition as well as wanting to become subjects in their own right. The safe route, or at least the way of limited conflict, is to imitate the dominant society whose acceptance they crave. In a very real sense, the consciousness of members of marginalized communities becomes submerged. They become unable, or unwilling, to see how the operating interests and values of the dominant culture are internalized. As long as we refuse to critically analyze how deeply Latinx minds are colonized, and how complicit we are in *el chismeteo*, the gossip, we will never create *comunidad*.

Despite the above assessment and the reality of many disappointments, there still is the possibility of *comunidad* and *teología en/de conjunto*. At the risk of being narcissistic, the reality that Edwin and Miguel are working together after all these years is a testimony of the genuine *comunidad* that exists between the two of us. And despite the pain and disappointments experienced with the passing of time, there is real community beyond the two of us. One of the hard truths learned and relearned is that *comunidad* becomes reality not in the saying but in the doing. The fact is that we still are working together and have

---

[4] Paulo Freire, *Pedagogy of the Oppressed, 50th Anniversary Edition*, trans. Myra Berman Ramos (New York: Bloomsbury Academic, 2018), 69.

produced this re-vision of *teología en conjunto*. This is not just self-absorbed navel-gazing, because there are many examples of *teología en conjunto* beyond the two of us. Despite disappointments there also is collaboration and honest critique between Latinx scholars of religion and theology. We have experienced solidarity with those going through professional difficulties. We have experienced *comunidad* with colleagues beyond the fuzzy boundaries of who is Latinx with African American, white, Native American, and Asian American colleagues. The experiences of the years have reinforced the reality of what we asserted in 2001, which is that *comunidad*/community is relational, with all the messiness of life that interpersonal interaction implies. When *comunidad* is evoked without relational commitments and the associated risks, then it can become highly wrought mythological rhetoric, self-deception, and the basis of the oppression of others. When commitment perseveres through disappointments, misunderstandings, and persecution—and through the bad times as well as good—then the reality of *comunidad* is experienced and the potential for working toward the good and just is unlimited.

We can talk about *comunidad* as if it will occur ex nihilo and never achieve it, or we can labor to make it a reality in daily life. We choose and commit to the latter. *Comunidad* is not some utopian concept; it can be authentic if approached with a good dose of humility and achieved through hard work when accompanied by a willingness to recognize past faults and failings not conducive to creating *comunidad*.

We recognize the many times when we personally have fallen short of true *comunidad* and were complicit with oppressive structures. For those times when we failed, when we refused to critically analyze how deeply our minds were colonized, and when we were complicit in spreading gossipy scandal that tore down *comunidad*, we offer our sincere apologies to whomever we offended and look forward to making amends—with a deep resolve to do better going forward, to cultivate *una rosa blanca*, and to begin reconciliation and perhaps model better what Latinx *comunidad* should look like (Mt 5:23–24). And for those who prefer not to reconcile but who choose to pursue a different path and weave alternative realities, we both say, *cardo ni oruga cultivo, cultivo una rosa blanca*.

So, this multifaceted challenge is true and, like many things in life, not neat—namely, that *comunidad* among Latinx scholars of theology and religion may be experienced as a myth, but also as a reality. Both possibilities are running concurrently within the same communities, and even the same person may experience both simultaneously. Consequently, even this revision—this book—remains a collaborative product, but one in which we try to pass along what we have learned from a broad com-

munity of people with whom we share *comunidad* and accordingly who
have contributed to our ongoing formation, including the never-ending
surprises that community exists with people and in places we did not
anticipate previously. Likewise, this revision also reflects what we have
learned from the absence of *comunidad* or when *comunidad* was evoked
in ways that proved disappointing, unsatisfactory, destructive, and even
mythological.

We are many things, but certainly we are scholars whose interdisciplinary work has taken us in different but occasionally overlapping
directions as we address the intersections of race, ethnicity, gender, class,
privilege and oppression, desperation and hope. And therefore, even in
this revised edition, and despite the joys, disappointments, and—yes—
pain of the years, this book still is both about collaborative Latino/a-
Latinx theologies as well as being one example of it. Again, taking heed
of the insights of the great Paulo Freire we must remember the critical
importance of hoping against hope, even as we engage struggle. Therefore, in the midst of hopelessness, our humble hope is that this book will
help generate many other examples of such mutual theologies, as well
as encourage others within and outside of the Latinx-Hispanic/Latino-
Latino/a-Latin@-Latinoa community to take the risk and commit to
comunidad.

Edwin David Aponte
Louisville, Kentucky

Miguel A. De La Torre
Denver, Colorado

Fiesta de San Miguel, San Gabriel, y San Rafael (Feast of Saint Michael,
Saint Gabriel, and Saint Raphael), 2019

Preface to the 2001 Edition

A well-meaning scholar suggested that it might be in the best interest of our academic careers if we could identify those parts of this book that we each wrote. Such a separation would be desirable so that it could be determined who would get credit for which part. Yet such a suggestion flies right in the face of the nature of this work. This book is a collaborative product. It is about collaborative theology that emerges from communities of Latinas/os. In a very true sense it was written together by two persons of different backgrounds, learning to work together, and growing in their relationship with one another as scholars and *hermanos* (brothers), that is, growing in community together. Likewise, Hispanic theology is at its heart a communal endeavor. Therefore, this book is not just about collaborative Latino/a theology, but hopefully it is also an example of it. This is a book about theological cooperation emerging from, in the words of Dietrich Bonhoeffer, our "life together" as Hispanics in the United States.

Yet this is not solely the product of two people. As we come to the end of this project, we have discovered in a deeper way what we knew before: that we are part of a larger community. We are members of a community of Latina/o scholars of religion, from whom we have learned, who have guided and at times challenged us, sometimes chastised us, but with whom we have always maintained our connection as part of a *comunidad* (community). The influence of others is manifold, as can be seen from the notes and bibliography in the text. Furthermore, the input of these larger communities is present under the text as well. Countless conversations, sermons, lectures, church services, late-night talks, and e-mail correspondence influenced our thinking and writing.

We are aware that our perspectives on Hispanic theology and religious history have many sources that cannot be acknowledged adequately. At the same time there are some who gave particular help for this specific project, often giving invaluable comments even when there was disagreement in our approach. These *colegas* (colleagues) who commented on portions of the manuscript or provided other helpful comments include Efraín Agosto, María Pilar Aquino, Orlando Espín, Gastón Espinosa, Luis León, Luis G. Pedraja, Jeanette Rodríguez, and José David Rodríguez. We appreciated all the wise advice we received, even when we felt compelled to go down a different path. We also offer our thanks to all those who responded to the electronic survey on Latina/o theology. All of this input reminded us that we were not alone in this enterprise, and also that there are larger communities with which we need to keep faith. This book is better for it, and any final shortcomings are our responsibility and not that of our colleagues.

We would also like to express our appreciation to others who provided different types of technical help without which we would have been lost. To our editor at Orbis Books, Susan Perry, we owe a debt of gratitude that cannot be repaid. She saw the need for this project, gave us the opportunity to try our approach to the subject, and shepherded us from start to finish. Susan Perry shared with us her wisdom, editorial astuteness, and helped us to overcome any residual fear of the "red pen." Jonathan Schakel also provided editorial assistance for which we are deeply appreciative.

Librarian Anthony Guardado at Hope College helped us immensely in providing countless hours researching and checking census information. Dan Griswold, instructional technologist at Perkins School of Theology, provided help above and beyond the call of duty in setting up the online survey and providing technical help throughout the course of this project. Jeremy Latchaw, research assistant to Miguel A. De La Torre, performed outstanding work in helping us pull together material for the book. Frank Leib's work in proofreading sections of the text helped make this a better book. Finally, we would be remiss if we did not thank our collective classes of students who were the first exposed to the unpublished manuscript and gracefully provided feedback to improve its overall quality and readability. The contributions of all these people are another way in which this book is a collaborative effort.

The collaborative help we received for this work includes the wise counsel, support, and occasional nudge of our wives, Deborah L. De La Torre and Laura J. Aponte. Through their steadfast love and encouragement they have made this journey along with us and indeed have made its completion possible. It is not an overstatement that we could not have done it without them.

This book does not simply look at the past and present of Hispanic theologies in the United States; it is also deeply concerned with their future. That future will be characterized increasingly by new generations of Latinas/os born and raised in the United States, shaping their own identities in ways different from their parents, grandparents, and great-grandparents. The challenges that younger generations of Hispanics will face cannot be totally foreseen. It is with that future in mind and with the firm hope that it will be better, more peaceful, and filled with greater justice, that we dedicate this book to our children, Vincent and Victoria De La Torre and David S. Aponte.

Miguel A. De La Torre
Holland, Michigan

Edwin David Aponte
Dallas, Texas

Epifanía (Epiphany)
El Día de los Tres Reyes Magos (Day of the Three Magi Kings), *2001*

Introduction

Social and Cultural Contexts for Theology

In March 1981 a major urban ministries conference was held in New York City at the world-famous, interdenominational Riverside Church. Part of what makes Riverside Church so renowned is that it was built in the early twentieth century with the support of the extremely wealthy financier and philanthropist John D. Rockefeller Jr., working in collaboration with celebrated Northern Baptist minister and preacher Harry Emerson Fosdick.[1] Not only because of how it was established, Riverside Church is also famous because it was the pulpit home of several prominent twentieth-century Christian preachers, including of course its first senior minister, the progressive Fosdick, as well as social justice and antiwar activist William Sloane Coffin Jr., who was the senior minister at the time of the 1981 urban ministries conference.[2] It was at Riverside Church when, on April 4, 1967, the Rev. Dr. Martin Luther King Jr.,

---

[1] Harry Emerson Fosdick (1878–1969) is still reviled or revered today, depending where one is located on a theological continuum. Fosdick is usually recognized as one of the most prominent and influential liberal Protestant ministers of the early and mid-twentieth century in the United States. His most famous sermon is "Shall the Fundamentalists Win?" preached on May 21, 1922. Fosdick's ongoing influence is such that even some who revile him unknowingly may use the hymn he authored, "God of Grace and God of Glory."

[2] In 2008 the *New York Times* described Riverside Church as follows: "a stronghold of activism and political debate throughout its 75-year history, [it] has been visited by Nelson Mandela and United States presidents like Bill Clinton. It was an early opponent of the Vietnam War and both wars in Iraq and has long been influential on the nation's religious and political landscapes." Russ Buettner, "Committee Nominates a New Leader for Riverside Church," *New York Times*, August 4, 2008. See also Peter J. Paris, John Wesley Cook, James Hudnut-Beumler, Lawrence H. Mamiya, Leonora Tubbs Tisdale, and Judith Weisenfeld, *The History of the Riverside Church in the City of New York* (New York: New York University Press, 2004).

while expressing his own moral vision and advocacy for the poor, gave his famous and at the time controversial condemnation of the Vietnam War: "Beyond Vietnam: A Time to Break Silence."[3] In addition to well-known preachers, the interdenominational church has equally famous neighbors in Grant's Tomb, Columbia University, Union Theological Seminary, Jewish Theological Seminary, Teachers College, Barnard College, the Cathedral Church of St. John the Divine, and the Interchurch Center at 475 Riverside Drive, informally known as the "God Box" of historic mainline Protestantism.[4]

But given its location in the Morningside Heights neighborhood, Riverside Church has other neighbors also, including Harlem, itself a noteworthy neighborhood that has seen numerous transitions since the seventeenth century, when it was founded as a colonial Dutch village, through the ongoing gentrification of the early twenty-first century. Harlem became home to waves of immigrants as New York City grew, including new Jewish and Italian arrivals, and in the early twentieth century, partly as a result of the Great Migration from the South, the neighborhood became a major African American population hub and the heart of the famed Harlem Renaissance.[5] Not very far from Riverside Church is a part of East Harlem that became known as Spanish Harlem or El Barrio, a major site of the Latino(a) population of New York City.[6]

---

[3] See Clayborn Carson and Kris Sheperd, eds., *A Call to Conscience: The Landmark Speeches of Dr. Martin Luther King Jr.* (New York: IPM/Warner Books, 2001), 139–64. One of King's advisers, the late historian and activist Vincent G. Harding, drafted "Beyond Vietnam"; see Vincent Harding, "Introduction," in Martin Luther King Jr., *Where Do We Go from Here: Chaos or Community?* (Boston: Beacon Press, 2010), xx.

[4] At the height of the ecumenical movement of the 1950s the intent for the building at 475 Riverside Drive was to have a wide variety of Christian denominations house their national offices and agencies in the same facility as well as to house the main offices of the National Council of Churches. Construction on the Interchurch Center, which was started in 1958, was made possible through a number of gifts, including that of major donor John D. Rockefeller Jr. Beyond the religious significance, the wider social and cultural impact of the Interchurch Center at the time is illustrated by the fact that U.S. president Dwight D. Eisenhower laid the building's cornerstone on October 12, 1958.

[5] For a brief summary, see Cheryl A. Wall, *The Harlem Renaissance: A Very Short Introduction* (New York: Oxford University Press, 2016).

[6] In 1981 the majority of the New York Hispanic/Latino population was Puerto Rican, but in the decades since, the Latinx population has diversified as it has grown and spread geographically across the five boroughs. Estimates in 2017 had Latinos/as comprising 29 percent of the entire New York City population, with a breakdown of Puerto Ricans at 31 percent, Dominicans at 25 percent, the rapidly growing Mexican population at 14 percent, as well as peoples

Despite the fact that Spanish Harlem is not far from Riverside Church, the 1981 urban ministry conference did not include any Latinas or Latinos on the program. That deficiency was interpreted as yet another example of Latina/os being ignored by the dominant religious institutions and social organizations of that time. That exasperating oversight prompted a group of Hispanics calling itself the Coalition of Hispanic Christian Leadership to interrupt the conference and protest this astonishing omission. The group of men and women led by the Reverend Benjamin Alicea-Lugo read their statement of protest in what became known as the "Riverside Manifesto," specifically charging that Latino/a social issues were not sincerely considered, and that the contributions of Hispanics to the church in ministry, theology, and liturgy continued to be ignored. Furthermore, the manifesto charged that Latinas/os experienced discrimination in seminaries and schools of theology, and also that the U.S. religious establishment (defined in the document as "Mainline Protestants, Conservative Fundamentalists, and Establishment Evangelicals") shared some of the responsibility for the ongoing exclusion of Hispanics.[7]

In the year 2000, almost twenty years after the Riverside Manifesto, an indication of some social change took place when *Time* magazine published a special edition focused on important trends in the United States for the new millennium. Roman Catholic priest Virgilio Elizondo, a Mexican American from San Antonio, Texas, appeared in the piece as one of the "New Lights of the Spirit." The *Time* article described Elizondo as "a priest-academic [who] has taken the stigma of Hispanic otherness and transformed it into a triumphant Catholic theology of *mestizaje*."[8] By focusing in December 2000 on Elizondo and his work, *Time* highlighted the growing importance of Latinx religion in the United States, especially at that point in history when historical religious establishments concurrently seemed to be losing their social and cultural influence.

---

of Central and South American origin. See Sherrie Baver, Angelo Falcón, and Gabriel Haslip-Viera, ed., *Latinos in New York: Communities in Transition*, 2nd ed. (Notre Dame, IN: University of Notre Dame Press, 2017).

  [7] See Daniel R. Rodriguez-Diaz, "Teología en Conjunto," in *Hispanic American Religious Cultures*, vol. 2, ed. Miguel A. De La Torre (Santa Barbara, CA: ABC-CLIO, 2009), 764; Edwin David Aponte, "Riverside Manifesto," in De La Torre, *Hispanic American Religious Cultures*, 2:661; Eldin Villafañe, *The Liberating Spirit: Towards an Hispanic American Pentecostal Social Ethic* (Grand Rapids: Eerdmans, 1993), 70–71; and Orlando E. Costas, *Christ outside the Gate: Mission beyond Christendom* (Maryknoll, NY: Orbis Books, 1982), 115–16.

  [8] "New Lights of the Spirit," *Time*, December 11, 2000, 84–85.

In the years since 2000, the significance of the growing Latinx population as the nation's largest minority or "minoritized" ethnic group was recognized in other ways, including through the efforts of corporations marketing to them, the growth of Spanish-language media, and the two U.S. major political parties working to court their vote in presidential elections from 2000 through 2016. During the first Democratic debates in 2019 for the 2020 election, several of the candidates felt the need to address the audience in Spanish, not bothering to translate for their predominately English-only audience. But sadly, those election cycles from 2000 onward also saw an increase of discrimination and bigotry toward Latinx peoples, especially in the watershed 2016 presidential election, which had the winning Republican candidate scapegoating immigrants from Latin America, calling Mexican immigrants rapists and criminals, advocating building a wall between the United States and Mexico, and questioning the ability and loyalty of a federal judge who was born a U.S. citizen but of Mexican descent. Discrimination against U.S. Latinos/as and people of Latin American descent has increased further since the 2016 election and under the presidency of Donald Trump, particularly seen in the anemic federal response in Puerto Rico in the aftermath of the double whammy of Hurricanes Irma and Maria, and the growing humanitarian crisis of the Trump administration's zero-tolerance immigration policies and related family separation of Latin Americans seeking asylum in the United States. Such anti-Latinx political rhetoric can prove deadly, as seen in the mass shooting at a Walmart in El Paso on August 3, 2019, by a white supremacist who admitted to targeting Hispanics and echoed the rhetoric of a president who consistently spoke in terms of "an invasion."

But it is not solely in the political and social realms that Latinx people are marginalized and reviled. To be sure, some religious denominations recognize Latino/as as the demographic wave of the future. On this point Allan Figueroa Deck, distinguished scholar of theology and Latino studies at Loyola Marymount University in Los Angeles, stated that "Latinos are the leading indicators of the church's future. So if the bishops or anyone else is interested in the church's future, you have to pay attention to the Latinos. It's not rocket science."[9] Nevertheless, although the racial/ethnic composition of the U.S. population is expected to grow to majority status by 2040, and Latinx remains the largest racial/ethnic group in this country, Latina/os still are underrepresented on seminary

[9] Dan Morris-Young, "Fr. Figueroa Deck Says That the Latino Catholic 'Sleeping Giant' Is Awakening," *National Catholic Reporter*, March 8, 2018.

and religious studies faculties.[10] Latina/os continue to experience bias in schools of theology where Latinx enrollment hovers around 7.1 percent, compared to their comprising at least 18.1 percent of the U.S. population (58.9 million people), estimated to reach 111 million by 2060.[11]

Astoundingly, nearly forty years after the Riverside Manifesto and despite passionate rhetoric that claims the opposite, some theological schools seem to go out of their way to ensure that Latinx student bodies, curriculum, faculty, and staff are not found within their hallowed halls (actually or virtually). In a cultural context where corporations are increasing their diversity in products and marketing (with varying degrees of success—sometimes getting it right, while other times wrong), the diversity and inclusion efforts of many religious institutions are paltry by comparison.[12] Even more remarkable is that some of the same schools, unaware that they are not as progressive and welcoming as they market themselves, ask people of color, including Latinx, how white people are to identify and dismantle white supremacy, and how white people can be more inclusive and racially diverse. Stated another way, the objects and victims of racial injustices are being asked to name

---

[10] Again, *Time* magazine, in its cover article "The Latino Reformation" (April 15, 2013), predicted that Latinos would comprise 29 percent of the U.S. population by the year 2050.

[11] Among the institutions belonging to the Association of Theological Schools in the United States and Canada, the Hispanic student population increased from 3.5 to 7.1 percent over fifteen years, but still runs behind the percentage of the U.S. population that is Latino/a. See Eliza Smith Brown and Chris Meinzer, "New Data Reveal Stable Enrollment but Shifting Trends at ATS Member Schools," *Colloquy Online*, March 2017, Release Number CB18-FF.07, https://www.ats.edu/uploads/resources/publications-presentations/colloquy-online/new-data-reveal-stable-enrollment.pdf. Regarding the estimated Hispanic population in the United States prior to the 2020 Census, see U.S. Census Bureau, "Hispanic Heritage Month 2018," September 13, 2018, https://www.census.gov/newsroom/facts-for-features/2018/hispanic-heritage-month.html.

[12] In 2019 Nike planned to launch a special-edition sneaker called "Air Force 1 'Puerto Rico' 2019" in time for the New York City Puerto Rican Day Parade. As Carmen Nanko-Fernández observes, "The plan backfired when the design came under scrutiny amid charges of cultural appropriation and plagiarism. The pattern used on the shoe was not of Puerto Rican origin, it was a textile print distinctive of the indigenous Guna people of Panama! Called out on social media and chastised by an online petition, Nike was forced to cancel the release of the shoe and 'apologize for the inaccurate representation of the design origin.' With one sneaker, the company had managed to offend Puerto Ricans, Panamanians and violate the intellectual property of indigenous women" (Nanko-Fernández, "Sneakers Are Never Just Sneakers," *National Catholic Reporter*, July 12, 2019).

the solutions for their oppression. This outrage is compounded by the additional, patronizing microaggressions and microinvalidations when some of the same white colleagues discount what Latinas and Latinos testify about as life as a person of color in the United States and instead pontificate about the Latinx experience, as if they know more about Latinx contexts. With ongoing ignorance, discrimination, and exclusion, in many ways the critiques of the 1981 Riverside Manifesto sadly are still valid.

Despite racism both from those who are unaware of their own complicity and the increasingly unfettered open actions of white supremacists, there is no denying the growing social and cultural importance of Latinx peoples in the United States. A key aspect of Latinx American life and culture is religion and spirituality in all its variety of articulations, of which Christianity is a major expression. Expanding on Allan Figueroa Deck's observation, then, Latinx people are key to the future of Christianity in North America.

Therefore, in light of these stubborn facts and with desire for a better and more just shared future, the purpose of this book is to introduce Christian theological concepts and practices from the perspectives of Latinx peoples in the United States and to provide a foundation for more specific and advanced study of Latinx theologies, cultures, religions, and the variety of spiritualities. The intention here is not to unpack fully all the tenets of all Latinx theologies, nor to detail every stream of historical and current Latino/a theological discourse and practice. Rather, we hope to provide a basic orientation and suggest paths for more in-depth research, while simultaneously noting the importance of the organic connections of the personal and the communal contexts of Latinx theologies. Indeed, while there are numerous varieties of Latinx theologies, one thing that is common to many—if not all—is the importance of stories about the multifaceted life journeys of what it means to be Latinx-Hispanic/Latino-Latina/o-Latin@-Latinoa in the United States. Accordingly, it seems completely appropriate at the start of this theological exploration for us to briefly describe aspects of our own personal stories and journeys into Latinx theologies.

A Personal Journey: Edwin David Aponte

When we began working on what became the first edition of this book, I mentioned to faculty colleagues the possibility of my co-writing an introductory textbook to Latino/a theologies. Some of them expressed curiosity and surprise. "You're not a theologian!" one said emphatically and a bit dismissively. And from a certain technical perspective, that critic was absolutely correct in that I am not a trained systematic theologian. Certainly, I studied theology, but systematic theology was and is not my disciplinary focus. For the record, one of my professional identities is that I am a cultural historian educated in interdisciplinary religious studies who explores faith, spirituality, and culture in North America, especially the intersections of race, ethnicity, and religion. In particular, one of the areas of my specialized research and writing is in Latinx religion, spirituality, and culture.[13] As I do this type of interdisciplinary work, I occasionally venture into the specialized academic branch of theology known as historical theology, but not technically as a professional systematic theologian. However, while recognizing the traditional professional disciplinary distinctions in the study of religion and theology, from another perspective the work of theology, and especially Latinx theologies, is not solely the property or territory of the trained theological specialists but of whole communities, particularly as they negotiate their daily lives.[14] So this particular critic was correct in that I may not be a technical professional systematic theologian, but I am regularly engaged in theological interpretations, particularly on the beliefs and practices of various Christian communities in their social and cultural contexts. Increasingly I find that my life and work connect simultaneously with numerous fields of study, including theological interpretations, whether systematic or grassroots. But is that not the nature of life, in which we are all doing and being more than one thing at the same time? Doing theology in the broadest sense of that term is one piece of a multifaceted vocation and living life each day.

Furthermore, in addition to being a cultural historian I approach Latinx theologies from additional social and cultural perspectives, locations, and intersections. As a heterosexual male Latino, specifically a second-generation-diaspora Puerto Rican Protestant Christian and an ordained minister of the Word and Sacrament in the Presbyterian Church (U.S.A.), I do theology on a daily basis—individually, within my family, and as part of multiple larger Christian communities. In my calling as a Latino cultural historian, over the years I have done theology daily as a member of a theological faculty and as an academic dean at a seminary,

---

[13] See Edwin David Aponte, *¡Santo! Varieties of Latino/a Spirituality* (Maryknoll, NY: Orbis Books, 2012).

[14] This concept of "theological specialist" is similar to what Isasi-Díaz and Tarango referred to as the "theological technician," as opposed to the "grassroots theologian." See Ada María Isasi-Díaz and Yolanda Tarango, *Hispanic Women: Prophetic Voice of the Church* (1988; Minneapolis: Fortress Press, 1992), 104–9; Ada María Isasi-Díaz, *En la Lucha / In the Struggle: Elaborating a Mujerista Theology* (Minneapolis: Fortress Press, 2004), 185.

serving those preparing for and some already engaging in various types of ministry. And now in a different social location as a grant agency administrator, my work includes being part of a team helping others explore their own vocations to be theological educators, or awarding research grants and fellowships to scholars and pastors, many of whom do theology in their own social and cultural contexts. In all of that variety of work I bring theological perspectives that have been shaped by the reality, wisdom, and experiences of many Latinx communities over the years, including the enduring influence of those who are deceased. So, what are some of the specific factors that brought me to this project about Latinx theologies and an ongoing collaboration with Miguel A. De La Torre?

The De La Torre–Aponte partnership is influenced directly by my own complex cultural identity. For years now, I have described myself as a Puerto Rican Yankee, fully aware of the pejorative sense the word "Yankee" has for some people in southern sections of the United States as well as the anti-Americanism in Latin America associated with the Spanish version *yanqui*. Nevertheless, by calling myself a Puerto Rican Yankee I seek to describe the multilayered complexity of my being Latino in the United States of America. My being both Puerto Rican and Yankee is the result of decisions my parents made before I was born in response to larger social, geopolitical, and economic forces over which they had no control. After World War II my parents, both U.S. citizens from birth, as are all Puerto Ricans since 1917, migrated from the colonized *isla del encanto* (island of enchantment) to the mainland United States along with tens of thousands of Puerto Ricans, many of them impoverished like my parents, in the hope of a better life for themselves and their families.[15] The government implemented a major trade and industry development program called Operation Bootstrap, designed to transform Puerto Rico's economy from agricultural to industrial in a short period of time. One result of that transformation was that a major wave of the Puerto Rican diaspora took place from 1946 to 1953, encouraged by the Puerto Rican government. Some of this migration was part of formal agreements negotiated by the Puerto Rican Department of Labor for contract labor, including unemployed rural workers, in response to fluctuations in both the Puerto Rican and U.S. economies. Desperate and hopeful enough to leave their home, my parents, Domingo David and

---

[15] Puerto Ricans became U.S. citizens through an act of the U.S. Congress usually referred to as the Jones Act (Jones-Shafroth Act) passed March 2, 1917. Every Puerto Rican born on or after April 25, 1898, was made a U.S. citizen. One result of the Jones Act was that it enabled Puerto Rican males to be drafted into the U.S. Army as the United States entered World War I on April 6, 1917.

Ana Raquel, were part of that vast migration wave.[16] Like so many others from the island my father first worked on the farms of New Jersey, then through an acquaintance he spent time in New York City, and then finally settled in Bridgeport, Connecticut. Later, my mother with my two older Puerto Rican–born siblings joined my father in New England. I was born and raised in Connecticut, along with five of my seven brothers and sisters. I am a Connecticut Yankee by birth.

Although we were all born U.S. citizens, we were also all objects of bigotry and racism seen by some people as undesirable foreign immigrants in a racialized context of a black/white binary paradigm. Because of being the object of the prejudices of others and the accompanying oppression, my parents decided we would be an English-dominant household to enhance their children's chances of success. One unfortunate result of this well-intended decision (which many other Latinx parents also made) has been the continuing rejection by some within the Spanish-speaking Latinx community because we are deemed "not Hispanic enough." To varying degrees my sisters, brothers, and I all experienced some rejection by local Latinx communities through our school years and beyond. After primary and secondary education in Connecticut I went to college and seminary in Massachusetts near Boston. To that point of my life I had been inculcated with New England cultural ethos and values, while within the racialized context of the United States I repeatedly experienced discrimination and rejection by some of the other Yankees around me. This led to a growing awareness that I would never be fully accepted by many of my fellow Yankee New Englanders (curiously, I never felt this rejection from African Americans in New England).

At various points of my life I wanted to say to those who had marginalized me, European Americans and Latino/as, "Fine, I'll do without you!" Yet, despite the agony experienced, I realized I could not sever my roots and survive. Moreover, I recognized that my roots went in several directions, including to New England, the land of my birth, and

---

[16] See César J. Ayala and Rafael Bernabe, *Puerto Rico in the American Century: A History since 1898* (Chapel Hill: University of North Carolina Press, 2007), 196; Lorrin Thomas and Aldo A. Lauria Santiago, *Rethinking the Struggle for Puerto Rican Rights* (New York: Routledge, 2019), 8–9, 19–20. See also Teresa Delgado, *A Puerto Rican Decolonial Theology: Prophesy Freedom* (New York: Palgrave Macmillan, 2017), 36–39; Carmen Teresa Whalen, *From Puerto Rico to Philadelphia: Puerto Rican Workers and Postwar Economies* (Philadelphia: Temple University Press, 2001), 4–5; Virginia E. Sánchez Korrol, *From Colonia to Community: The History of Puerto Ricans in New York City* (Berkeley: University of California Press, 1983), 47–48; and Virginia Sánchez Korrol and Pedro Juan Hernández, *Pioneros II: Puerto Ricans in New York City, 1948–1998* (Charleston, SC: Arcadia Publishing, 2010), 115.

Puerto Rico, where my parents were born. Gradually, I came into a new awareness of who I am as a diaspora Puerto Rican Latino. One avenue for entering into this deeper understanding was connecting with Latinx theologies. Foundational in this awareness is that, although I might not fit any stereotype, indeed, I am still indeed a Puerto Rican, Hispanic, Latino, Latinx, Yankee, and American.

On this journey I also have had to consider my relationship to Latin America. Because my life experience as well as my citizenship is in the United States, I never saw myself as Latin American, although often other people do. I realize from my writing this may pain some of my friends and colleagues from Latin America, but I do not mean this as an insult or rejection; nor does this mean I do not have connections to Latin America, but my reality is much more complex than any one identity. My roots are in Puerto Rico, in New England, and in particular expressions of the Christian church. Accordingly, some people find it difficult to pigeonhole me. I knew that a stereotype was at work when, upon learning I was a Puerto Rican, a well-meaning person would comment (often in an attempt to connect or be helpful) that I was a *Nuyorican*, but, while I appreciate the effort, this is not accurate either. "Nuyorican" is a term that emerged to describe persons in the Puerto Rican diaspora from New York City, usually referring to those born and living in one of the five boroughs. Without a doubt I am a Puerto Rican, but I am neither from the *isla* (island) nor from New York City. A Nuyorican identity did not make space for my New England realities. Then at times another stereotype is at work, when upon learning I am Puerto Rican someone would say a version of, "You don't sound Puerto Rican," or "You don't seem Puerto Rican!" Sadly, for some Puerto Ricans I was not fully Puerto Rican for them. And yet for some non–Puerto Ricans I was too Latino. I was always something different. As a Puerto Rican Yankee, I am a New Englander without a doubt, but not someone who is considered a member of the dominant social networks of New England life and culture and who can trace his ancestry back to the *Mayflower*.

I was confronted with yet another stereotype when a fellow Latino Protestant Christian told me that I looked "too Presbyterian," as if there is only one way to be genuinely Christian and Latinx. That particular stereotype took no account of my own spiritual journey as casual Roman Catholic, fervent charismatic Catholic, naive Protestant fundamentalist, Baptist, disillusioned believer, explorer of the Reformed tradition of Christianity, ecumenist, embracer of the liturgical heritage of Christianity, and a grassroots postdenominational Christian.[17] Furthermore,

---

[17] Often in this book we use the term "Roman Catholic" instead of simply

in our own personal understandings of God, the Divine, religion, and spirituality, my sisters and brothers and I might seem to some people like different kinds of Latinas and Latinos, given the variety of expressions and practices that exist among this one set of siblings. But actually, ours is not a unique story, rather one experienced across the United States and retold by other Latinx persons of second, third, and later generations. Any attempt to talk about Latinx theologies ought to take into account all these generational, linguistic, and contextual multilayered diversities.

My reconnection with Latinx communities began in an odd way. In my first career in higher education, while working as a university financial aid administrator, I attended a conference where a plenary speaker informed us about the growing Latino/a population of the United States, how the corporate and business worlds were taking steps to address this phenomenon, and how colleges and universities should do the same— certainly for reasons of inclusion and equity, but if for no other reason at the very least for their own institutional survival and future. The speaker's comments seemed reasonable to me, and I thought that someone in the church should also focus on the growing Latinx population. Unexpectedly, from that very moment I consciously started down a path that included Latinx theologies, although I began the journey with a great deal of ignorance, anxiety, and fear. I had only the vaguest idea of where to start since I was disconnected from and still feeling the pain of prior rejections from parts of the Latinx community. It was then that I began doctoral studies in religion and culture at a large public university, embarking on a journey that included finding out about Hispanic/Latino theologies.

Thankfully, early in my doctoral studies I was introduced into the vibrant community of Latinx scholars of religion and theology. It was refreshing, overwhelming, frightening, exhilarating, unnerving, and encouraging to discover many others who had blazed the trail with their diverse, wide-ranging, and innovative scholarship: scholars including María Pilar Aquino, Arturo Bañuelas, Orlando Costas, Allan Figueroa Deck, Ana María Díaz-Stevens, Virgilio Elizondo, Orlando Espín, Ada María Isasi-Díaz, Alejandro García-Rivera, Roberto Goizueta, Justo González, Otto Maduro, Ana María Pineda, Gary Riebe-Estrella, Luis Rivera Pagán, Jeanette Rodríguez-Holguín, Jean-Pierre Ruiz, Samuel Solivan, Anthony Stevens-Arroyo, Fernando Segovia, Yolanda Tarango,

---

"Catholic," not because we are trying to revive the religious wars of Europe during the sixteenth and seventeenth centuries, but in recognition of other Catholic communities besides the one connected to the pope in Rome. See Julie Byrne, *The Other Catholics: Remaking America's Largest Religion* (New York: Columbia University Press, 2016).

and Eldin Villafañe. It was both humbling and reassuring that others had started before me and many others were also traveling the path with me. Additionally, it was inspiring to join with grassroots practitioners who were seeking to make connections between scholarship and daily life and who challenged the stereotype of an unbridgeable divide between church and academy. It was an additional pleasure to be welcomed into informal but very real communities of Latinx scholars of Latinx religions, theologies, and all types of spirituality. Like any human community, there is no platonic perfection, and yet these overlapping communities of scholars, colleagues, and practitioners are constant sources of encouragement, inspiration, and motivation, as well as dialogue partners, friends, and in some cases *compadres* and *comadres*. Surprisingly, encountering Latino/a theologies became a way of coming home—a way to discover who I am called to be and what I am called to do.

My growth as a scholar of religion and culture led to my personal discovery of Latinx theologies, and in turn I came to a new appreciation of the importance and reality of Latinx communities of faith and spirituality in the United States. As a second-generation Puerto Rican Yankee Latino, the study of Latinx theologies and spiritualities is simultaneously personal, communal, historical, contextual, creative, visionary, and essential for understanding Latinx peoples in the United States, but also indispensable for the common good of all society. Latinx theologies nurture people spiritually and culturally, both as individuals and as communities, and empower people for their daily interactions with the world. Latinx theologies without a doubt impact other people beyond Latinx communities. For many Latinx peoples, their day-to-day understanding and articulation of theology is a resource for navigating dominant public spheres where they might be despised and regularly at risk, seeking to provide for themselves and their families what they need to live. Therefore, Latinx theologies are not merely an academic articulation of theological specialists or pious banalities of people unmoored from reality, but are a means and expression of survival, meaning, and agency at the grassroots levels, with real-world outcomes. As such, Latinx theologies at their best are the work of the people as they negotiate daily life.

A Personal Journey: Miguel Angel De La Torre

I was not always a Southern Baptist. In fact, before I ever learned what the word "hybridity" meant, I had experienced spiritual hybridity since I was a child. Belonging to more than one faith tradition with contradictory doctrines and beliefs, I would argue, is very common among those of us who hail from the Caribbean. Holding in tension diverse and inharmonious religious beliefs develops an ambiguous methodology by which to approach the metaphysical. I was the first Latino to ever attend Blessed Sacrament Catholic School in Jackson Heights, New York—and to prove it, I still have the well-deserved ruler marks across my knuckles administered by the Grey Nuns of the Sacred Heart. I was baptized at the Catedral de San Cristóbal in la Habana, Cuba, by Bishop Eduardo Boza-Masvidal and confirmed in the Holy Mother Church at Blessed Sacrament. The De La Torres were so Catholic that my paternal grandfather was a Catholic priest. Apparently, lucky for me, he met my grandmother while serving her Communion. It was a tradition for the firstborn De La Torre to attend the Catholic seminary in Camagüey. If I had stayed in Cuba, I very well might have been a Roman Catholic priest. I attended Blessed Sacrament while Vatican II was convened, witnessing firsthand the radical changes that took place in our parish. During my confirmation I first discovered (in a very elementary way, of course) the social teachings of the church. Today, any perusal of my books or writings demonstrates how the social teachings of the church, Vatican II, and liberation theology are central to my theological thinking.

Although I was a good Catholic boy during the day, at night my family and I would offer up sacrifices to *Obatalá* (my mother's *santo*), *Changó* (my father's), and of course *Elegguá* (my *santo*). My parents were a priest and priestess of the Cuban religious tradition known as Santería. I was a child of Elegguá, best known as the trickster. I wore his *elekes* (beaded necklaces), kept his image in a dish behind my front door, and was in line to become a *santero*, a priest of the faith. And as contradictory as Roman Catholicism and Santería are, there was no confusion in my mind, my parents' minds, or that of their house congregation as to the difference between what was done at the church and what was done in our apartment. My parents cautioned me from revealing to the Irish priests and nuns the rituals in which we participated, because the religious were "confused" about how God works. My parents feared that if they discovered we had *el conocimiento* (the knowledge), I might be expelled from school. When I asked what we were, my parents replied, as if by rote, "We are apostolic Roman Catholics, but we believe in our own way." Like many Latinx, I grew up within a hybrid spirituality where I could be a good Catholic boy who prayed the rosary and a faithful Santería devotee who made offerings to Elegguá. Although theologian purists will be quick to point out the contradictions of my religious practices, those of us who participate in the faith of the people recognize and hold a more fluid understanding of spirituality. Today, to read any of my books or writings is to recognize how the trickster image is central to my theological thinking.

In my early twenties, I walked down a Southern Baptist church aisle and gave my heart to Jesus. I became a Southern Baptist for two reasons. First, the young Anglo woman I wanted to date would only go out with me on Saturday night if I went to church with her on Sunday morning. Second, being a successful businessman I wanted to assimilate to the dominant culture, even referring to myself as "Mike." Converting to Protestantism was a way of converting to whiteness. Eventually I would go to Southern Baptist Theological Seminary and pastor a rural church in Kentucky. I embraced concepts like "the priesthood of believers," "the autonomy of the local church," and "no creed but the Bible" (concepts that, I might add, have been discarded by today's Southern Baptist Convention). I was influenced by an evangelical zeal to share the good news. As an ordained Southern Baptist minister, I did more than simply put aside my previous religiosity; I became fundamentalist in my views, seeing Roman Catholicism as idol worship and the pope as akin to the antichrist. As to my Santería background, this was clearly satanic. All of the *santos*, I was taught, were demons. I accepted these interpretations without question and to my detriment turned my back on my spiritual and cultural roots with the fervor of a new convert. Today, to read any of my books or writings is to recognize how the passion to share the good news of salvation (understood as liberation from institutionalized and personal sins) is core to my theological thinking.

With a certain degree of apprehension I signed up for the required theology course during my first year as a seminarian while attending Southern Baptist Theological Seminary. Having drunk the assimilation Kool-Aid, I anticipated a rational and systematic approach to understanding the mysteries of the Divine. Theology, the study of God, would elevate my rudimentary comprehension of the Deity learned in my Sunday school classes. Throughout the course I took meticulous notes as we reviewed the work of intellectual giants of the faith, the men who "pierced into God's truth," men like Luther, Calvin, Troeltsch, Barth, Brunner, and Bultmann. I sat at the feet of my Euroamerican professors, drinking fully from the cup of their wisdom as they contributed to the formation of my theological outlook.

Then, while exploring the "harmartiological question"—a term referring to the flawed nature of fallen humanity, or sin—I experienced a shift in my theological thinking. Our professor attempted to enlighten us as to the fourfold essence of sin. He walked to the blackboard and wrote the numeral 1, followed by the word *hubris*, "pride." I copied it into my notebook. Then he wrote 2, *harmartia*, "rebellion." Amen, sounded good to me. Then he wrote 3, *concupiscentia,* "greed." *Preach on,* I thought. Finally, he wrote 4, the foundation of sin, *acedia,* "sloth." *Sloth?* Isn't that laziness? Grant you, sloth is no virtue, but is sloth the foundation and essence of sin? The fact that we only studied Eurocentric male theologians never bothered me at the time. Instead, what did disturb me was the inclusion of sloth in this list as foundational to a Christian understanding of sin. It sounded exaggerated to me. But why was I so perturbed?

Thanks to the cartoon character Speedy Gonzales, part of the Warner Brothers' Looney Tunes series, the image instilled in the minds of children throughout the United States was of the stereotypical Mexican, leaning against a cactus, taking a siesta under his large sombrero. This is the offensive image that flashed through my mind as I wrote the word "sloth" in my notebook. Contributing to this image of Latinx peoples is the fact that the United States celebrates the so-called Protestant work ethic as a basic element of its ethos. This work ethic has led many in the dominant culture to see indolence and sloth as the common denominator of all Latinx culture. Part of the North American myth is that if (any) body can become a (some)body through hard work, then a (no)body cannot blame (any)body but themselves for failing to do so. Latinx "laziness" then becomes a fatal flaw, defining us as a sinful people, responsible ourselves for the economic privation we face in this country.

Was this fourfold essence of sin perhaps chosen by the dominant culture to define themselves and their other? Would not a culture whose salient characteristic is hyperindividuality produce a list of sins devoid of any communitarian dimension? As so defined, this fourfold essence of personal sin requires personal repentance to a personal Savior in order to establish a personal relationship with a solitary God. Absent from this construction of sin is its role as a source of social injustice and human oppression. The privatizing of sin led our theology class to consider it a purely private affair. Nevertheless, any exclusively private sin is never actually personal. All sins are communal. While the Eurocentric theologies I was studying in seminary taught me to categorize sin as an essentially private affair, Latin American theologians like Gustavo Gutiérrez and Jon Sobrino showed how sin always negatively affects the whole community. My assimilation project began to develop cracks.

I lacked the philosophical terminology at the time to articulate what I was feeling. Theology, I was beginning to understand, was but a philosophical construct that justified the way of being of those defining the theology. Why was I so surprised to discover that a society that defines itself first and foremost as "industrious" would use the antonym "sloth" as the foundation of all sins? "Sloth," then, characterizes groups seen by the prevailing culture as nonindustrious. Additionally, sloth becomes the foundational sin that fatally threatens the dominant ethos of the culture. Thus, the dominant culture offers salvation for Latinx only through hard work (as defined by the dominant culture), the capitalist solution for all socioeconomic ills. For Latinx peoples to become productive citizens who share in the North American Dream, they must first pull themselves up by their bootstraps, according to dominant social attitudes, most particularly the North American version of the Protestant work ethic. The dominant culture's need to protect itself from the threat of sloth finds its justification by creating a theological perspective that puts any blame on the victims of socioeconomic abuses. "They bring drugs, they're rapists, and they have many problems" is what we hear from the highest office in the land. I concluded that theology had just as much to do with understanding *who we are*—or better yet, who we want to be—as it did with understanding who God is.

Anyone examining or forging theological texts does so from a particular context, what is termed a "social location." The idea of studying God or reading a biblical text from a position of complete objectivity is a myth. In fact, neither theology nor biblical interpretation occurs in a social vacuum. We are all born into an ongoing society that shapes us. When we turn our attention to the biblical text as the source of our theological perspectives, we participate in a dialogue between the written word and the meanings our community taught us to give to this word. We inform the text with the presuppositions we bring to the reading. We become part of the reading done through our own eyes. And then we are informed by the text. Such a reading inevitably shapes a theology tied to our particular community.

How then does my location as an exilic Cuban Latinx influence my theological perspective? When I was in seminary I was a former practitioner of an African Cuban religion known as Santería. Does this background in Santería affect my understanding of the Divine? Does the fact that I am a cisgender male, possess cultural capital, and am seen by fellow Latinx as white (though I am seen by the dominant culture as a person of color) influence how I define the Divine? As I struggled with questions like these, I sought guidance from the teaching assistant assigned to my seminary class. I shared with him these concerns, asking how a theology from Latinx perspectives might differ from that of Euroamericans. He laughed, stating that we do not need any more "chicken-bone theologies," a reference, no doubt, to the rituals of Santería.

I could not understand why the teaching assistant was hostile to my inquiries. Until then, I had assumed a theologian had to have a Eurocentric worldview. Now I began to question this presupposition. I attempted to perceive the Divine, not as a Euroamerican wannabe, but as a Latinx person. The process of decolonizing my mind began. My first order of business was to research the works of Latinx thinkers. Knowing little about Latinx theologies, I went to the seminary library and began to check out the few books in the collection written by individuals with Latinx-sounding surnames—not knowing who Bonino or Gutiérrez or Assmann were. During this time, I became exposed to liberation theologies as done in the Two-Thirds World and the United States.

Today, attempting to undo the damage of my quest to assimilate, I unapologetically refer to myself as a Southern Baptist, Roman Catholic child of Elegguá, fully embracing the hybridity of my being. Decades of commitment with the marginalized within these different manifestations of faith have informed my understanding of that which is beyond my understanding. As I reclaimed the hybrid spirituality of my people, I moved away from a rigid understanding of doctrine and instead now boldly wrestle with and against faith concepts that bring oppression to the most vulnerable. Yet I find that some of my fellow Latinx religious scholars' emphasis on orthodoxy leads them to refusing to join me in the orthopraxis struggle for justice. Recently I was refused membership as a Catholic to a Latinx Catholic association because some refuse to accept me as Catholic, even though I am probably more faithful than those who are cultural Catholics—Catholic in name only. It's fine if some Latinx Catholic groups refuse to recognize my Catholicism, because frankly I don't necessarily recognize their authority in naming what I am and what I believe. But I'm not just a Catholic: I am also a Protestant evangelical sharing the good news that God has called all of us to life and life abundantly (Jn 10:10), not in some hereafter, but in the here and now. I dedicated my life as a scholar-activist to the struggle for a justice that can provide an abundant life. And just as I can speak with authority as a Catholic and as an evangelical Protestant, so too can I speak with authority as a child of Elegguá—*porque lo que me dio Elegguá no hay quién me lo quite* (because what Elegguá gave me, no one can take away).

Getting to embrace the fullness of my Latinx identity was a long and painful journey, one that has yet to end. At the start of my journey, not many books were available, which is why Edwin and I set out to pen the first edition. Those books that were available assumed that the reader possessed a fundamental understanding of Latinx thought. What I needed when I was a seminary student was a systematic review of how Latinx theologies developed and of their common denominators. I needed a survey of the formation and challenges of these theologies. I needed a chicken-bone book like this one.

Goals for a Common Journey

Why is a book like this still important? When we wrote the first edition there were still few Latinx religious studies scholars who had published introductory texts dealing with Latino/a Christianity in the United States. Happily, since 2001 there have been numerous contributions in a variety of areas of theology, biblical studies, sociology of religion, history, ethics, and religious studies from Latinx perspectives and related to the richly diverse faiths and practices of Latinx peoples in the United States; these volumes serve well both as introductions and for deeper study.[18] The expressions and articulation of Latinx theolo-

---

[18] Works appearing since 2001 include Raimundo Barreto and Roberto Sirvent, eds., *Decolonial Christianities: Latinx and Latin American Perspectives* (New York: Palgrave Macmillan, 2019); Efraín Agosto and Jacqueline M. Hidalgo, eds., *Latinx, the Bible, and Migration* (New York: Palgrave Macmillan, 2018); Natalia Imperatori-Lee, *Cuéntame: Narrative in the Ecclesial Present* (Maryknoll, NY: Orbis Books, 2018); Teresa Delgado, *A Puerto Rican Decolonial Theology: Prophesy Freedom* (New York: Palgrave Macmillan, 2017); Francisco Lozada Jr., *Toward a Latino/a Biblical Interpretation* (Atlanta: SBL Press, 2017); Mark T. Mulder, Aida I. Ramos, and Gerardo Martí, *Latino Protestants in America: Growing and Diverse* (Lanham, MD: Rowman and Littlefield, 2017); Orlando O. Espín, ed., *Wiley/Blackwell Companion to Latino/a Theology* (Malden, MA: John Wiley and Sons, 2015); Néstor Medina and Sammy Alfaro, eds., *Pentecostals and Charismatics in Latin America and Latino Communities* (New York: Palgrave Macmillan, 2015); Daniel Ramírez, *Migrating Faith: Pentecostalism in the United States and Mexico in the Twentieth Century* (Chapel Hill: University of North Carolina Press, 2015); Gastón Espinosa, *Latino Pentecostals in America: Faith and Politics in Action* (Cambridge, MA: Harvard University Press, 2014); Loida I. Martell-Otero, Zaida Maldonado Perez, and Elizabeth Conde-Frazier, *Latina Evangélicas: A Theological Survey from the Margins* (Eugene, OR: Cascade Books, 2013); Timothy Matovina, *Latino Catholicism: Transformation in America's Largest Church* (Princeton, NJ: Princeton University Press, 2012); Carmen Nanko-Fernández, *Theologizing en Espanglish: Context, Community, and Ministry* (Maryknoll, NY: Orbis Books, 2010); Benjamín Valentín, ed., *In Our Own Voices: Latino/a Renditions of Theology* (Maryknoll, NY: Orbis Books, 2010); Oscar García-Johnson, *The Mestizo/a Community of the Spirit: A Postmodern Latino/a Ecclesiology* (Eugene, OR: Pickwick Publications, 2009); Harold J. Recinos and Hugo Magallanes, eds., *Jesus in the Hispanic Community: Images of Christ from Theology to Popular Religion* (Louisville, KY: Westminster John Knox Press, 2009); Luis G. Pedraja, *Teología: An Introduction to Hispanic Theology* (Nashville: Abingdon Press, 2003); María Pilar Aquino, Daisy L. Machado, and Jeanette Rodríguez, eds., *A Reader in Latina Feminist Theology: Religion and Justice* (Austin: University of Texas Press, 2002); Miguel A. De La Torre, ed., *Encyclopedia on Hispanic American Religious Culture*, vols. 1 and 2 (Santa Barbara, CA: ABC-CLIO, 2009).

gies have both grown and developed since the first edition of this book. We have benefited from the many creative insights and methodological richness in analysis, all accompanied by continued interest in the beliefs and practices of grassroots Latinx communities. Given these changes and new resources since 2001, why the need for this revised edition?

In the intervening years there has been ever greater diversity within the U.S. Latinx population, even as the population of the United States itself becomes more diverse, with projections that the national population will be majority-minority by the year 2044, some of whom are foreign-born, but also increasingly those who are 1.5-generation, second-generation, and later.[19] Many cities already have become majority-minority in population, including Atlanta, Baltimore, Boston, Charlotte, Chicago, Cincinnati, Dallas, Houston, Los Angeles, Memphis, Miami, Milwaukee, New Orleans, New York City, Philadelphia, Phoenix, San Antonio, San Francisco, St. Louis, and Winston-Salem. The states of California, Hawaii, New Mexico, and Texas are ahead of the national trend with a population majority composed of minoritized people. Moreover, it should be noted that even in its attempt to be inclusive, this majority-minority designation still reflects the dominant binary construction of racial identity in the United States.[20] Increasingly, people are openly embracing their multiple identities and could be of both "majority" and "minority" heritage.

Simultaneously and contributing to this, the majority-minority demographic shift the world is experiencing consists of major transnational migrations of people unlike anything seen in history. One result of this movement of peoples is that undocumented immigrants arrive in the United States from all over the world for all kinds of reasons, including humanitarian and economic. Unfortunately, some people in the United States have chosen to see these new arrivals as illegal criminals and call their very humanity into question. Ongoing racial profilings of black and brown people represent expressions of contempt for Latinx generally and Latin American undocumented immigrants specifically.

---

[19] Sandra L. Colby and Jennifer M. Ortman, *Projections of the Size and Composition of the U.S. Population: 2014–2060*, Current Population Reports, P25-1143, U.S. Census Bureau, Washington, DC, 2014. See also William H. Frey, *Diversity Explosion: How New Racial Demographics Are Remaking America* (Washington, DC: Brookings Institution, 2018), 1–10.

[20] For various analyses of the social construction of race and racial identities in the United States, see Daniel Martinez HoSang, Oneka LaBennett, and Laura Pulido, eds., *Racial Formation in the Twenty-First Century* (Berkeley: University of California Press, 2012); and Michael Omi and Howard Winant, *Racial Formation in the United States*, 3rd ed. (New York: Routledge, 2015).

These anti-immigrant attitudes and actions are concurrent with new waves of racism, discrimination, and oppression under the guise of U.S. nationalism, in which civil rights once considered settled are again in question. White supremacy has reasserted itself with an aggressiveness that finds encouragement and support at all levels of government. Persons of color (citizens and noncitizens) find their lives cut short by police officers sworn to protect and serve the public. In 2015, African American Christians at Mother Emanuel African Methodist Episcopal Church in Charleston, South Carolina, welcomed a young white visitor to their prayer meeting, who then shot and killed nine people, wounding several others, thus carrying out his premeditated racist attack. Remarkably, at the very moment when the country is becoming more and more diverse, an open racial struggle is emerging in which xenophobic white supremacists, neo-Nazis, and members of a resurgent Ku Klux Klan openly march through city streets with torches ablaze. We are in a time when a racist former Arizona county sheriff violated the constitutional rights of Latinx people, was voted out of office by his constituents, and convicted of criminal contempt by a federal judge, but then was shockingly granted a presidential pardon and chose to run for the U.S. Senate with presidential endorsement. The U.S. population is not only becoming more diverse, but also younger: over eight hundred thousand young people brought to the United States as children by their immigrant parents are at risk of being deported from the nation that is their home.

If the majority of the church in the United States is going to be Latinx, Asian, and African, it is all the more important to understand their theologies, spiritualities, and spiritual outlooks and practices. In such a multifaceted and volatile context, we still see the need for an introduction like this survey that intentionally engages these multifaceted contexts and their challenges for Latinx theologies. A confluence of revisionist intellectualism, backward-looking forces, deniers of history, and anti-intellectual movements are trying to undo social advances in the United States of the period from 1954 to 1990.[21] In the midst of this hatred, death, and the increasing struggles, the premature claims in 2008 of the United States being a postracial society are proven false and foolish. In such a time as this, knowing our contexts is desperately needed,

---

[21] The year 1954 was chosen for the *Brown v. Board of Education* Supreme Court decision that declared racially separate public schools to be unconstitutional and was so significant in the civil rights movement, and 1990 was chosen for that year's passage of the Americans with Disabilities Act. Choosing these two years as *terminus a quo* and *terminius ad quem*, respectively, does not mean that there was an uncontested constant advance in civil rights, rather that significant progress did occur in that thirty-six-year period.

and understanding Latinx theologies is more relevant than ever.

Therefore, we offer this revised and expanded basic introductory text on the fundamental principles and various perspectives of how Latinx people from different faith traditions do theology. This book is not solely De La Torre's or Aponte's perspectives on Latinx theologies (although admittedly there is some of that). Rather, we seek to explore the numerous perspectives of many Latinx—some perspectives are complementary, others conflicting. In the first edition and in this revision, we made a conscious commitment to inclusiveness of perspectives in order to be as representative as possible. This book strives to inform and challenge. With this in mind, we invite you to read about the theological, religious, and spiritual perspectives of the diverse peoples collectively called by many terms: Hispanic, Latino/a, Latinx, and Latin@. Included are marginalized, so-called chicken-bone, vibrant theologies that confound stereotypes, but at the same time provide their adherents with resources as they fight in the struggle for life, contending with both hope and hopelessness, confident in the presence of the Divine who accompanies them on the journey.

I

Who Are Latinx Peoples?

Constructing Identities

Take a moment to look at Figure 1.1. What do you see? Not surprisingly, you probably will respond with "a map of the world." In fact, such an answer is expected. Most of us grew up seeing this type of map on our classroom walls, our church bulletin boards (with red pins demarcating where the church-sponsored missionaries live), in our educational textbooks, in the back of many airline magazines, and on many Internet sites. This particular map is a version of the so-called Mercator projection of the Earth, based on the work of sixteenth-century mapmaker Gerardus Mercator (1512–1594), who produced the first version in 1569.

Surprisingly, this sixteenth-century view of the world is still quite common in the twenty-first century.

The map in Figure 1.1 is considered normal and legitimate only because we have been taught to "see" the world in this fashion. There is a "top" and "bottom" to the map, and by extension a top and bottom to the world and what looks "right." North is the "top" of the map, South is the bottom, East is on the right-hand side, and West is on the left-hand side. Additionally, this particular rendering of the map is centered on North America and actually distorts the actual size of the landmasses the farther one moves from the equator. This traditional way of seeing masks the power and privilege of those who made this particular type of map. We are conditioned to view the world in this way, even if it fails to accurately represent the geographic configuration of landmasses.

For example, look at Greenland and then look at South America. Which one seems larger? According to Figure 1.1, Greenland has a greater landmass than South America, yet Greenland contains 840,000

1

Figure 1.1. *Mercator Projection of the Earth*

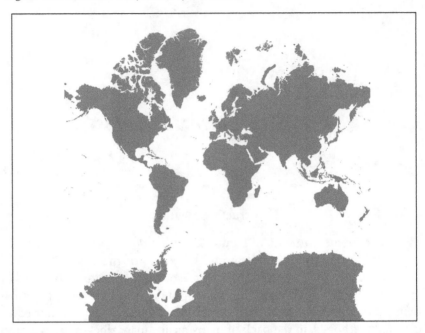

square miles while South America has 6.9 million square miles. In other words, South America is almost nine times larger than Greenland, a fact not obvious from this map. Greenland, the world's largest island in terms of landmass, could easily fit within the boundaries of Brazil—at least three times. Another example of this distortion of perspective in terms of land size is the continent of Africa, which appears modest in size according to the Mercator projection of the Earth. Actually, the continental United States, China, India, Pakistan, and several other countries could easily fit within the boundaries of Africa.

Particularly since the 1970s many people and organizations have recognized the shortcomings of the Mercator projection and endeavored to find a way to see the world as it really is in terms of actual landmasses relative to each other. The map in Figure 1.2 is one response. This map, based on the Winkel Tripel projection of the Earth, tries to better represent how the world actually is. Figure 1.1 centers North America and Europe, forcing other areas to be disproportionately represented. Figure 1.2, on the other hand, tries to correct the distortion of sizes of landmasses.

Figure 1.2 *Winkel Tripel Projection of the Earth*

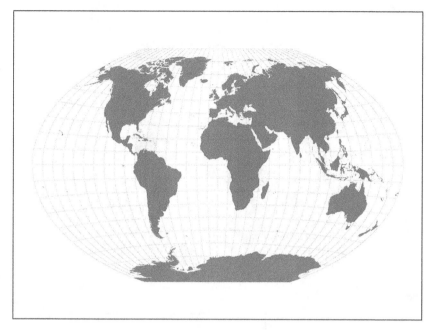

For most of us, the view of the world represented in Figure 1.2 still appears unnatural, even if it is closer to geographic reality. It appears strange because it has not been adjusted for the dominant consensus of what is "normal." It also appears strange because there is still some distortion, both of the actual geography of the Earth and with the way we are conditioned to see things. In a way, recognizing both the distortion and the discomfort help in understanding the difference between how dominant cultures gaze upon Latinx bodies and how Latino/as see themselves. Once the perspective of a dominant culture is decentered, there is a possibility for alternate and inherent homegrown ways of seeing to develop, though they may at first seem abnormal since they depart from how we are accustomed to viewing the world.

Before we get too comfortable with Figure 1.2, we need to realize that this representation is still arbitrary. Why is the North chosen as top and the South as the bottom? Is there an implicit bias about what is top and what is bottom? Why must the North Atlantic countries be "on top"? If the sixteenth-century explorers and mapmakers came from the Southern Hemisphere, would the South be up? When seeing the planet from outer space, there is no sign stating, "This Side Up"; there is no top or bottom. Hence, Figure 1.3 also represents the Earth but literally upends what we have been taught is normal.

Figure 1.3 *Upended Projection of the Earth*

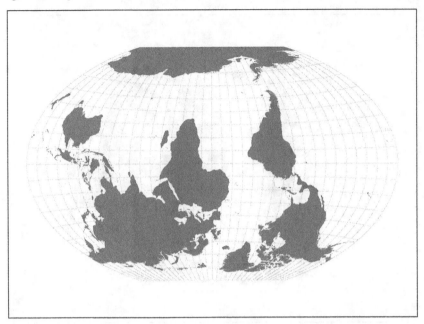

Seeing is not an entirely innocent physiological phenomenon involving the simple transmission of light waves. Visual perceptions also include modes of thought that transform the object being seen into a concept for intellectual assimilation, interpretation, and possession. Recognizing the importance of perspectives and viewpoints, this book focuses on seeing Latinx peoples and their religious and spiritual beliefs, practices, and interpretations, concentrating primarily but not exclusively on Latinx Christianity. Like the world of Figure 1.1, Christian theology has been legitimized and normalized through the eyes of certain dominant "white" Euroamerican cultures that declare the expected standard—in effect, what is acceptable and normal. But as with maps of the Earth, there are multiple ways to see theology.

Seeing the religiosity of any group of people, in our case Latina/os, contradicts Émile Durkheim's sociological, Sigmund Freud's psychological, and Karl Marx's economic functionalism, each of which insists that overarching societal structures powerfully determine religious beliefs. As historian and philosopher of religion Mircea Eliade reminded us, the faith of a people, as the irreducible sacred, resists being reduced to an effervescence of the so-called underlying social reality. Instead the reverse is claimed: religion shapes society; it is not simply a dependent variable of other forces. Eliade asserts that society, psychology, and economics affect religion, but that their influences are neither dominant nor determining.[1] Theologian Orlando Espín is even more explicit in grounding society and culture in actual people, stating, "I insist that the people's faith be taken seriously as a true *locus theologicus* and not solely or mainly as a pastoral, catechetical problem."[2]

Our studies of Latinx religions, spiritualities, and related practices show not only that peoples' own faith and practices should be taken seriously as legitimate sources of theology, but also that what is usually called "religion" and "theology" profoundly affects society, psychology, and economics, as well as the other way around. As scholar of religion and society Manuel A. Vásquez observes, "It behooves scholars of religion to take seriously the native actor's lived world and to explore the biological, social, and historical conditions that make religious experience possible as well as the effects these experiences have on self, culture, and nature."[3] With this exhortation in mind, the intention of this book is to explore how dominant cultures see Latino/as, but also how Latinx peoples see themselves, and more importantly, how Latinx see the Divine, the biblical text, other sacred texts, formal and informal theological traditions, their faith communities, spiritual practices, and the rituals that impact their understandings of self, society, culture, and nature.

Seeing Identity

There is no such thing as a "typical" or "pure" Hispanic. They are white with blond hair and blue eyes, they are black with curly hair, and they are everything in between. They have Native American features or Asian features or both. They are Catholics, Protestants, worshipers of the Orishas (African quasi-deities), Jews, atheists, spiritualists, and followers of indigenous religious traditions. Some speak "pure" Spanish, others speak Spanglish, and still others only speak English. Some converse only in Cholo, Mayan, Náhuatl, or Pocho. Some have recently arrived in this country, while the ancestors of others were here centuries before the formation of the United States. Some cross borders, while others had borders cross them. Some live in poverty, while others live in multimillion-dollar mansions. They live in the blank despair of the barrio

---

[1] Mircea Eliade, *Patterns in Comparative Religion*, trans. Rosemary Sheed (New York: Meridian Books, 1963), xii.

[2] Orlando O. Espín, *The Faith of the People: Theological Reflections on Popular Catholicism* (Maryknoll, NY: Orbis Books, 1997), 2.

[3] Manuel A. Vásquez, *More Than Belief: A Materialist Theory of Religion* (New York: Oxford University Press, 2011), 5.

and in the comfortable illusions of the suburbs. Some pick apples and grapes; others pick stocks and bonds.

But when members of the U.S. dominant culture, shaped by a white Euroamerican perspective, gaze upon Latinx peoples, what do they see? This question of the perceived image is significant because the seeing done by many in the dominant Euroamerican culture impacts the existential selves of Latinx peoples; it affects the way Latino/as internalize who they are, and it may compel them to behave and act according to ways in which the dominant culture seeks to construct and delineate reality for them. More specifically, when a so-called true American gazes upon a Hispanic, the former often perceives a deficient person who is dark, lazy, immoral, and backward. Fernando Segovia compiled a popular conception of Latina/os as seen through the eyes of North American dominant culture. For a large number of people of a variety of backgrounds but influenced by the dominant Euroamerican culture, Hispanics are

(a) lazy, unproductive, unenterprising—the sleeping Mexican with the wide *sombrero*, drinking tequila and whiling away the day against a wall, or a bunch of open-shirted Caribbean men drinking beer and playing dominoes at a local, rundown park; (b) carefree, fun-loving, romantic/sensual—latin-lover types with bushy mustachios and beguiling *señoritas* in bright-colored, low-cut dresses; *maracas*-swinging trios and voluptuous vendettas with plenty of flowers or fruits upon their heads; (c) disorderly, undisciplined, violent—uncontrolled progenitors, breeding like rabbits, and knife-wielding gangs, killing one another like animals; (d) vulgar, unintelligent, unteachable—short, swarthy, and primitive people, with funny broken accents and happily occupying the most menial and servile of occupations.[4]

Unfortunately, such racist judgments have not diminished since Segovia's 1995 observation. Federal documents filed in U.S. District Court in Tucson in 2019 testify that a U.S. Border Patrol agent in Nogales, Arizona, in text messages called undocumented Latin American migrants "disgusting subhuman [expletive] unworthy of being kindling for a fire" and urged President Trump to "PLEASE let us take the gloves off . . . !"[5]

---

[4] Fernando F. Segovia, "Two Places and No Place on Which to Stand," in *Mestizo Christianity: Theology from the Latino Perspective*, ed. Arturo J. Bañuelas (Maryknoll, NY: Orbis Books, 1995), 31.

[5] Reis Thebault, "A Border Patrol Agent Called Migrants 'Subhuman.' Then He Purposefully Hit One with His Truck" *Washington Post*, August 13, 2019,

The same former Border Patrol agent accepted a guilty plea that he hit a Guatemalan migrant with a Border Patrol truck on December 3, 2017. In short, some still see Latinx peoples as inferior, ignorant, uncouth, and even in some cases nonhuman. Such assumptions, racist judgments, and accompanying evil actions of some white Euroamericans toward Latinx peoples also contribute to self-definitions of white superiority, intelligence, and cultural sophistication.

In such a social and cultural context, even accomplished Latinx persons are seen as less than adequate, and in some cases perceived as less than normal. Take, for example, the role played by stereotypes during the confirmation of Supreme Court justice Sonia Sotomayor. Former Speaker of the House Newt Gingrich and popular radio show host Rush Limbaugh insisted that then-nominee Judge Sotomayor should withdraw from being considered for the Supreme Court because she is "a Latina woman racist." Sotomayor was attacked for lacking sufficient intelligence (apparently graduating summa cum laude from Princeton University and earning a law degree from Yale University was not enough for such critics) or for being too abrasive (translated as a nondocile Latina who speaks her mind). Some of the comments bordered on the absurd. Take, for example, former Colorado congressman and Republican presidential candidate Tom Tancredo, who in 2009 in his opposition to Judge Sotomayor's nomination both misrepresented a speech she made and called the civil rights organization the National Council of La Raza (NCLR, now known as UnidosUS), a "Latino KKK without the hoods or the nooses"—that is, a version of the notoriously racist and violent Ku Klux Klan.[6]

While certainly an outrageous charge, it was reignited in 2016 when then–Republican presidential candidate Donald Trump repeatedly accused federal judge Gonzalo P. Curiel, who was born in Indiana of Mexican immigrant parents, of making biased decisions against Trump and of being a "hater of Donald Trump" and a "Mexican," and called

---

https://beta.washingtonpost.com/immigration/2019/08/14/border-patrol-agent-called-migrants-subhuman-then-he-purposefully-hit-one-with-his-truck/.

[6] Tancredo made his statement in an appearance on CNN on May 28, 2009. The National Council of La Raza (NCLR) changed its name to UnidosUS in July 2017. See UnidosUS, *UnidosUS 50: Fifty Years of an American Institution* (Washington, DC: UnidosUS, 2018), 47. The actual words of then-judge Sotomayor's 2001 speech at the University of California, Berkeley, were, "I would hope that a wise Latina woman with the richness of her experiences would more often than not reach a better conclusion than a white male who hasn't lived that life." Those who accused Sotomayor of being a racist and bigot used a truncated version of what she said, "a wise Latina woman . . . would more often than not reach a better conclusion than a white male."

into question Judge Curiel's association with the San Diego La Raza Lawyers Association, which some of Trump's supporters linked to the National Council of La Raza.[7]

For some communities in the United States, what it means to be an American is defined by emphasizing the perceived differences of Latino/as. The power of seeing becomes internalized, naturalized, and legitimized in order to mask the dominant culture's position of power. Rarely are the self-perceptions of Latinx peoples solicited. One of the first modern and still influential Euroamerican presentations of a Latino was the television character Ricky Ricardo, played by Desi Arnaz, in the popular 1950s' sitcom *I Love Lucy*, which also starred Lucille Ball. *I Love Lucy* continues to be shown in television reruns and is constantly available through Internet video-streaming, allowing new viewers to become acquainted with this fictional but archetypal person. Although the character of Ricky Ricardo was Cuban, dominant and nondominant cultures watching the show saw him as part of an overall homogeneous group of exotic "Latin" others, later labeled during the 1970s in the popular imagination as "Hispanic."

The second episode of *I Love Lucy*, "Be a Pal," first broadcast on October 22, 1951, demonstrates how Hispanics were and continue to be seen as one monolithic cultural group. In this episode, Lucy, fearing her husband, Ricky, is losing interest in her, transforms the living room of their apartment to resemble Ricky's Cuban homeland, but what is seen has very little to do with Cuba. The viewer gazes upon icons that include a chicken coop, a donkey, bananas, palm trees, and a woman (Lucy's friend and neighbor Ethel) dressed as a Mexican man wearing a serape under a sombrero. Five children run out of the bedroom, emphasizing the fecundity of people from south of the border. At one point Lucy appears with fruit in her hair performing as the Brazilian Carmen Miranda, lip-syncing "Mamãe eu quero" (Mama, I want), a Brazilian song in Portuguese asking Mama for a *chupeta*, literally a "sucker." Without any apparent distinction between very different cultural types, Brazilian and Mexican symbols in the popular imagination are merged indiscriminately to create a sucker's reflection, not only of Ricky's Cuban homeland but also of all so-called Hispanic homelands of origin.

This episode illustrates that under the racialized, white Euroamerican gaze, all Latina/os are seen as the same, as one monolithic group, where the distinctions between the Spanish and Portuguese languages are not even worth mentioning, and the differences existing between a Puerto Rican, a Brazilian, an Argentinean, or a Chicano are deemed

---

[7] Reuters, "Judge Orders Documents Unsealed in Trump University Lawsuit," *New York Times*, May 30, 2016.

irrelevant. But in fact, Latinx peoples in the United States are also often perceived as a *mestizaje* (racial mixture) or combination of ethnicities, a mestizaje of races. As some have noted, the Latinx cultural mixing in the United States is the result of a complicated and sometimes violent history, summarized by historian Daisy Machado as "not only about borders crossed, but also very much about racial mixture that includes the *mestizaje* of Indian and Spanish blood, the *mulatez* of Spanish and African, the whiteness of *criollos*, and the brown tones of the indigenous peoples, as well as other racial mixtures that are the reality of human pigmentation in the Americas."[8]

While there are challenges with using the concepts of mestizaje, and especially *mulatez*, including romanticized and ahistorical appropriations, nevertheless they still provide helpful theological insights.[9] Christian theologian Gilberto Cavazos-González observes, "Mestizaje recalls the foundation of our Christian faith. . . . The spiritual theme of mestizaje takes seriously the incarnation of the Word made flesh, making Jesús a divine/human mestizo."[10] Likewise, seeing Latinx peoples as a mestizaje of cultures provides illumination. Latinx as a mestizaje or mulatez of kitchens, a dense stew of distinct flavors, brings a different perspective to the still common image of a melting pot. That paradigm typically pictures all immigrants to the United States from all nations placed into one pot where they all combine into a new American culture that curiously remains essentially Eurocentric. In contrast, the Latina/o mestizaje stew always retains the differing flavors of its diverse roots (varieties of European, indigenous, and African) while enriching all elements of the mix. Some ingredients may dissolve completely in the blend while others remain more distinct, and new ingredients are constantly added—all providing flavor to the simmering stew that is always in a state of change. For this reason, the Latinx stew, whether it is called an *ajiaco* or a *sancocho*, is unapologetically an authentic reality, a *locus theologicus* (theological location), a Latinx setting for approaching the wider world.

---

[8] Daisy L. Machado, "History and Latino/a Identity: Mapping a Past That Leads to Our Future," in *The Wiley Blackwell Companion to Latino/a Theology*, ed. Orlando O. Espín (Malden, MA: Wiley Blackwell, 2015), 36.

[9] A milestone work on this topic is Néstor Medina's *Mestizaje: (Re)Mapping Race, Culture, and Faith in Latina/o Catholicism* (Maryknoll, NY: Orbis Books, 2009). An extremely helpful summary and examination of the challenges is found in Jorge A. Aquino, "*Mestizaje*: The Latina/o Religious Imaginary in the North American Racial Crucible," in Espín, *Wiley Blackwell Companion to Latino/a Theology*, 283–311.

[10] Gilberto Cavazos-González, OFM, "The Study of Spirituality," in Espín, *Wiley Blackwell Companion to Latino/a Theology*, 430.

Being Latinx in the United States is a complex reality. Latino/as are heirs of several different indigenous cultures (such as Taíno, Mayan, Aztec, Zapotec, etc., depending on the particular context) of medieval Catholic Iberia (influenced by centuries of Muslim and Jewish presence in Al-Andalus or the period of Islamic rule from 711 to 1492 CE), of enslaved African peoples (primarily in the Caribbean and Brazil, but certainly throughout Latin America), of Asia (the result of European empires and the movements of colonized people), and due to our continuing presence in the United States, of various non-Iberian European backgrounds. Latino/as are truly a multicultural people, the heirs of many cultural traditions, yet fully accepted by none of them. Although their presence *aquí* (here) in the United States binds them together in the constructed identity of Hispanics, they remain unwelcome by many in the country, as resurgent white nationalism since 2016 demonstrates. Also, because of their geographic absence from the cultural land of their births or the birth of their progenitors, in one sense they cease to belong *allá* (there). Exilic Cuban Lourdes Casal captures poetically the difficult task of constructing a U.S. Hispanic ethnic identity in such a context:

This is why I will always remain on the margins,
a stranger among the stones,
even beneath the friendly sun of this summer's day,
just as I will remain forever a foreigner,
even when I return to the city of my childhood
I carry this marginality, immune to all turning back,
too *habanera* to be *newyorkina*,
too *newyorkina* to be
—even to become again—
anything else.[11]

But for many Latinx, identity is even more complex than the existential space between *aquí* and *allá*. For example, for those who identify as Mexican American or Chicano/as, there is no *allá*; the entire existence for generations has been here in what is now called the United States. Although seen as foreigners by some, Mexican Americans are actually dwelling in their ancestral lands with roots going back to the Spanish conquest and, before that, indigenous peoples. From these existential, in-between spaces, Latino/as construct the theological bases upon which they reconcile their several selves to their theological beliefs and practices.

---

[11] Lourdes Casal, "For Ana Veldford," trans. David Frye, in *Bridges to Cuba/ Puentes a Cuba*, 20th ann. ed., ed. Ruth Behar (Ann Arbor: University of Michigan Press, 1995, 2015), 22.

The widespread Euroamerican vision of Hispanics, as portrayed in *I Love Lucy*, can easily delude us into assuming there can be only one homogenized Hispanic religious expression. But because Hispanic cultures and contexts are so varied, we cannot speak of one Latino/a perspective. Instead we must speak of perspectives. While some commonalities exist, divergences flourish, depending on the group's gender, race, economic class, ethnic identity, national background, sexual preference, years in this country, and geographic location. Latinx theological reflections are neither imported nor created by theological professionals for the uniform consumption of Latina/os. The various expressions of Latinx religious thought, at their best, reflect believing communities seeking to understand their own locations and everyday realities, while remaining strangers and exiles in a foreign land that may also be home.

Again, poetry helps to better understand this multilayered, complex reality that being Latinx is not just one thing but can be several concurrent identities. Aurora Levins Morales provides a good illustration of these complex cultural identities in her poem "Child of the Americas":

I am a child of the Americas,
a light-skinned *mestiza* of the Caribbean,
a child of many diaspora, born into this continent at a crossroads.
I am a U.S. Puerto Rican Jew,
a product of the ghettos of New York I have never known.
An immigrant and the daughter and granddaughter of immigrants.
I speak English with a passion: It's the tool of my consciousness,
a flashing knife blade of crystal, my tool, my craft.
I am *Caribeña*, island grown, Spanish is in my flesh,
ripples from my tongue, lodges in my hips:
the language of garlic and mangoes,
the singing in my poetry, the flying gestures of my hands.
I am of *Latinoamerica*, rooted in the history of my continent:
I speak from that body.
I am not african. Africa is in me, but I cannot return.
I am not taína. Taíno is in me, but there is no way back.
I am not european. Europe lives in me, but I have no home there.
I am new. History made me. My first language was spanglish.
I was born at the crossroads
and I am whole.[12]

---

[12] Aurora Levins Morales, "Child of the Americas," from *Getting Home Alive* (Ithaca, NY: Firebrand Books, 1986), 50. Reprinted with the permission of the The Permissions Company, LLC, on behalf of the author, auroralevinsmorales. com.

In a sense each Latinx person in the United States is a child of the Americas. Consequently, there is no such thing as a typical or pure Hispanic. On this point the U.S. Census Bureau may have it right in that "Hispanic origin can be viewed as the heritage, nationality, lineage, or country of birth of the person or the person's parents or ancestors before arriving in the United States. People who identify as Hispanic, Latino, or Spanish may be any race."[13]

What's in a Name? Hispanic, Latino, Latino/a, Latin@, Latinoa, Latinx

Nearly equal to the challenges of describing the nature of Latinx reality in the United States are the collective terms used to represent that compound life experience, the most common candidates being Hispanic, Latino, Latino/a, Latin@, Latinoa, and Latinx. All the terms have their own rationale—and their advocates as well as their critics. For some, using the "wrong" terminology can be insulting or a sign of betrayal; as a result, considerable debate has taken place over ethnic self-identification. In some contexts, it is difficult if not dangerous to determine who uses what term and why. In a few words, the etymology of the word "Latino/a" and its variants is rooted in Latin, the dominant language of ancient Rome, while the term "Hispanic" is connected in some fashion with Spain, being from Spain or Spanish language and culture.

The word "Hispanic" can refer to one of the nations that were former colonies of Spain. Hence "Hispanic America" is another term used for Latin America. Curiously, in the United States, "Hispanic" usually does not refer to the African or Asian-Pacific parts of the former Spanish Empire, so Filipinos typically are not counted as Hispanics. The term "Hispanic" is seen as overemphasizing the European/Spanish element of the heritage, ignoring the legacies of non-Spanish Europeans, Africans, Asians, and indigenous peoples. *Hispanos*, the Spanish equivalent of Hispanics, is a term long used by the inhabitants of New Mexico for self-identification. Starting with the 1970 U.S. Census, "Hispanic" was employed as an official term imposed by U.S. governmental agencies to officially identify people of Latin American and Spanish descent living in the United States. As a governmental construction, "Hispanics" lumped everyone who comes from a Spanish-speaking culture together in one group. People with Brazilian or Portuguese backgrounds do not usually

---

[13] U.S. Census Bureau, *Hispanic Origin*, https://www.census.gov/topics/population/hispanic-origin.html.

use the term "Hispanic" since they do not trace their roots to a Spanish-speaking country.[14]

As an alternative, "Latino" became popular among many who reject the term "Hispanic," as did the dualistic gender-sensitive label "Latino/a" and related terms. It is often argued that "Latino/a" emphasizes the importance of the Latin American context and origins, while also allowing for greater inclusion from the legacies of indigenous, African, Asian, Spanish, Portuguese, and other European heritages. However, it can also be seen that, linguistically, Latino/a emphasizes a Latin (European) culture while overlooking other groups. Like the term "Hispanic," "Latino/a" or "Latina/o" is a catch-all label that still can homogenize diverse groups.

In recent years, as greater awareness of issues related to gender and sexual identity has become more widespread, the limitations of binary-gendered formulations such as "Latino/a," "Latina/o," and "Latin@" are becoming more apparent. In response to these concerns, another term has emerged, "Latinx," that tries to address the problem of exclusionary language and seeks to be more inclusive. In describing the appeal of this term, journalist Ed Morales asserts,

> The growing movement to embrace *Latinx* highlights how it dispenses with the problem of prioritizing male or female by negating that binary. The real power of the term and its true meaning, however, erupts with its final syllable. After years of Latin lovers, Latin looks, Latin music, and Latin America, the word describes something that is not as much Latin—a word originally coined by the French to brand non-English- and Dutch-speaking colonies with a different flavor—as it is alternative America, the unexpected X factor in America's race debate.[15]

Moreover, as others have noted, part of the appeal of using "Latinx" is that it acknowledges and makes space for "the complex realities of the peoples, nationalities, and sexualities represented by US Latina, Latino, and transgender, non-binary individuals, many of whose ancestors migrated to the confines of current US borders or were already 'here' when 'the border crossed us,' and many of whom are more recent immigrants."[16]

---

[14] Edward Murguia, "On Latino/Hispanic Ethic Identity," *Latino Studies Journal* 2 (September 1991): 11.

[15] Ed Morales, *Latinx: The New Force in American Politics and Culture* (New York: Verso, 2018), 4.

[16] Efraín Agosto and Jacqueline M. Hidalgo, "Introduction: Reading the Bible

Although any racial/ethnic label is an abstraction from reality and each comes with its own set of problems, the necessity of using a collective term leads this book's authors to favor "Latinx" for its inclusion as well as for reminding us of the multifaceted reality we are examining. At the same time, while we favor the use of "Latinx," the appearance of other terms in this book acknowledges that there is no consensus on this point and that all the other terms are still in use. Often multiple terms are used interchangeably. In any case, few Latinx people ordinarily use the collective terms in everyday conversation for self-reference. When Latinx persons talk among themselves, they seldom use labels like "Hispanic" and "Latina/o," nor do they use compounded identities that attempt to reconcile two distinct and separate cultures into one being. Instead, they commonly identify themselves by their or their family's country of origin: Mexican, Cuban, Salvadoran, Dominican, Puerto Rican, and so forth. But even within subgroups there is a dispute regarding self-identifying terminology. For decades many Mexican American self-identified as Chicano/a/x, but in 2019 some local chapters of the Movimiento Estudiantil Chicanx de Aztlán (MEChA) chose to stop using the words "Chicanx" and "Aztlán" in their names, explaining that

> Chicanx, which directly translates to Mexican-American, is exclusionary. Although some identify with the political connotations Chicanx can have, it has not traditionally been used in that way. We recognize that it would be wrong to force non-Mexican-Americans, Indigenous Mexicans who cannot identify with this term, and Black Mexicans whom this term has historically excluded to use this term to describe their political philosophy.[17]

Again, this shows that whatever collective terms are used, they are ultimately both contextual and provisional to the extent that they are helpful in describing present reality.

---

and Latinx Migrations / The Bible as Text(s) of Migration," in *Latinx, the Bible, and Migration*, ed. Efraín Agosto and Jacqueline Hidalgo (New York: Palgrave Macmillan, 2018), 17n10.

[17] Katherine Chiu, Emilio Balderas, and Gabriela Guillén (MEChA's National Board 2019–20), "A Message from ME(ChA)'s National Board: Why We Decided to Change the Name of Our Movimiento," https://remezcla.com/features/culture/mecha-national-board-statement-on-name-change/, April 5, 2019.

Challenges of Pan-Latinx Identity

Collective terms reinforce a pan-Latinx identity, which can explain their appeal but also why some of these terms are barely acceptable to some of the population.[18] No doubt, many commonalities exist among different Latinx groups. In fact, the very purpose of a book like this is to explore some of these shared characteristics as they relate to religious discourse and practice. Nevertheless, caution is needed to avoid constructing some mythical Latinx "umbrella" that ignores or simplifies major contextual differences among Latinx peoples while essentializing their very being. Even as commonalities are identified, one should remember that there is no such thing as a Latinx homogeneous whole.

At times, those who engage in discourse about Latinx religious thought have also advanced a type of singular pan-Latinx theological identity. This was very popular during the early development of Hispanic theological thought in the 1980s and 1990s when some of the original architects of the theological discourse were of Cuban descent, many of whom either wrote on pan-Latinx themes or on the religious symbols of other Latinx groups—for example, discussing the Mexican *Virgen de Guadalupe*—rather than the Cuban *Virgen del Cobre*.[19]

While most scholars today recognize the importance of naming the unique features of each Latinx group, some academics still identify common or shared themes and characteristics, frequently using terms like "*latinamente*," as in "doing theology *latinamente*" or "evangelizing *latinamente*," or doing something in a distinctive Latinx way. Such pan-Latinx terms can become more of an academic construct than anything existing within the grass roots of Latinx religious thought. There is always the danger that all-encompassing terms such as *latinamente* and *latinidad* could be used to do the very opposite—that is, to exclude some and privilege others—so the question should be asked: Who is included in such descriptions? In a similar vein, when talking about doing theology *latinamente*, caution must be exercised to avoid insisting on there being only one type of Latinx religious trajectory, which submerges if not silences other religious perspectives. If indeed every theological and

---

[18] For further discussion on pan-ethnic Latinx-Latino/a identity, see Edwin David Aponte, *¡Santo! Varieties of Latino/a Spirituality* (Maryknoll, NY: Orbis Books, 2012), 67–77.

[19] One of the first studies focused on Cuban religious and social location is Miguel A. De La Torre, *The Quest for the Cuban Christ: A Historical Search* (Gainesville: University of Florida Press, 2002). Another work in this area that in particular compares Cuban American and African American religiosities is Michelle A. Gonzalez, *Afro-Cuban Theology: Religion, Race, Culture, and Identity* (Gainesville: University of Florida Press, 2009).

religious reflection is contextual, then it is imperative to be open to multiple Latinx theological or religious perspectives. The task before us is to recognize the shared commonalities that show up in different Latinx contexts without ignoring very real differences.

If the author of a religious perspective happens to be a Latinx person, does that make their theological view Latinx? Can an Anglo, African American, or Asian American writing about the Latinx religious social location produce a Latinx perspective? Are religious views based on a right-wing fundamentalist worldview that accepts unfettered capitalism as the God-ordained plan for humanity representative of Latinx religiosity? What about theological perspectives that are neither Catholic nor Protestant, but rather based on Islam, Santería, humanism, or Buddhism? Who gets to determine—or better yet, has the power to determine—what is a so-called *latinamente* way of doing theology from a Latinx perspective?

Such questions go to the heart of any attempt to write a definitive book (the present volume included) on what is and what is not Latinx religiosity and, more importantly, who gets to call themselves "Latinx." If a matrix of religious voices exists within diverse Latinx communities, how can it be discussed without silencing some of those voices? Which perspectives are created in the academy and then imposed upon Latinx peoples as if they are native to the cultures and arise from the grass roots? Do more formal theological assessments of grassroots Latinx religiosity published in academic books allow for the spiritual hybridity that seems more commonplace? For example, one of the authors of this book, De La Torre, as mentioned earlier, self-identifies as a Roman Catholic, Southern Baptist child of the Santería Orisha Elleguá.[20]

These questions shouldn't imply that we must say nothing about what constitutes Latinx religious and theological conversations. Nor does it mean that we as authors are offering ourselves as experts on what is genuinely Latinx. What it means is to be open about a preferential option as to which voices will be heard, and to be aware that such choices always are being made either implicitly or explicitly. The focus of what we are calling the different expressions of Latinx religiosity and theological perspectives are the marginalized and disenfranchised Latinx communities within both the overall dominant culture shaped by Euroamerican sociopolitical culture, as well as Latinx communities themselves.

As we think about what constitutes Latinx perspectives, and who gets to name their perspectives as Latinx, we conclude that no one

---

[20] See also Miguel A. De La Torre, "I'm a Southern Baptist, Roman Catholic Child of Elegguá—Deal with It," *Cuba Counter Points*, November 2, 2015, https://cubacounterpoints.com/archives/2633.

simple way of looking at Latinx religious life in the United States exists. Terms like *latinamente* may be used as long as the existing diversity is not obscured. Just as it is possible to look at a world map from different viewpoints, so too can observers see Latinx religious thought from different perspectives. Many factors are involved in achieving a clear picture of Latinx religious and theological thought.

Latinx Demographics

Chances are you know a Latina or Latino, or have heard people speaking Spanish in an elevator, in a grocery line, or on campus. According to the U.S. Census Bureau, as of July 1, 2018, the Hispanic population of the United States was 59.9 million people, making people of Latinx origin the nation's largest ethnic population group (or "minority group," as the Census Bureau called it). Of the nation's total population, Latinx people constituted 18.3 percent, with Mexicans comprising 11.1 percent; Puerto Ricans, 1.7 percent; Cubans, 0.7 percent; and other Hispanics or Latinos, 4.1 percent.[21] Another way to look at it is that the vast majority of Latinx are of Mexican origin (63 percent), followed by Puerto Rican (9.2 percent), Cuban (3.5 percent), Salvadoran (3.3 percent), and Dominican (2.8 percent).[22] States with a population of 1 million or more Latinx residents in 2018 were Arizona, California, Colorado, Florida, Georgia, Illinois, New Jersey, New Mexico, New York, and Texas.[23] According to U.S. Census Bureau projections, the Latinx population may reach 24 percent by the year 2065.[24]

Missing in the Census Bureau's Hispanic count are Puerto Ricans who live on the island of Puerto Rico (the population is fluctuating in response to the devastation wrought by Hurricanes Irma and Maria in 2017) and undocumented Latinx immigrants. No one knows how many undocumented immigrants are presently in the United States, although it is estimated that of the roughly 11.1 million undocumented

---

[21] U.S. Census Bureau, 2013–2017 American Community Survey 5-Year Estimates, https://factfinder.census.gov/.

[22] David Garoogian, ed., *The Hispanic Databook*, 3rd ed. (Amenia, NY: Grey House Publishing, 2012), 7.

[23] U.S. Census Bureau, "Annual Estimates of the Resident Population by Sex, Age, Race, and Hispanic Origin for the United States and States: April 1, 2010 to July 1, 2018," https://factfinder.census.gov/.

[24] Pew Research Center, "Modern Immigration Wave Brings 59 Million to U.S., Driving Population Growth and Change through 2065: Views of Immigration's Impact on U.S. Society Mixed" (Washington, DC: Pew Research Center, 2015), 10.

immigrants, about 8.99 million are Hispanic (71.6 percent of whom are of Mexican origin). After Mexicans, the next two largest groups are Guatemalans and Salvadorans.[25] This situation is further complicated by the Census Bureau's own admission of underrepresenting Hispanics (and other minority groups) by as much as 1.5 percent.[26] All this is to point out that if a true count of Latino/as were to be conducted, rather than a population of 59.9 million, the number would be closer to 73.2 million, or about 22 percent of the 2018 U.S. population. Undercounting Hispanics denies Latina/os hundreds of millions of dollars per year in federal money for health, social services, community development, and other governmental programs, as well as greater legislative representation. Misrepresented in the national consciousness, Hispanics also become misrepresented demographically.

It is common to hear Spanish spoken throughout the United States. In fact, Spanish is the second-most-spoken language, surpassed only by English (other languages in common use in the United States following Spanish are Chinese, French, Tagalog, and Vietnamese).[27] According to a 2015 report issued by the Instituto Cervantes, the United States had 41 million native Spanish speakers and 12 million who were bilingual Spanish and English. Uncounted in those numbers are the millions of undocumented immigrants from Latin America who might be native or bilingual Spanish speakers and who also speak an indigenous language. Among the nations in the Western Hemisphere, the United States has the fourth-largest Spanish-speaking population. Only Mexico, Colombia, and Argentina (in order) claim more Spanish-speaking people.[28]

While it is important to be aware of the role the Spanish language plays in Latinx religion and culture, speaking English is also part of being Latinx in the United States. In a 2015 report, the Pew Research Center stated that in 2013 approximately 33.2 million Hispanics in the

---

[25] Mary Seaborn, "By the Numbers: How America Tallies Its 11.1 Million Undocumented Immigrants," Pew Research Center, April 11, 2013, https://www.pewresearch.org/hispanic/2013/04/11/by-the-numbers-how-america-tallies-its-11-1-million-undocumented-immigrants/.

[26] U.S. Census Bureau, *Census Bureau Releases Estimates of Undercount and Overcount in the 2010 Census* (Washington, DC: U.S. Department of Commerce, 2012), http://www.census.gov/.

[27] U.S. Census Bureau, "Top Languages Other Than English Spoken in 1980 and Changes in Relative Rank, 1990-2010," https://www.census.gov, last revised August 2019.

[28] Claudio Iván Remeseira, "US Is 5th Largest Spanish-Speaking Country: New Census Interactive Map," NBCLatino News, August 7, 2013, http://nbclatino.com/2013/08/07/us-is-5th-largest-spanish-speaking-country-new-census-interactive-map/

United States speak English proficiently; 89 percent of U.S.-born Latinx do so, an increase of 17 percent since 1980. The segment of Latinx people who speak English proficiently is growing, while the percentage speaking Spanish at home is declining.[29] Such social and cultural shifts add another dimension to questions about how to define "Latinx."

To see Latinx and understand their religious perspectives, one must understand their present locations as well as their social, cultural, and religious roots. Drawing upon these broad demographic data concerning Latinx, we can make some initial observations about how Latinx peoples construct theological perspectives. These brief observations are explored in greater detail in subsequent chapters.

- Latinx people often are seen and experience life as "exiles, aliens, and outsiders." They are commonly seen through the eyes of the dominant culture, which is shaped by Euroamerican perspectives, as the marginalized "other," or outsider. This acutely influences Latinx approaches to religiosity and understanding of faith in alternative cultural spaces, drawing upon Latinx faith and life experiences and resources.
- Theology does not exist in a social vacuum but rather reflects specific sociopolitical locations. Consequently, any Latinx theology tends to represent the social, economic, political, and religious struggles of its people. As Elieser Valentín observes, "In many ways the political is tied to the theological."[30]
- Many Latinx come from conservative religious backgrounds that affect their moral and ethical decisions. A still-prevalent cultural tradition that celebrates early marriage and large families may contribute to a younger ethnic group when compared to the rest of the nation. As global capitalism continues to expand, the future workforce of the United States will have a disproportionately greater number of Latinx who nevertheless may face greater economic struggles than previous generations.
- Latinxs have disproportionately lower levels of educational attainment. Not surprisingly, this underrepresentation is also evident in formal theological education, where Latinx account for less than 3 percent of the total enrollment in accredited graduate seminaries. The low number of Latinx faculty serving as mentors and

---

[29] Jens Manuel Krogstad, Renee Stepler, and Mark Hugo Lopez, "English Proficiency on the Rise among Latinos; U.S. Born Driving Language Changes" (Washington, DC: Pew Research Center, May 2015), 4–5.

[30] Elieser Valentín, "Latino/a Religion and Politics," in Espín, *Wiley Blackwell Companion to Latino/a Theology*, 471.

advisers makes it difficult for institutions to offer curricula with a genuine Latinx component, thus contributing to a monolithic and Eurocentric education that ignores the variety of religious life within the United States. This in turn continues a vicious cycle of discouraging some Latinx from pursuing formal theological education.

Mapping the Religious Background of U.S. Latinx Theologies

Understanding the social locations and religious life and practices of Latino/as in the United States involves considering a wide range of rich and diverse multicultural backgrounds and roots. Religion in both Latin America and among U.S. Latinx is not exclusively Christian, and those U.S. Latina/os who are Christian are not exclusively Catholic or Protestant. Various Latinx groups often practice religious faith in ways that vary from dominant mainstream cultures. Generally speaking, the diversity of cultural and religious roots of Latinx falls into four main categories: (1) European; (2) numerous and diverse Indian or indigenous cultures of the Americas; (3) the complex and innovative beliefs and practices of Africa, primarily West Africa; and (4) Asian, to a smaller degree, a result of various empires transnational migration of peoples such as Filipinos to the United States, or Chinese to Mexico and the Caribbean.[31] These streams are brought together historically and culturally into a Caribbean and Latin American synthesis with profound regional differences. They then undergo further development and innovation in the context of North America, with the outcome that while there are discernible links between Latin American religions and Latinx religions in the United States, each is a distinct phenomenon.

Christians

The growing Latinx population and their distinct spiritual manifestations are transforming the U.S. religious landscape. According to a 2013 Pew Research Center study, more than 80 percent of Latinx identify with a specific Christian tradition. As Table 1.1 shows, approximately 55 percent of Latinx identified as Roman Catholics and 22 percent as Prot-

---

[31] See Freddy González, *Paisanos Chinos: Transpacific Politics among Chinese Immigrants in Mexico* (Oakland: University of California Press, 2017); Kathleen López, *Chinese Cubans: A Transnational History* (Chapel Hill: University of North Carolina Press, 2013); Robert Chao Romero, *The Chinese in Mexico, 1882–1940*, 2nd ed. (Tucson: University of Arizona Press, 2012).

estant—with 16 percent of Latinx Protestants identifying as evangelical and 3 percent identifying as Other Christian. The next-largest category is born-again or evangelical Hispanic Protestants (15 percent). While their numbers are growing, they remain disproportionately smaller than for non-Hispanic whites and blacks.[32] Complicating the religious map are Latinx Millennials and Generation Z, who, like other young U.S. adults, have lower rates of religious affiliation and commitment compared with older generations.[33]

Table 1.1. *Religious Affiliation of Hispanics*

U.S. Hispanic Adults		U.S. General Public	
Catholic	55%	Catholic	22
Protestant	22	Protestant	48
Evangelical	16	White evangelical	18
Mainline	5	White mainline	15
		Black Protestants	8
		Other Protestants	7
Other Christian	3	Other Christian	3
Jehovah's Witness	2		
Mormon	1		
Orthodox	*		
Other faiths	1	Other faiths	6
Unaffiliated	18	Unaffiliated	20
Atheist/agnostic	3	Atheist/agnostic	6
Nothing in particular	15	Nothing in particular	14
Don't know	*	Don't know	1

Source: Pew Research Center survey of Hispanic adults, May 24–July 28, 2013. Based on FORM12 and FORMNCO, N=4,080 (margin of error for FORM 12 and FORMNCO +/–2.4). Figures may not add to 100% due to rounding. U.S. general public figures from aggregated Pew Research surveys, May–July 2013. White evangelical, white mainline, and black Protestants are non-Hispanic. Other religious groups include some Hispanic respondents. In the figures for the general public, Jehovah's Witnesses are included in the Protestant category. Previous Pew Research surveys find that Jehovah's Witnesses make up 1% of the total U.S. adult population.

[32] Roberto Suro et al., *Changing Faiths: Latinos and the Transformation of American Religion* (Washington, DC: Pew Hispanic Center, 2007), 1, 17.

[33] Jessica Martínez and Michael Lipka, "Hispanic Millennials Are Less Religious Than Older U.S. Hispanics," Pew Research Center, May 8, 2014, https://www.pewresearch.org.

While the majority (82 percent) of Hispanics continue to participate in the same faith tradition as their parents, a growing minority (18 percent) changed their faith affiliation. Because most Latinx are Catholics, it shouldn't be surprising that many of these converts are former Catholics. For every Latinx who converts to Catholicism, four leave the faith. Of the 18 percent of Hispanics who converted, 13 of the 18 percent had been Catholics (3 of the 18 percent were Protestant and 2 percent indicated no religious affiliation).[34]

Roman Catholics

One of the most enduring myths about Latinx religiosity is that *all* Latinx are Catholic; certainly the majority are Catholic. In 2013 the majority (55 percent, or 19.6 million) of the estimated 35.4 million U.S. Latinx adults self-identified as Catholic, a decline from 67 percent in 2010. At the same time, the percentage of all U.S. Catholics who are Latinx is increasing, with researchers indicating that the percentage of U.S. Roman Catholics who are Latinx rose from about one-quarter in the 1980s to approximately 40 percent in 2014. The growth of the Latinx share of the U.S. Catholic population is attributed to the overall growth of the Latinx population itself. "If both trends continue, at some point in the future, it is possible that a majority of U.S. Catholics will be Hispanic, even though the majority of Hispanics will no longer be Catholic."[35]

Among Latinx Roman Catholics, approximately one-half self-identify as being charismatic (compared to only one-eighth of non-Latinx Catholics). A majority (68 percent) are foreign born, and most (55 percent) claim Spanish as their primary language. These Catholic Latinx tend to occupy a lower socioeconomic status, with roughly one in two (46 percent) having a total household income of under thirty thousand dollars a year, and a substantial minority (42 percent) not graduating high school.[36]

Some Latinx Catholics see themselves as "born-again," a term used mainly by some evangelicals and some Protestant groups. Cursillos de Cristiandad is a movement influential among Catholic Latinx. Originating in Franco's Spain and focusing on the sacraments, this conservative

---

[34] Miguel A. De La Torre, "Conversion," in *Encyclopedia on Hispanic American Religious Culture*, vol. 1, ed. Miguel A. De La Torre (St. Barbara, CA: ABC-CLIO, 2009) 156–59.

[35] Cary Funk and Jessica Martínez, "Fewer Hispanics Are Catholic, So How Can More Catholics Be Hispanic?" Pew Research Center, May 7, 2014, https://www.pewresearch.org.

[36] Ibid., 1, 7, 11.

and hierarchical lay movement had spread to the United States by the mid-1960s. These cursillos are retreat-type events where participants renew their faith commitment, thus providing Catholics with born-again-type experiences.[37]

Many Latinx Catholics link popular movements (e.g., sociopolitical movements for human rights and dignity) with ecclesiastical authority. Commitments to social justice, shaped by papal encyclicals and everyday struggles, are seen as expressions of faith. This development of a Latinx perspective of Catholic thought views the hierarchical nature of the church with suspicion, for at times it imitated the race and class divisions existing within the culture.[38]

Protestants, Evangélica/os, and Pentecostals

Latinx leaving Catholicism historically take one of two paths, either becoming born again as evangelical Protestants, or as pentecostal or charismatic Protestants, who sometimes also identify as being evangelical. Complicating the categorization is that all three groups—mainline Protestant, evangelical, and pentecostal/charismatic—use the Spanish term *evangélico/a*, which has a broader connotation than the English "evangelical." Some Latinx for generations now have never left Catholicism and have in addition always been some type of *evangélico/a*. Historian Juan Martínez notes that one sign of the arrival of Latinx Protestantism into the dominant culture's consciousness was the April 15, 2013, *Time* magazine cover story, "The Latino Reformation."[39] In that issue, *Time* profiled prominent Latino Protestant leaders Sammy Rodríguez, president of the National Hispanic Christian Leadership Conference (NHCLC), which claimed at the time to serve 40,118 churches; and Wilfredo "Choco" de Jesús, pastor of the New Life Covenant Church, the largest Assemblies of God church in the United States. A few years earlier, *Time* featured Luis Cortés, president of Esperanza USA as one of "The 25 Most Influential Evangelicals in America."[40]

For purposes of analysis we say a few words about each grouping of Latinx Protestants, acknowledging the overlap and that a Latinx in some

---

[37] Anthony M. Stevens-Arroyo, "Latino/a Catholic Theology," in *Handbook of Latina/o Theologies*, ed. Edwin David Aponte and Miguel A. De La Torre (St. Louis: Chalice Press, 2006), 175–76.

[38] Ibid., 169–76.

[39] Juan Francisco Martínez, *The Story of Latino Protestants in the United States* (Grand Rapids: Eerdmans, 2018), 1; "The Latino Reformation," *Time*, April 15, 2013.

[40] "The 25 Most Influential Evangelicals in America," *Time*, February 7, 2005.

cases may have multiple religious identities, for example, as a member of a mainline denomination who has had a born-again experience and also is charismatic.

In writing about his mainline Protestant (*protestante*) experience as a Methodist, David Maldonado observed, "To be Hispanic and Protestant means to exist in the margins of two realities, a Hispanic world in which being Protestant means being at the margins of a Catholic context, and a Protestant world in which being Hispanic means being at the margins of a non-Hispanic context."[41] Some Latinx Protestants may feel marginalized within a larger Latinx context, due in part to how mainline Eurocentric Protestant denominations came in contact with the Latina/o world. The first phase of contact occurred in the early 1820s, culminating with Texas's declaration of independence from Mexico and the subsequent Mexican-American War. During this time, a gradual increase began of Protestant evangelistic endeavors aimed at Mexican Catholics living in the newly conquered territories. Motivating factors for conversion included the opportunity of social mobility, continued grievances over both Roman Catholic doctrine and Spanish oppression, and the perceived social and economic benefits of assimilating to the dominant culture. The second phase began in the aftermath of the 1898 Spanish-American War. The opening of new territories in Central America and the Caribbean through conquest (Cuba and Puerto Rico) and economic exploitation (gunboat diplomacy) provided Protestants with greater opportunities for mainline Protestant evangelism.

Among Latinx Protestants, no denomination can claim exclusivity in the incorporation of Latinx into their congregations.[42] Conversion to Protestantism does not exclude Latinx converts from the prevalent racism and classism within the overall U.S. culture. The most significant challenges that Latinx mainline Protestants face are congregations tending to be poorer than Euroamerican Protestant churches within the same denomination, racial discrimination and limited resources from regional and national levels of the mainline denomination, and limited access to higher education, which contributes to a more working-class congregation led by non-seminary-trained clergy.[43] Although most Latinx Protestants identify as evangelicals or Pentecostals, or sometimes both, one in twenty (5 percent) identify as mainline Protestants. They tend to be native born (65 percent) and primarily speak English (45 percent).

---

[41] David Maldonado, ed., *Protestantes/Protestants: Hispanic Christianity within Mainline Traditions* (Nashville: Abingdon Press, 1999), 16.

[42] Suro et al., *Changing Faiths*, 1, 11.

[43] Alberto Hernández, "Historic Mainline Protestants," in Aponte and De La Torre, *Handbook of Latino/a Theologies*, 184–90.

Many (68 percent) have a high school diploma and a smaller percentage (29 percent) have a household income under thirty thousand dollars.[44]

Loida I. Martell-Otero, Zaida Maldonado Pérez, and Elizabeth Conde-Frazier define *evangélica/o* as "a particular popular Protestantism that arose in the Americas originally colonized by Spain and Portugal as a result of religious and spiritual influences of Iberian Catholic, African, and indigenous beliefs and their late encounter with various Protestant influences."[45] This understanding recognizes a type of hybridity inherent in *evangélica/o* persons. Latinx who identify as evangelicals may be more native born than Catholics (46 percent versus 32 percent); nevertheless, more than half (55 percent) are foreign born. Evangelicals have a slightly higher socioeconomic status than Catholics, with about two-thirds (64 percent) having a high school diploma and only 39 percent with total household income under thirty thousand dollars. Most (63 percent) say English is their primary language or that they are bilingual.[46] *Evangélico/as* view the Latinx church as empowered to usher in personal conversion and social transformation.

For the most part, the Latinx *evangélico/as* proclaim what they call "the entire gospel," so that the world can be transformed. The good news they hope to share is the liberating message of Christ, who died outside the gate, outside of church power and doctrines, outside the realm of privilege. Change within a sinful world is brought about through the repentance of sins (personal and public) and faith in Jesus Christ. Although hot-button issues like abortion, gay marriage, immigration, or family values may at times drive the political agenda of *evangélico/as*, only a liberating gospel, in their view, can transform and provide a public witness to the movement of God's hand among God's people.[47]

More than half of Latinx Protestants self-identify as being "Spirit-filled" pentecostal Christians.[48] Latinx Pentecostalism is a tradition grounded in an evangelical Christianity that stresses the gifts of the Spirit along with the baptism of the Spirit, manifested by speaking in tongues (glossolalia). A belief in *sola scriptura* (Scripture alone) is amplified by contemporary experience of the Spirit of God. There have been Latinx Pentecostals since the emergence of modern Pentecostalism in the early twentieth century, right

---

[44] Suro et al., *Changing Faiths*, 11.

[45] Loida I. Martell-Otero, Zaida Maldonado Pérez, and Elizabeth Conde-Frazier, *Latina Evangélicas: A Theological Survey from the Margins* (Eugene, OR: Cascade Books, 2013), 140.

[46] Suro et al., *Changing Faiths*, 1, 11.

[47] David Traverzo Galarza, "Evangélicos/as," in Aponte and De La Torre, *Handbook of Latino/a Theologies*, 193–97.

[48] Suro et al., *Changing Faiths*, 1.

through the present global pentecostal phenomenon in which so many U.S. Latinx and Latin Americans are leaders and participants.[49] The Latinx faith community attempts to enter the reality of the Holy Spirit's presence in the everyday, a presence that can be marked by physical or emotional healing, deliverance from a life-controlling problem, or miraculous deliverance from everyday obstacles. When poverty prevents proper medical care, the laying of hands to secure a healing fills a need for the believer. But healing encompasses more than simply physical ailments. It also encompasses deliverance from issues including drug or alcohol dependency. Healing services prove crucial in leading some Catholics to convert to Pentecostalism.[50]

Other Christian Traditions

Some Hispanics practice within faith traditions that emerged in the U.S. context, specifically Jehovah's Witnesses and Latter-Day Saints / Mormons. These faith traditions are categorized as "Other Christian" based on the research of many social scientists examining the U.S. religious landscape. Some people among the mainline Protestants, *Evangélica/os*, and Pentecostals just reviewed may argue that these religious communities are not Christians at all—a theological discussion that is beyond the scope of this book. To be sure, those Latinx who are Jehovah's Witnesses or members of the Church of Jesus Christ of Latter-Day Saints self-identify as Christians.

Jehovah's Witnesses

Worldwide, there are an estimated 2 million Jehovah's Witnesses representing Spanish-speaking nations. Within the United States, more than eight hundred thousand Latinx worship in more than twenty-two hundred Spanish-speaking congregations, making the Jehovah's Witnesses the largest non-Catholic faith tradition among Christians. This growth is expected to continue due to the organization having the highest conversion rate among Latinx immigrants. Jehovah's Witnesses' expansion within Latinx communities is similar to their expansion among other ethnic and racial groups. Their work among U.S. Latinx can be traced to 1932, when John Wahlberg, the only Witness living in Puerto Rico

---

[49] See Gastón Espinosa, *Latino Pentecostals in America: Faith and Politics in Action* (Cambridge, MA: Harvard University Press, 2014); Daniel Ramírez, *Migrating Faith: Pentecostalism in the United States and Mexico in the Twentieth Century* (Chapel Hill: University of North Carolina Press, 2015).

[50] Arlene M. Sánchez Walsh, "Pentecostals," in Aponte and De La Torre, *Handbook of Latino/a Theologies*, 199–205.

at the time, was joined by a married couple from the United States to evangelize the island. Ambrosio Rosa was the first Latinx convert in 1938. Today, twenty-seven Spanish translators, based in Puerto Rico, are responsible for rendering from English to Spanish all the Jehovah's Witnesses' literature distributed globally.[51]

Latter-Day Saints / Mormons

The first Latter-Day Saints, commonly known as Mormons, fled the United States after the arrest and murder of their prophet, Joseph Smith, in 1844 and settled as illegal aliens on then-Mexican territory in present-day Utah. By the second half of the nineteenth century, Mormons launched their first missions to Latin America. They were particularly interested in preaching to mestizos who were seen as the descendants of Lamanites, whom the Book of Mormon describes as descendants of the lost tribes of Israel who lapsed into barbarism and settled the Western Hemisphere, but whose conversion would usher in Christ's second coming. When Utah became a state and outlawed polygamy, Anglo Mormon polygamists fled, establishing colonies in Mexico. In the early twentieth century, three Latina sisters (Augustina, Dolores, and Domitila Rivera) launched missionary efforts among Latino/as moving to Utah to work in Mormon-owned industries, specifically sugar beet farms. The Lucero Ward, which they help established, is the oldest ethnic Mormon congregation within the United States. By 1939 Mormon literature was being translated into Spanish.[52] Mormons rank eighth among the Latinx's largest religious tradition.[53]

Other Expressions of the Faiths of People

If U.S. Latinx religious thought uses the existential lived faith of the Latinx people as a major starting point and resource, then the faith of U.S. Latinx naturally takes on a wide variety of forms and expressions. Other Latinx institutional and grassroots religious practices and devotions do not fit into the rubrics of any form of Christianity in their outlook or practice, yet they may form parts of the U.S. Latinx everyday

---

[51] Virginia Loubriel-Chévere, in "Jehovah's Witnesses," *Encyclopedia on Hispanic American Religious Culture*, vol. 1, ed. Miguel A. De La Torre (Santa Barbara, CA: ABC-CLIO Publishers, 2009), 312–13.

[52] John-Charles Duffy, "Mormons/Latter-Day Saints," in De La Torre, *Encyclopedia on Hispanic American Religious Culture*, 1:375–76.

[53] Miguel A. De La Torre, "Conversion," in De La Torre, *Encyclopedia on Hispanic American Religious Culture*, 1:157.

reality. Some of these expressions draw more heavily upon indigenous traditions or African sources. These alternatives are also manifestations and expressions of the grassroots faiths of Latinx, and they form other ways with which Latinx connect their concrete realities with doctrine, discipline, liturgy, and personal action. Through these alternatives, Latinx and their communities access routes of knowledge and understanding, pursue ways toward health and healing, and find accessible paths that furnish a sense of holistic balance in life.

Certain of the better-known alternative expressions and practices include *curanderismo*, a path of folk healing and medicine, different types of *espiritismo* or spiritism, and different types of African diaspora traditions and practices. Furthermore, some Latinx and their communities connect with several traditions simultaneously and in doing so create a hybrid spirituality that fails to see any contradiction or mutual exclusion in their multiple allegiances. Many persons in Latinx communities are in touch with all or part of these alternatives and still view themselves as members of Christian communities. Indeed, these multiple avenues appear as complementary and acceptable combinations for faith and life. Carlos Cardoza-Orlandi relates the story of a Dominican family in New York City who were members of a Protestant church that he pastored. When their child was gravely sick, the family asked the Protestant congregation for prayer and visited a *santero*, a healer. The child regained health. Cardoza-Orlandi relates, "In a moment of confusion and surprise, I asked the father, 'Whose miracle is it? Is it your *orisha*? Is it Jesus Christ?' The father, puzzled by the question, looked at me and said, 'It was God, Pastor, it was God. It is your problem to decide whose miracle it is, not my problem.'"[54]

Curanderismo

Curanderismo, or folk healing and medicine, has many expressions. The name finds its roots in the Spanish verb *curar*, "to heal, cure." Mexican American or Chicano/a/x *curanderismo* is a dynamic and fluid combination of indigenous Mesoamerican and Spanish popular religious outlooks and orientations to the physical world and spiritual realms, expressed in healing and health practices. Mexican American *curanderismo* developed into an extensive health-care system that assumes sickness can have either natural or supernatural causes, and may require

---

[54] Carlos Cardoza-Orlandi, "Drum Beats of Resistance and Liberation: Afro-Caribbean Religions, the Struggle for Life, and the Christian Theologian," *Journal of Hispanic/Latino Theology* 3, no. 1 (1995): 56.

a natural or supernatural cure, or a combination of both. For many, it serves as an alternative to modern medical services that are not available. Luis León describes community-based healing *curanderismo* as including "somatic techniques of power; from home remedies such as herbal teas and ointments, to spiritual or symbolic open-heart surgery, and other spiritual operations conducted to heal cancer, for example. Social ills and family problems are also addressed in *curanderismo*."[55]

Curanderismo contains an extensive collection of rituals and customs, explanatory stories, and a symbolic system for understanding sickness, health, and life. *Curandero/as* are specialized healers who are from the people but also are recognized as having received special supernatural abilities—a gift or *el dón* from God for discernment and healing. The healers inherit and transmit the ancient ways and knowledge to the next generation, including the remedies for a variety of sicknesses, physical complaints, and injuries. Rather than independent agents, each healer really is part of a sophisticated alternative worldview with a hierarchy of healers and a complex way of understanding the world.

Curanderismo involves a complex interplay between material and immaterial worlds. *Mal de ojo* (the evil eye) and *susto* (loss of spirit and deep profound discouragement and hopelessness) are considered afflictions on several levels: material, spiritual, and mental. Physical symptoms are believed to have supernatural or spiritual causes. *Limpias* (cleansing rituals) are common practices performed to restore balance to the body, or the *curandera/o* may prescribe an herbal remedy. The cure may employ a type of counter-magic, herbal remedies, potions, or rituals, depending on the illness, and may use ordinary religious symbols like the crucifix, rosary, or holy pictures.[56]

As a spiritual specialist, a *curandero/a* is the healer who can treat *mal puesto* (illnesses caused by evil spell or hex), usually as the result of the work of a *brujo* or *bruja* (witches). Spiritual interpretation is important to the people who come to *curandera/os*; thus it is not uncommon that the local Catholic priest may be the second choice of a person for consultation. Catholic pastoral workers vary in their attitudes toward *curanderismo*, whereas there is widespread opposition among Latinx Protestants (especially evangelicals and Pentecostals), who view *curanderismo* as the work of the devil.

---

[55] Luis D. León, *Religious Movement in the United States–Mexico Borderlands: Toward a Theory of Chicana/o Religious Poetics* (Ph.D. diss., University of California, Santa Barbara, 1997), 187.

[56] Fernando A. Ortiz and Kenneth G. Davis, "Curanderismo," in De La Torre, *Encyclopedia on Hispanic American Religious Culture*, 1:179–85.

Espiritismo

Founded by Hippolyte Rivail, who wrote under the pseudonym Allan Kardec, *espiritismo* originated in France and spread to the Western Hemisphere in the mid-nineteenth century. Kardecism, or spiritism, was considered by its adherents to be a combination of positive science, progressivist ideology, Christian morality, and mysticism. As spiritism spread, it developed unique manifestations that were quite adaptable to local contexts. The *espiritismo* practiced in Puerto Rico differed considerably from that practiced in Mexico, Argentina, or Brazil. In fact, even within the same country, different social classes or races practiced *espiritismo* differently. *Espiritismo* has absorbed into its practice elements of Spanish folk religion, herbalism, African religious practices, and indigenous healing practices.

Espiritismo first took the form of small groups of mediums assisting their clients in communicating with the spirits of the dead. It was believed that good and evil spirits existed that can affect a person's life. Séances became a central practice and were called *misas* (masses) that would center on an altar called a *boveda espiritual* or *mesa blanca* (white table). Believers would gather in a home, sit around a table, and make specific invocations. This simple table with a white linen would have from one to nine glasses filled with cool water (each glass representing an ancestor or spiritual guide), flowers with sweet basil, a crucifix, incense and/or perfume, Kardec's book of prayers, and a lit candle. Offerings, such as food, candy, rum, or cigars, were left for the dead. By gazing at the glasses of water and reciting the prayers, the medium was able to create a spiritual environment where the medium could be possessed by the dead to become a conduit to the spirit world.[57] The mediums insisted that their practice was pure experimental science, and the practitioner verified the experience by speaking with the dead through the medium, who provided immediate solutions to what ailed them; hence they were called *científicos* (scientists).

Among the first to be attracted to this movement were the Creole middle and upper classes, from which spiritism spread to other urban groups of less power and privilege, eventually reaching the rural countryside. The poorer segments of society turned to *espiritismo* for help and guidance with the struggle of daily life, specifically in areas of material depravity or health problems. In the Spanish Caribbean—particularly in Cuba and Puerto Rico, which were still under Spain's colonial yoke—

---

[57] George Brandon, *Santería from Africa to the New World: The Dead Sell Memories* (Indianapolis: Indiana University Press, 1997), 85–87; Miguel A. De La Torre, "Espiritualismo," in De La Torre, *Encyclopedia on Hispanic American Religious Culture*, 1:220–24.

independistas (freedom fighters) found in *espiritismo* an alternative to the Roman Catholic Church, which was perceived to be in league with the Spanish monarchy. Amid suppression of political organizations that challenged the colonial authority, *espiritismo* served as a political space for liberal ideas to flourish. For those who considered themselves Catholic even though they seldom visited a church or a priest, the practice of *espiritismo* did not conflict with their religious worldview. Others found in *espiritismo* a progressive ideology advocating science, modernity, and democracy. Still others connected to their pre-Christian past of ancestral spirits that encouraged different religious practices historically that the official church repressed.

Santería

During the 1950s the character of Ricky Ricardo in the seminal television sitcom *I Love Lucy* sang his signature song, "Babalu-Aye." Most viewers did not know that Ricky Ricardo was singing to one of the semigods or Orishas of the Afro-Cuban religion known as Santería. In reality, several religious-cultural structures, all originating in Africa, live within the Latinx cultures. They are *palo monte* of Kongo origin; the *regla Arará* of Ewe-fon origin; the *Abakuá* Secret Society containing *Ejagham, Efik, Efut,* and other Calabar roots; and the *regla de Ocha* of Yoruba. The last of these, in the form of Santería, is the most popular among U.S. Latinx.

Santería, also known as *Lukumí,* "is a Cuban religion of African roots. It is a direct descendant of the Yoruba traditional religion of colonial Nigeria."[58] Santería, from the Spanish word *santo* (saint), literally means "the way of saints" that was originated when enslaved Africans were brought from their homeland to colonial Cuba and forced to adopt Catholicism. They recognized existing parallels between their Yoruba religious beliefs and this new religion of their slave masters. Santería recognizes the existence of one supreme God, Olodumare. This transcendent supreme being is a world force or "current" known as *ashé.* This sacred energy becomes the power, grace, blood, and life force of Olodumare and nature, embracing all mystery, all secret power, and all divinity. "So, everything and everyone has *ashé,* lives by it and because of it, and needs it to survive. . . . The essence of Santeria, then is the concern for *ashé.* This *ashé* is the essence and the 'substance' of God."[59]

---

[58] Orlando Espín, "Santería," in *An Introductory Dictionary of Theology and Religious Studies,* ed. Orlando O. Espín and James B. Nickoloff (Collegeville, MN: Liturgical Press, 2007), 1218.

[59] Ibid., 1219.

Adherents of Afro-Cuban Santería/*Lukumí* religion believe in the existence of intermediary beings involved in daily life called Orishas (*orichas* in Spanish). Orishas are considered by some as quasi-deities serving as protectors and guides for every human being. They were the first to walk the earth, and from them all humans are descended. The Orishas are the first ancestors, created by the supreme God, Olodumare, and are the specific parts, forces, or manifestations within Olodumare, governing certain parts of the universe. Because the universe is so vast, Olodumare is not directly involved in the daily affairs of humans. Consequently, when an animal is sacrificed to Babalu-Aye (who governs the sphere of illness), the practitioner is worshiping the part of Olodumare exemplified in this particular Orisha.

Catholic saints were interpreted as outward manifestations of African Orishas. So, while the believer bent their knees to venerate Saint Lazarus, in reality, the believer was invoking the African Orisha known as Babalu-Aye, who revealed himself to the white Catholic masters as Saint Lazarus. These Orishas, manifested as Catholic saints, are recognized as the power brokers between the most high God and humanity. Orishas personify the forces of nature; manifest themselves as amoral powers; can be virtuous or exhibit vices as they express emotions, desires, needs, and wants; and can have either positive or negative implications for humans.

A *santero/a*, who also serves as priest, is consecrated to a specific Orisha, becoming representative of that specific divine force. This reflects the era when the inhabitants of each Yoruba city-state served as "priest" to a sole Orisha, the one who protected that particular city. Santería's components consist of an Iberian Christianity shaped by the Counter-Reformation and Spanish folk Catholicism blended together with African Orisha worship as practiced by the Yoruba of Nigeria and as modified by nineteenth-century Kardecan spiritualism. Santería can best be understood as the product of a shared hybrid sacred space caused by the cultural mix of Christianity and African beliefs, brought about by the introduction of slaves in the Americas.[60]

As the faith system of the marginalized, Santería has always been an underground religion in Cuba and the United States, due to its historical persecution. It was a slave religion that strengthened an oppressed people's will to survive. With the exodus of Cubans immediately following the Cuban Revolution of 1959, Santería was brought to the United States by new refugees. It was recognized as a legitimate religion on June 11, 1993, when the U.S. Supreme Court ruled that Santería prac-

---

[60] Miguel A. De La Torre, *Santería: The Beliefs and Rituals of a Growing Religion in America* (Grand Rapids: Eerdmans, 2004), xi–xiv.

titioners had a constitutional right to sacrifice animals in connection with their rituals.[61]

Santería is an amorphous and practical religion that promises power in dealing with life's hardships, power that is manifested in a variety of ways depending on the believer's situation. Santería has been an expression of a people's attitude toward finding harmony between one's life and one's environment, community, and the spiritual realm. In a very real sense, Santería is created by the disenfranchised to resist their annihilation, a religious expression that protests their subjugation and provides a way of cultural resistance.[62]

Recognizing Latinx Hybridity

Due to persecution, many practitioners of *curanderismo, espiritismo,* and Santería maintained an outward appearance of belief in the dominant social religion. For example, Orishas in Santería can appear as male or female, such as Changó, the male warrior, as Saint Barbara; or Obatalá, the father of the Orishas, as Our Lady of Mercy. Over time, official faith traditions began to share quite similar sacred spaces with these so-called unorthodox religious expressions. Some in the Catholic Church see these expressions as an authentic search of believers to grasp the reality of the Divine and the priest's role to be one of gently correcting practitioners of the unofficial religion. Others voice harsher criticism, claiming that *curanderismo, espiritismo,* and Santería adulterate the purity of Catholicism. For Protestants, specifically *Evangelico/as* and Pentecostals, these religious expressions represent Satanic cults. For those attempting to assimilate to Euroamerican culture, they become a source of embarrassment, appearing as backward and primitive.

Christians usually portray *curanderismo, espiritismo,* and Santería as the dialectical product of an indigenous belief system and Iberian Roman Catholicism, in which a "confused" and idiosyncratic merging of the traditions occurred. Throughout the Americas, however, the phenomenon of cultural groups simultaneously participating in two diverse, if not contradictory, religious systems is widespread. Christianity, when embraced under the context of colonialism or slavery, created a threat to the indigenous beliefs of the marginalized group, which, to resist annihilation, needed to adopt to the new dominant religion. The vitality of African belief systems found expression through Catholicism as *Vodou* in Haiti, *Shango* in Trinidad and Venezuela, *Candomblé* in Brazil, *Kumina* in Jamaica, and Santería in Cuba.

---

[61] Church of Lukumi Babalu Aye, Inc. v. City of Hialeah, 508 U.S. 520 (1993).
[62] De La Torre, *Santería,* 179–81.

For practitioners of Santería who were raised in homes where this religious expression flourished generally consider themselves also as good and faithful Catholics. Such persons may have been initiated into Santería yet still attended parochial school, participated in receiving First Communion, practiced weekly confession, and were confirmed by the church. At nights crowds would still visit their home to consult the Orishas. In these cases, no internal confusion exists among the participants as to the difference between what was done at the Catholic Church and in their home. Different practices take place in different settings. There are *santera/os* who declare, "*Somos católicos romanos, y apostólicos* [We are apostolic Roman Catholics], *creemos a nuestra manera* [We believe in our own way]." While both religions shared the same sacred space, there was no confusion among those practicing Santería—or *curanderismo* or *espiritismo*, for that matter—concerning the differences between them and *los curas y monjas* (priest and nuns).

So, are *curanderismo*, *espiritismo*, and Santería popular forms of Christianity? Indeed, is a Christian categorization needed for them? While such a label may help elucidate their genesis, it hinders understanding them as present-day hybrid and transcultural phenomena. As genuinely popular religious expressions, rooted in the violent contact of separate religious faiths, they contribute on their own terms to a U.S. Latinx theological view. Some people see that one can be a Catholic and a *santero*, or a Baptist and an *espiritista*, or even a Catholic and a Protestant. As U.S. Latinx religious expressions continue to evolve, new hybrid manifestations of what it means to be spiritual are developing that are as hybrid as Latinx identity.

Non-Christian Expressions of the Faith of the People

Even though less than 1 percent of the U.S. Latinx population identify as belonging to a non-Christian faith tradition, it is still important to explore these different manifestations of the faith of the people.[63] Eight percent of Latina/os identify as having no religious affiliation or self-identify as agnostic or atheist.[64] Those self-identifying as secular were financially better off, with about a third earning in excess of fifty thousand dollars (compared to only 17 percent of all Hispanics). The majority are native born (54 percent) and either are primarily English speakers or are bilingual (68 percent). Additionally, 20 percent had a college diploma, compared with 10 percent of all Latino/as).[65] Also, a

---

[63] Suro et al., *Changing Faiths*, 7. See also Table 1.1 in this chapter.

[64] Suro et al., *Changing Faiths*, 7.

[65] Miguel A. De La Torre, "Conversion," in De La Torre, *Encyclopedia on Hispanic American Religious Culture*, 1:158.

small but growing number of Latino/as are turning to Buddhism, engaging its religious practices with their experiences of marginality and suffering, seeking healing. In 1992 the Shambhala Meditation Center was established in San Antonio, Texas, by Elisa Gonzalez. In the economically disenfranchised community of Westside in San Antonio, a Spanish-speaking Vajrayana study group meets.[66] Although Latinx people can be found participating in a multiple of faith traditions, for purposes of this chapter, we concentrate on two: Judaism and Islam.

Latinx Jews

With the expansion of the Roman Empire, Jewish communities existed in every corner of the empire, including the Iberian Peninsula. There they flourished. Although periodically persecuted by both Christian and Muslim rulers, a large and culturally thriving Jewish community sustained itself. They were so successful that, to this day, a significant portion of the Jewish world is known as Sephardi, which means "Spanish." In spite of persecutions, many Iberian Jews served as advisers, linguists, and financiers in Muslim and Christian courts.

Today, estimates show approximately one hundred thousand Hispanic Jews within the United States, most coming from Mexico and Argentina. However, these numbers are skewed when we recognize that in some cities, like Los Angeles, 95 percent of Latina/o Jews self-identify as white and/or Caucasian.[67] Any discussion of U.S. Hispanic Jews must start profiling the historical significance of the Jewish *conversos* (converts). Throughout much of the Middle Ages, Iberia, the region now consisting of Spain and Portugal, was home to a significant Jewish community. As the Christian kingdoms of Iberia embarked on a campaign of *reconquista* (reconquest) of lands under Moorish (Muslim) control, Jews within those lands often faced the choice of conversion, expulsion, or worse. Many tried to escape persecution in Spain by going to the "Indies" (the Americas). Some changed their names to very Christian-sounding names (e.g., Jesús de la Cruz) to circumvent the royal decree that Jews could not immigrate to the new lands. Nevertheless, the Inquisition pursued them into the New World. Records of the Inquisition in New Spain (Mexico), Peru, and New Granada (Colombia, Venezuela, and Panama) show the surnames of *conversos* who were tried for relapsing into Judaism. Several *conversos* fled to the north, the farthest

---

[66] Oswald John Nira, "Buddhism," in De La Torre, *Encyclopedia on Hispanic American Religious Culture*, 1:90.

[67] Anna Adams, "Jews," in De La Torre, *Encyclopedia on Hispanic American Religious Culture*, 1:314–15.

reaches of the empire, into what is now California, Texas, New Mexico, and Arizona, where many of their descendants still live. For descendants of these exiles from Latin America, Judaism has been an uninterrupted faith, while for many others it has been a well-kept but persistent secret in family histories.

In recent years, particularly in the U.S. Southwest, Hispanics who have followed Catholicism for generations are investigating their possible family heritage as Jews from Spain or Portugal. Many times, clues in the popular religiosity of a family prompt searches for roots and a spiritual home.[68] For instance, a particular dialect of Spanish used in devotion is discovered to actually be *Ladino*, the common language of Sefarad. Or Latinx members of a family realize that they have never owned a crucifix despite their tradition of Roman Catholicism. Some families have the tradition of never eating shellfish or pork. A grandmother might teach her daughters to light candles on Friday nights. Another person remembers that a grandfather may have had the habit of going off to a remote location with other men for weekly prayers. There are reports of grandmothers telling a granddaughter that the family had always been Jewish.

Family rites, rituals, stories, objects—all the elements of popular religiosity are the clues that some Latinx are following to rediscover their Jewish heritage. Once the family secret becomes known, some New Mexican Hispano/as have decided to lay aside the religion in which they were raised in favor of the religion of their ancestors. As they seek a new place in their community, these Latinx converts find opposition from Jews who believe they are not authentically Jewish, while some Christians charge them with abandoning their faith.

In addition to those reconnecting with Jewish heritage, some Latin American Jewish communities have struggled as a marginalized people. Latin American Jewish communities were supplemented by later arrivals from Eastern Europe after World War II who settled in Argentina, Bolivia, Brazil, Colombia, and Mexico, bringing their cultural influences to the Latin American mix. As some of their members have come to the United States and become part of Latinx communities, they bring their religion and popular religiosity with them. As an example, Cuba has long been a major site for settlement of Jews who were refugees from persecution.

---

[68] See Stanley M. Hordes, *To the End of the Earth: A History of the Crypto-Jews of New Mexico* (New York: Columbia University Press, 2005); Cary Herz, Ori Z. Soltes, and Mona Hernandez, *New Mexico's Crypto-Jews: Image and Memory* (Albuquerque: University of New Mexico Press, 2007); and Ilan Stavans and Steve Sheinkin, *El Iluminado: A Graphic Novel* (New York: Basic Books, 2012).

Spanish and Portuguese Jews arrived either with the conquering Spaniards as *conversos* and crypto-Jews (secret Jews) or in later migrations from the island of Curaçao, the center of Sephardic culture in the Caribbean. In the late nineteenth and early twentieth centuries, migrations of Jews to Puerto Rico and Cuba took place.[69] There were additional migrations of European Jews prior to World War II, although in 1937 a ship called the *St. Louis*, carrying 937 Jewish refugees from Germany, was turned away from both Cuba and the United States. Today, one identifiable Latinx Jewish community exists in Miami Beach, composed of Cuban Jews, known as "Jubans" by the Miami exilic community.

Latinx Muslims

An additional manifestation of the faith of the Latinx people is members of Islam, the second-largest religion in the world. This includes both historical factors and the more recent embracing of Islam by Latinx in the United States.[70] While still small in numbers, the U.S. Latinx Muslim population is rapidly increasing.[71] The historical echoes of contemporary Latinx Muslims can be traced to 711 CE, when a small army crossed the Straits of Gibraltar to spread the new faith into Western Europe via the Iberian Peninsula. These Muslims were eventually stopped at the Battle of Tours by Charles Martel in 732 CE. Still, they took possession of most of Iberia. From the very start of the Muslim presence in Iberia, a concerted Christian effort started to reclaim lost lands under the rubric of the *reconquista*. This idea of holy war had a significant impact on the development of the Spanish kingdoms and the subsequent colonization of Latin America. The seven-hundred-year-old struggle to reclaim the land merged nationalism with Catholicism, whereby holy war became an expression of faith.

The formal presence of Islam in Iberia, lasting nearly seven hundred years, left a profound and sometimes forgotten influence on Spanish and Portuguese culture. This imprint was transferred to the Americas with

---

[69] Ruth Behar, *An Island Called Home: Returning to Jewish Cuba* (New Brunswick, NJ: Rutgers University Press, 2007).

[70] In 2015 the estimates of U.S. Latinx Muslims were between 52,000 and 198,000. See Harold D. Morales, *Latino and Muslim: Race, Religion, and the Making of a New Minority* (New York: Oxford University Press, 2018), 7; and Hjamil A. Martínez-Vázquez, "Islam," in De La Torre, *Encyclopedia on Hispanic American Religious Culture*, 1:306.

[71] Hjamil A. Martínez-Vásquez, *Latina/o and Musulmán: The Construction of Latina/o Identity among Latina/o Muslims in the United States* (Eugene, OR: Pickwick, 2010), 2–3.

migration and is an element in the mestizaje of Latin America and in the United States. Spanish literature, music, and thought are filled with African and Islamic themes. In fact, some people see a Moorish influence in Mexican American *curanderismo*.

Just as some Latinx are exploring the possibility of Iberian Jewish roots, others are finding a connection with their Muslim heritage from Spain. With roots in the 1970s, the Latinx Alianza Islámica, a mosque and community center, emerged in New York City's El Barrio (Spanish Harlem) in the 1980s and 1990s. There are sizable communities of Latinx Muslims in major metropolitan areas like Chicago, Houston, Los Angeles, Miami, Newark, and New York City. In recent years a small but growing number of Latinx are "converting" to Islam, although some of these Latinx Muslims do not use the language of conversion, but rather "reversion," as in "going back" to their historical, cultural, and spiritual Moorish roots. Many describe their reversion or conversion as an intellectual, emotional, and spiritual journey spanning years. Harold D. Morales summarizes the experience of those who came from a Christian background and converted to Islam: "Like many other Latinos who leave the church, Latino Muslims cite a desire for a more direct experience of God as a central motive for conversion along with finding the tenets and practices of Islam more appealing, the Islamic critique of class- and race-based inequality compelling, and their familial and intermarriage connections as significant."[72]

Seeing and Mapping Latinx Theologies

According to sales figures, in 1992 ketchup ceased being the favorite condiment in the United States, losing out to salsa. But taste buds are not the only thing the growing Latinx presence is affecting. Many in the United States cheer for Latinx sports personalities like baseball figures Miguel Cabrera, Manny Machado, or Albert Pujols. Boxing legends include Oscar de la Hoya and Wilfredo Gomez. The literary works of Julia Alvarez, Sandra Cisneros, Junot Díaz, Christina Garcia, Oscar Hijuelos, and Esmeralda Santiago are widely read. People move to the Latin rhythms of Pitbull, Celia Cruz, Marc Antony, Shakira, and Gloria Estefan. Moreover, the hip-hop songs of Lin-Manuel Miranda's musical *Hamilton* are sung around the world. Countless lives in the United States have been improved by the contributions made by Nobel Prize winners like Luis Walter Alvarez, Mario Molina, and Severo Ochoa. Every aspect of American life has been influenced by the Latinx presence, including

---

[72] Morales, *Latino and Muslim*, 9–10.

religion—specifically, how Americans conduct rituals, understand doctrinal truths, or do church. To ignore Latinx contributions to the public and private discourses of U.S. religiosity and culture is to ignore a major segment of the American population's religion and spirituality.

There is no one simple way of looking at Latinx religious life in the United States. Whatever perspective one adopts, as one gazes at Latinx Christianity in the United States, it becomes abundantly clear that the terrain is richly varied, with many important features. Myriad factors need to be considered to obtain undistorted pictures of Latinx religious and theological thought.

The subsequent chapters present a particular way of mapping Latinx theologies. We consider the full complexity of Latinx cultural life along with its religious expressions. The map we want to construct recognizes other, equally legitimate ways of seeing Latinx religions and spirituality. Of particular concern to this volume is how Latinx in the United States see the Divine, sacred texts, their churches and other faith communities, their own stories, and their rituals, particularly as these perspectives appear in some of the shared features of Latinx theologies.

2

Common Cultural Themes within a Community-Based Theology

"Theology" is often defined as "the study of God," and from the eighteenth century through the present, many theologians have increasingly emphasized God as the object of their analysis and scholarship rather than concentrating on themselves as practitioners of the theologies they articulate. This distancing of those who do and write formal theology from those who try to live out a theology can be problematic. Yet to understand the nature and functions of theology, we first need to focus upon the unmentioned subject of this definition: Who is doing the studying? Why are they doing the theology? What are the motivations that compel anyone to do this type of work? Theology may aspire toward eternal and universal truths about the nature and essence of God and the meaning of human existence, or theological study can be solely a descriptive enterprise done with a dispassionate detachment. Whatever the reasons one might choose to engage in theological study, all theology is done by human beings, limited by their finite identities and their place in society, culture, and history. Catholic theologian Orlando Espín asserts, "Theology is not a monologue or a parroting exercise. Theology is crafted and engaged *en conjunto*, whether we are aware of it and want to admit it or not."[1] Consequently, rather than some intellectual soliloquy, to do theology holistically is to participate in an ongoing communal process arising from actual people and communities, particular places, and specific contexts.

Theology as done primarily by men (of all races) working within the parameters of the dominant hegemonic Eurocentric culture necessarily

---

[1] Orlando O. Espín, *Idol and Grace: On Traditioning and Subversive Hope* (Maryknoll, NY: Orbis Books, 2014), ix.

differs from the types of theology done by African Americans, Asian/ Pacific Americans, Native Americans, or Latinx peoples. Eurocentric-based theologies have positioned themselves historically and socially as the center in worldwide theological thought, as though they were more objective, self-evident, and legitimate. Any theology constructed by others not in the self-appointed theological center is delegated to the periphery, automatically becoming a response to, or a dialogue with, or even an exotic add-on special topic, in relation to the issues that the center deems most important. Any attempt by marginalized people to study God apart from any self-appointed center risks ridicule and being disregarded as nonscholarly. Unless established authorities such as those found in the mainstream Eurocentric tradition are mentioned, such as Augustine, Anselm, or Thomas Aquinas, theologies from the supposed margins are often considered lightweight and irrelevant. However, theology done at the self-appointed center is still considered to be relevant to all communities without ever having to mention, discuss, or understand other voices in the history of the church whom Latinx theologians draw upon, such as Teresa de Ávila, Juan de la Cruz, or Sor Juana Inés de la Cruz, to just name a few.

The family of Latinx theologies can be understood as the study of God and ultimate meaning from alternative places sometimes called "the margins" of North American society and culture. Latinx theologies are shaped by myriad sources and contexts. At their very best, Latinx theologies accomplish many different tasks while seeking to be relevant to Latinx's daily lives. As scholars continue to investigate, enumerate, and identify all of these sources, there is agreement that the Latinx experience in the ordinariness of the everyday is paramount for developing their theological perspectives. While it may seem trite, it is nevertheless true that if there were no Latinx communities, there would be no Latinx theologies. Thus, Latinx theologies become a distinct type of God-talk arising from specific community contexts whose functions are as follows:

- To understand the Divine from within Latinx social, cultural, political, religious, and spiritual locations
- To seek God's liberative will in the face of cultural, social, political, and economic oppressions and injustice
- To search for a common voice that proclaims salvation, liberation, justice, and reconciliation to the most diverse segments of the Latinx cultures
- To create theological coordination between the U.S. Latinx condition, scriptural narratives, received traditions (both institutional and grassroots), and life experiences

- To struggle against the way Latinx are perceived and conceived by culturally dominant cultures
- To provide prophetic voices that unmask the racism, classism, sexism, and political and economic oppressions implicit in the theologies of dominant white cultures

If Latinx theologies are the theological reflections of diverse peoples labeled "Latinx," we must begin with an effort to understand how the communities see, define, and understand themselves while avoiding the temptation of essentializing a people. We must discern the variety of Latinx social and cultural locations to comprehend these conceptions of and dialogue with God. This is accomplished when the study of Latinx theologies begins by elucidating their own Latinx *comunidad*, their community in all their distinctiveness and complexity. *Comunidad* becomes a touchstone by which to comprehend Latinx's perception of God and themselves, the starting point in developing specific and con-textualized Latinx theological perspectives in relationship to their social and cultural realities.

Since Latinx are not a monolithic group, any attempt to define their *comunidad* by listing superficial, stereotypical denominators—positive or negative—does violence to the realities and dignity of Latinx, who, after all, are of many races, ethnicities, national origins, and generations who live across the entire United States and Puerto Rico. Latinx communities are as different as the colors of the rainbow. When the practice and discussions of Latinx grassroots communities are consulted, common themes do recur in the shared attempt to understand God. As one of the authors has written elsewhere, "The job of the scholar is to translate this grassroots praxis to a more general audience in an accessible matter (oblique writing does not equal brilliance) so to raise the consciousness of society."[2]

While these recurring themes are neither universal nor applicable to every Latinx group found in the United States, they do serve as impor-tant clues, exposing the basic foundations that underlie and support the multiple perspectives existing in Latinx theologies. Theologian Nancy Pineda-Madrid reflects on the importance of community as being some-thing more than an informal gathering of people without "a shared his-tory or vision of itself. Rather, a body of people becomes a community as a result of a particular process of *interpretation*. Interpretation is *the way* community is formed and sustained. Ultimately, salvation in history

---

[2] Miguel A. De La Torre, *The U.S. Immigration Crisis: Toward an Ethics of Place* (Eugene, OR: Cascade Books, 2016), xiv.

is actualized through a particular kind of community."[3] Without a doubt, Latinx cultural roots help shape the community-based interpretations and theologies of Latinx, including how Latinx regard aspects of Christian theology such as God and the personhood of Jesus Christ, how they read and interpret the Bible and other sacred texts, how they worship and praise God, and how they understand and practice the justice-based teachings of the gospel. This chapter lays the groundwork for grasping how Latinx do theology by first exploring the cultural roots that influence the construction of Latinx theology, and then reviewing some of the significant aspects of the resulting theologies.

Cultural Roots Influencing Latinx Theologies

Since the Spanish language was introduced into the Western Hemisphere during the time of European exploration, exploitation, and colonization, those who speak Spanish in the United States today are nonetheless viewed as newcomers. Yet a glance at a U.S. map demonstrates long-term Hispanic influences in the nation's geography. States carry the names Nevada, Florida, and Colorado instead of Snow, Flowered, and Red-Colored. Cities and towns across the nation are named Los Angeles, Santa Fe, San Antonio, Española, and El Paso instead of The Angels, Holy Faith, St. Anthony, Spanish Lady, and The Pass. There are even Spanglish place names, such as St. Augustine in Florida. These geographic place names bear witness to the Latinx heritage and presence. Regardless of the fact that the majority of the first European settlers in what was to become the United States came from Spain, their descendants—who are part of the contemporary Latinx people after some five hundred years—are still seen by the dominant culture as exiles, aliens, outsiders, and unwelcome intruders.

Even though the population of the United States is becoming increasingly diverse, in recent years, and especially since the 2016 presidential election, certain unprincipled politicians and media commentators have encouraged open resentment and animosity toward Latinx. Latinx persons and communities, whether U.S. citizens or recent migrants, have been characterized as untrustworthy and biased; as violent gang members; and as undocumented, job-stealing immigrants unwilling to learn English, seeking to cheat the American people and the U.S. government. But those negative stereotypes do not reflect the history of the emergence of Latinx in the United States. Some Latinx trace their presence to

---

[3] Nancy Pineda-Madrid, *Suffering and Salvation in Ciudad Juárez* (Minneapolis: Fortress Press, 2011), 133.

overt military conquests by the United States (such as Mexicans, Puerto Ricans, and Panamanians).[4] Others, such as Cubans, Dominicans, and Central Americans, can trace the pathways of U.S. Latinx presence as a result of late-nineteenth-century gunboat diplomacy and twentieth-century imperial capitalism.[5] Still others are the victims of geopolitical struggles played out in their homelands, in which the United States participated in or covertly supported regime change (Chileans, Argentines, Venezuelans, and Colombians).[6]

Mexicans (some who self-identify as Chicana/o/x) and Puerto Ricans, whose presence is a direct consequence of U.S. territorial expansion, are treated as foreigners and aliens in their own lands. Chicana/o/x occupied the land that would eventually be known as the United States for centuries before the European invasion. Virgilio Elizondo stated that Mexicans did not cross the border; rather, the border crossed them. The same can be said about Puerto Ricans, whose land the United States invaded in 1898.[7] Both were and are the consequences of the doctrine of Manifest Destiny—the idea that the United States was destined by

---

[4] On the U.S. invasion of Mexico, see Timothy J. Henderson, *A Glorious Defeat: Mexico and Its War with the United States* (New York: Hill and Wang, 2007), 177; Amy S. Greenberg, *A Wicked War: Polk, Clay, Lincoln, and the 1846 U.S. Invasion of Mexico* (New York: Knopf, 2012), 247–63. Regarding U.S. colonial involvement in Puerto Rico, see Teresa Delgado, *A Puerto Rican Decolonial Theology: Prophesy Freedom* (New York: Palgrave Macmillan, 2017), 30–33; Ed Morales, *Fantasy Island: Colonialism, Exploitation, and the Betrayal of Puerto Rico* (New York: Bold Type Books, 2019), 20–22; Nelson A. Denis, *War against All Puerto Ricans: Revolution and Terror in America's Colony* (Nation Books: New York, 2015), 13–17.

[5] On U.S. involvement in Cuba, see Louis A. Pérez Jr., *Cuba in the American Imagination: Metaphor and the Imperial Ethos* (Chapel Hill: University of North Carolina Press, 2008). Regarding U.S. involvement in Central America, see Michel Gobat, *Empire by Invitation: William Walker and Manifest Destiny in Central America* (Cambridge, MA: Harvard University Press, 2018); Stephen Schlesinger and Stephen Kinzer, *Bitter Fruit: The Story of the American Coup in Guatemala*, rev. ed. (Cambridge, MA: Harvard University Press, 2005); Jeffrey L. Gould and Aldo A. Lauria-Santiago, *To Rise in Darkness: Revolution, Repression, and Memory in El Salvador, 1920–1932* (Durham, NC: Duke University Press, 2008); Russell Crandall, *The Salvador Option: The United States in El Salvador, 1977–1992* (New York: Cambridge University Press, 2016).

[6] See Tanya Harmer, *Allende's Chile and the Inter-American Cold War* (Chapel Hill: University of North Carolina Press, 2011); Jeffrey A. Taffett and Dustin Walcher, eds., *The United States and Latin America: A History with Documents* (New York: Routledge, 2017).

[7] Virgilio Elizondo, *The Future Is Mestizo: Life Where Cultures Meet*, rev. ed. (Boulder: University Press of Colorado: 2000), 44–45.

God to expand and govern the regions beyond its own borders. Nine-teenth-century Manifest Destiny fed the impulses for the global expansion of the United States and its relationships with the nations of Latin America. Cubans, on the other hand, had their independence struggle against Spain interrupted due to the intervention of the United States in the Spanish-American War. That war did not result in immediate Cuban independence, but in the nation being a U.S. protectorate until 1902 and in continued American intervention in Cuban internal affairs until the overthrow of the government of dictator Fulgencio Batista in 1959. Also, in 1898 the United States invaded all of Puerto Rico, becoming its new colonial overlord at the end of the Spanish-American War. Note how the Puerto Rican and Cuban wars for independence transformed these islands into the spoils of war by the very name of the conflict—Spanish-American War—that signified the military struggle between the declining and emerging empires.

Likewise, Central Americans from various nations find themselves in this country because of civil wars sponsored by the United States in their homelands, as with the U.S. Contra war in Nicaragua during the Reagan administration, or because of some nations' political instability. With ongoing violence and extreme poverty in parts of Central America, people are compelled to take the risky journey to the United States, even given the aggressive anti-immigrant policies of the Trump administration, in the hope of better life for their families. Territorial invasions and the exploitation of people and natural resources by U.S. corporations like the United Fruit Company contributed to Latin America's underdevelopment and internal unrest. Ironically and tragically, many now find themselves refugees in the same country that is responsible for their flight from home. In all of these cases, these U.S. Latinx are separated from the land that previously defined them. In such challenging contexts, how then do those who become Latinx in the United States construct and understand their ethnicity and new contextual identities while separated from the land of their roots?

People often define their ethnic identity by the land of their birth. Interestingly, no questions are asked when some Americans identify themselves as Irish, Italian, German, or Swedish, even if it has been generations since their grandparents, great-grandparents, or even great-great-grandparents arrived from those lands. This is not the case with people of Latinx heritage, whose connections to the United States may be held suspect. Often in self-identification Puerto Ricans or Cubans refer to themselves as such, in part because they or their parents were born on those particular Caribbean islands. But what happens when the land that defines them is no longer available to them as it was for their parents and grandparents? How do they understand themselves in a foreign and, at times, hostile land? How do those born in the United States forge an identity, specifically a religious identity, when they are treated as foreigners? What if love for their homeland remains stronger than their allegiance to the land where they presently reside? How do they remain faithful to the land they love and the land they adopted? How does their outsider status affect their theological understandings?

These questions and others like them go to the heart of their sense of otherness. Cultural anthropologist James Clifford wrote of one of the challenges of otherness, "Perhaps there's no return for anyone to a native land—only field notes for its reinvention."[8] While Clifford's anthropological musings are helpful, the cultural condition is more complicated when people are still treated as the other in their land that is their home. Drawing on his studies of indigenous peoples Clifford developed his thinking further and contends that the cultural adaptations of indigenous people contributed to their persistence and survival despite dire predictions to the contrary, arguing that "they reach back selectively to deeply rooted, adaptive traditions: creating new pathways in a complex postmodernity. Cultural endurance is a process of becoming."[9] This insight is helpful in understanding the cultural condition of Latinx in the United States (many of whom, incidentally, have indigenous roots); as a designated other individually and in their communities, Latinx construct adaptive theological understandings in a complex and sometimes threatening world.

Additional insight about the complex Latinx cultural condition can be gained by drawing upon Mieko Nishida's astute study of Japanese Brazilians. Nishida concluded, "The image of Japanese immigrants became a commodity that other people own. Japanese immigrants and their descendants have no ownership of their own image, which is divorced from reality. This is another illustration that Japanese Brazilians are not completely in control of how their identity is constructed or represented under hegemonic power."[10] Similarly, this is the experience of Latinx peoples, who, like the Japanese Brazilians, have their own sense of image, identity, and community but at the same time must contend with "how their identity is constructed or represented under hegemonic power."

---

[8] James Clifford, *The Predicament of Culture: Twentieth-Century Ethnography, Literature, and Art* (Cambridge, MA: Harvard University Press, 1988), 173.

[9] James Clifford, *Returns: Becoming Indigenous in the Twenty-First Century* (Cambridge, MA: Harvard University Press, 2013), 7.

[10] Mieko Nishida, *Diaspora and Identity: Japanese Brazilians in Brazil and Japan* (Honolulu: University of Hawai'i Press, 2017), 231–32.

The vileness of the hegemonic power in the United States reveals itself when Latinx persons and communities whose families have been in the United States for generations are told, "Go back to where you came from!" An incredibly blatant racist and public expression of the construction of image and identity as other appeared on July 14, 2019, at 5:27 a.m., when U.S. president Donald Trump tweeted the following:

> So interesting to see "Progressive" Democrat Congresswomen, who originally came from countries whose governments are a complete and total catastrophe, the worst, most corrupt and inept anywhere in the world (if they even have a functioning government at all), now loudly and viciously telling the people of the United States, the greatest and most powerful Nation on earth, how our government is to be run. Why don't they go back and help fix the totally broken and crime infested places from which they came. Then come back and show us how it is done. These places need your help badly, you can't leave fast enough. I'm sure that Nancy Pelosi would be very happy to quickly work out free travel arrangements![11]

Given the public discourse at the time, it was clear that Trump was referring to four first-term U.S. congressional representatives, all women of color and all members of the Democratic Party who were also well known for their progressive views: Representatives Alexandria Ocasio-Cortez of New York, Ilhan Omar of Minnesota, Ayanna Pressley of Massachusetts, and Rashida Tlaib of Michigan. All four women are U.S. citizens, and all of them except Omar were born in the United States. Omar was originally from Somalia, arriving in the United States as a refugee, and then subsequently being granted asylum along with her family. In the year 2000, Omar became a U.S. citizen at age seventeen. She and Representative Tlaib are the first two Muslim women to serve in the U.S. Congress. Representative Pressley is African American, and Representative Ocasio-Cortez is of Puerto Rican descent. The U.S. Equal Employment Opportunity Commission (EEOC) lists the phrase "Go back to where you came from" as an example of "harassment based on national origin." Trump's tweets and later public statements were widely condemned as racist and as encouraging white nationalism. Nevertheless, Trump's words also unleashed a new wave of public racist rhetoric with chants of "Send her back!" at Trump political rallies. People of color,

---

[11] https://twitter.com/realdonaldtrump/status/1150381396994723841?lang=en.

including Latinx, were targeted and once again had to deal with negative constructions and representations of their identities and communities.

In such contentious and even sometimes physically violent contexts, Latinx adaptively reach back to deeply rooted traditions. By doing so, Latinx of all generations craft life-sustaining pathways in a complex and racialized United States. Latinx cultural, social, and religious endurance is part of the process of constructing adaptive theological understandings. Some of that creativity may mean remembering, some of it doing something new, and sometimes the creativity comes from reinventing the past. Reinventing the past allows older adults of the first generation of migration to the United States to live within their dismembered memories. This reinvention enables them to try to deal with the pain of displacement, even when surrounded by constant reminders that they now reside on foreign soil. Concurrently, younger Latinx adults and adolescents of the second and subsequent generations must live in multiple worlds, negotiating the tension of trying to reconcile the constructed ideal of a former homeland, or one they never personally knew, with the present reality of their complex present. Latinx children and infants of the 1.5 generation who hold few or no memories of their (former) homeland live within the memories constructed for them by their parents and grandparents. Those Latinx were born U.S. citizens of migrant parents; their native land is thus the United States even though they also have roots in Latin America. Latinx exiles, aliens, and outsiders must struggle with multiple definitions of their humanity and ethnicity.

Exiles, Aliens, and Outsiders

Exiles, aliens, and outsiders are three separate ways Latinx are categorized, even though many if not all Latinx groups experience all three types of otherness. For example, many Salvadorans entered the United States as exiles during the U.S.-sponsored civil wars of the 1970s and 1980s, having left El Salvador in order to preserve their lives. Once hostilities ceased, later refugees were not fleeing tyranny as much as seeking economic stability. In 1992 the Salvadoran government and the Frente Farabundo Martí para la Liberación Nacional (FMLN [Farabundo Martí Liberation Front]) signed peace agreements to end the twelve-year civil war. The agreements were followed by years of political challenges and economic fluctuations that eventually saw an increase in organized crime in El Salvador and the emergence of organized Salvadoran transnational gangs such as Mara Salvatrucha (also known as MS-13) and the 18th Street Gang (also known as Barrio 18), which were linked with violence, drug trade, and human trafficking. The violence of the gangs has compelled new waves of immigration to the United States.[12] As these Salvadoran families settled in the United States, their children, born in this country, grew to adulthood experiencing the pain of being treated like outsiders. Neither being birthed here, speaking the dominant language, nor eating hamburgers provides acceptance or fosters belonging.

Declared aliens by the hegemonic power in the United States, the Salvadorans closely resembled "classic immigrants," such as the Irish, who were "pulled" by the allure of economic opportunities found in the United States, as opposed to being "pushed" by warfare. The economic lure of the United States complicates the reductionist argument that the sole reason for immigration is political. It ignores the natural flow of people from so-called underdeveloped into developed countries. While the basic reason for an individual to leave any country may be dissatisfaction with the current situation, it is often impossible to discern any clear dividing lines between political, economic, psychological, and religious reasons.[13]

Within most Latinx communities, individuals have multiple existential experiences as exiles, aliens, and outsiders. All three of these groups experience the pain and difficulties of being treated as strangers in one's land of residence. The myth of a melting pot has proven to be an empty and selective promise. For purposes of exploring these three categories in greater detail, we focus on the Cuban community when discussing exiles, the Mexican community when discussing aliens, and the Puerto Rican community when discussing outsiders, recognizing that these three specific groups serve as representatives of other nationalities.

Exiles

Although there have been Cuban migrants in the United States since the early nineteenth century, in the popular imagination Cubans are perceived as political refugees who sought asylum following the Cuban Revolution of 1959. Many Cuban Americans identify with the identity construction of *el exilio* (the exile) even if they are too young to have personally experienced an actual exile from Cuba. This includes people who trace their roots to family members who went into exile after Fidel

---

[12] T. W. Ward, *Gangsters without Borders: An Ethnography of a Salvadoran Street Gang* (New York: Oxford University Press, 2013); Susan Bibler Coutin, *Exiled Home: Salvadoran Transnational Youth in the Aftermath of Violence* (Durham, NC: Duke University Press, 2016), 83–84, 90–91.

[13] María Cristina García, *Seeking Refuge: Central American Migration to Mexico, the United States, and Canada* (Berkeley: University of California Press, 2006).

Castro seized power in 1959, the second wave of exiles airlifted in the 1965–1973 period, or the third wave of exiles in the Mariel Boatlift of 1980 and the Balsero (Cuban Rafters) Crisis of 1994.[14] Accordingly, the sense of exile can be not only a historical experience but also a state of mind. Deeply embedded in the psyche of many first- and 1.5-generation Cubans in the United States is a realization that they have lost the land of their birth and that when their bodies are finally laid to rest, they will be interred as foreigners in alien soil. *El exilio* is a term mainly used by exilic Cubans to name their collective identity. The term connotes the involuntary nature of their displacement and constructs them as sojourners in a foreign land. *El exilio* is an in-between place where one can wait and hope for a return to the homeland, a process that with each passing decade becomes less feasible. More than a geographic separation, the exile encompasses disconnection, displacement, and disembodiment. In Miami, longing for Cuba, or the "rhetoric of return," becomes the unifying characteristic of Cubans who construct *el exilio* as a sacred space in which religion and morality become synonymous with nationality.

For many Cubans in Florida, *el exilio*, although literally a geographic reality, is a culturally constructed artifact imagined as a landless nation complete with its own history and values. From this imaginary land(lessness), those in *el exilio* have evolved theological perspectives within which ethnic identity assumes religious significance. For example, on December 2, 1973, in order to rectify an exilic existence, connect with Cuban cultural roots, and help shape the community-based interpretations and theologies, a shrine for *La Virgen de Caridad*, the Virgin of Charity and patroness of Cuba, was dedicated on Biscayne Bay in Miami. The tentlike building serves as sacred space, but also as cultural and political space. Upon this sacred ground, exilic Cubans re-created the image of their homeland on foreign shores. In this shrine, religious zeal marries Cuban patriotism, merged with shifting expressions of Cuban American patriotism as the generations change. With a mural behind the altar and a sacred icon before it, the building is but a replica, a weak substitute for the original shrine still in Cuba. Standing in the shrine, which faces Cuba, one can simultaneously occupy space in both *la Cuba de ayer* (yesteryear's Cuba) and the contemporary Miami. The religious illusion created by this reproduction of an authentic Cuban shrine on U.S. soil only masks the reality and pain of the exilic condition.

---

[14] Albert Hernández, "Cuban Americans," in *Hispanic American Religious Cultures*, vol. 1, ed. Miguel A. De La Torre (Santa Barbara, CA: ABC-CLIO, 2009), 165.

For older Cubans, the Our Lady of Charity National Shrine constructs and glorifies a Cuba that never was and never could be, yet somehow by simply worshiping in this space, one can be transported to that other place and time. For those who arrived in Miami as infants or children and are now busy paying mortgages, climbing the corporate ladder, or planning for retirement, the shrine is a physical representation of the dreams of their parents—dreams about which they feel a strong, yet fading, sense of loyalty. The shrine provides a space where exiles can safely display their patriotism without having to commit to any action to make those dreams a reality. For children born and raised in this country, the shrine only confirms that their parents' dreams of Cuba amount to little more than an artificially constructed fantasy island.

Generations of exilic Cubans have heard the internationally renowned Celia Cruz (1925–2003) sing the popular tearjerker "Cuando salí de Cuba" (When I left Cuba). The song summarizes the pain of existential location: "Never can I die, my heart is not *here*. Over *there* it is waiting for me, it is waiting for me to return *there*. When I left Cuba, I left my life, I left my love. When I left Cuba, I left my heart buried." This popular Cuban ballad, written by a Chilean and sung as a hymn of faith, illustrates a denial of reality by many exiled Cubans: the reality is that they are living and probably will die on foreign soil.

Like the Jews captive in Babylon, Cubans must deal with this incomprehensible pain of being torn from their promised land. In Babylon, out of their pain, the Jews questioned the sovereignty of a God who would tear God's people from their homes and plant them in an alien land. A major concern for those in exile is their status as deportees. Does removal from the promised land, by which their identity is constructed, indicate a divine rejection, voiding any future participation in God's plan? Does resettlement in a foreign land mean assimilation to a culture perceived as inferior? Surely names given to children like Jordan Perez or Jennifer Gomez reveal the changing Cuban ethnic identity and the pain caused in assimilating. These children will grow old as new "Americans." They are no more Cuban than their grandparents are "American." They exist in two different worlds, connected only by an in-between generation. Cuban sociologist Rubén Rumbaut has labeled this in-between space the "1.5 generation." While the first generation, consisting of the parents from the "old" world, faced the task of acculturation, managing the transition from one sociocultural environment to another, the second generation, consisting of the children from the "new" world, faces the task of managing the transition from childhood to adulthood. People caught between these two spaces are forced to cope with both crisis-producing and identity-defining transitions.

Aliens

Terms like "exile" and "alien" are often used interchangeably. Yet the term "exile" has political connotations and suggests an inability on the part of the exile to return to the homeland. "Alien," on the other hand, reflects a different type of otherness, regardless of the cause of expatriation. Aliens may reside in a new land for political or economic reasons and accordingly may receive official asylum from the federal government. In theory, however, the alien can always return "home," if only for a visit.

The United States Citizenship and Immigration Services (USCIS) has an official category of "resident alien," with three subcategories. Basically, for the U.S. federal government, "alien" refers to "non-U.S. citizens currently residing in the United States." While the vast majority of Mexican Americans are U.S. citizens, many Mexicans live the life of resident aliens in this country while others, even though they are citizens of the United States, are treated as aliens. The assumption of some people that all Mexicans are aliens is tied to one of the major misconceptions about Mexicans in the United States that Laura Gómez discusses: "that Mexican Americans are a 'new' group that consists primarily of recent immigrants and their children . . . While the Mexican American group continues to grow due to ongoing immigration from Mexico, it includes a large proportion of people whose American roots go back many generations."[15]

When Donald Trump announced his candidacy for the presidency of the United States on June 16, 2015, he launched it with this accusation as part of his justification: "When Mexico sends its people, they're not sending their best. They're not sending you. They're not sending you. They're sending people that have lots of problems, and they're bringing those problems with us. They're bringing drugs. They're bringing crime. They're rapists. And some, I assume, are good people." Trump never retreated from his inflammatory words; indeed he added to them with more racist comments and actions, which encouraged other racist and white supremacist rhetoric to come out into the open. For white supremacists and some in the dominant culture, Trump's accusation is in line with their views of all who have Mexican roots. To them, all Mexicans are undesirable aliens.

Obviously, not all Mexicans in the United States are aliens, either resident aliens or undocumented immigrants (for whom many prefer to use the racist term "illegals"). Many Mexican Americans can trace

---

[15] Laura Gómez, *Manifest Destinies: The Making of the Mexican American Race*, 2nd ed. (New York: New York University Press, 2018), 1–2.

their connection to what was to become the United States through their Spanish ancestors for more than five centuries. The indigenous population of Mexico is significant, numbering in the millions, and includes the Nahuatl, Yucatec Maya, Zapotec, Mixtec, and Yaqui (Yoeme) peoples. Many continue to speak their indigenous languages, and some do not even speak Spanish.

Twelve years before the 1620 landing of the *Mayflower* at Plymouth Rock, Santa Fe, New Mexico, was founded as a colonial Spanish settlement, having been explored years earlier by Francisco Vásquez de Coronado. In fact, the first European flag to be raised in what was to become the United States was the flag of Spain with the establishment of St. Augustine (in Florida), founded in 1565 by Spaniards as San Agustín. St. Augustine predates the first English settlement of Jamestown, Virginia (in 1607), as the oldest continuously inhabited settlement established by Europeans in what became the continental United States. These are inconvenient historical facts often ignored by those who view Latinx solely as recent and unwelcomed aliens. From Latinx perspectives, Anglos were the more recent arrivals and are the aliens in the southwestern portion of the United States through their immigration into the Mexican border area of Texas (which was part of the Mexican state of Coahuila y Tejas), and the gigantic land grab of the Mexican-American War (Intervención Estadounidense en México [United States Intervention in Mexico]) of 1846–1848. In 1848, as a result of the related Treaty of Guadalupe Hidalgo in addition to Texas's annexation, the United States acquired 54 percent of Mexico. Ironic that the latest immigrants to the land reconstruct themselves in the historical narrative and political imagination as the natives. By painting all Mexicans as aliens, the power and privilege of the dominant white culture are preserved and legitimized while masking the historical reality that Mexican territory once included Texas, New Mexico, Arizona, California, Nevada, Colorado, Utah, and portions of Kansas, Oklahoma, and Wyoming.

The justification for this massive land acquisition was a theology that conceived of the dominant Euroamerican culture as especially chosen and as God's new Israel. The previously mentioned romantic form of jingoism known as "Manifest Destiny" taught that God had manifestly intended Euroamericans to spread their eagle wings over the entire Western Hemisphere, starting with the northern continent. To deny this concept was not only treasonous but also blasphemous. The popular theological doctrine of the early 1800s concerning how the world would end, a type of millennialism, suggested that God's kingdom would be realized through the history of the United States. Christ's second coming would commence once the United States executed its apocalyptic mission of manifesting its territorial destiny. This so-called divine mandate extended not only "from sea to shining sea" but also from the snowy lands of the Arctic to the tropical charms of the Isthmus of Panama.

The U.S. expansionist war against Mexico is a prime example of Manifest Destiny at work. In July 1845 General Zachary Taylor encroached on Mexican territory by deploying his troops to bait the Mexicans. Once Mexico mobilized to meet its adversary, President Polk (who was elected for his explicit support of the annexation of Texas and a war with Mexico) had the opportunity to request a declaration of war from Congress. A military onslaught by the powerful United States led to Mexico's capitulation and to the 1848 Treaty of Guadalupe Hidalgo, which ceded half of Mexico's territory to the United States. This land included gold deposits that would be discovered in California in 1849, silver deposits in Nevada, oil in Texas, copper deposits in New Mexico and Arizona, and all of the natural harbors (except Veracruz) necessary for commerce. John Quincy Adams denounced the government's naked act of aggression against Mexico in his well-known caustic remark to Congress: "The banners of freedom will be the banners of Mexico; and your banners, I blush to speak the word, will be the banners of slavery."[16] Even Ulysses S. Grant, who served in this conflict, viewed the war—so obviously forced upon Mexico for the sake of acquiring land—as unjust.[17]

With the acquisition of land, the "Mexican question" in the United States developed. What would be done with the "alien" inhabitants? First, the U.S. government ignored treaty agreements and historic land titles and denied justice in the courts. Second, Mexican Americans were further marginalized due to their economic value. They represented a reserve army of laborers, allowing the overall southwestern economy to develop and function. The new Euroamerican settlements profited by the labor surplus extracted from the barrios. Cities throughout former north

---

[16] *Speech of John Quincy Adams, May 25, 1836* (Washington, DC: Gale and Seaton, 1838), 119.

[17] Ulysses S. Grant, in *Personal Memoirs*, 2 vols. (New York: Charles L. Webster and Company, 1885), wrote, "The occupation, separation and annexation [of Texas] were, from the inception of the movement to its final consummation, a conspiracy to acquire territory. . . . Even if the annexation itself could be justified, the manner in which the subsequent war was forced upon Mexico cannot. The fact is, annexationists wanted more territory than they could possibly lay any claim to, as part of the new acquisition. . . . The Southern rebellion was largely the outgrowth of the Mexican War. Nations, like individuals, are punished for their transgressions. We got punished in the most sanguinary and expensive war of modern times" (1:54–56).

Mexico developed by utilizing these "illegal immigrants." Third, in the binary black/white social construction of race in the United States, the segregation of "nonwhite" U.S. Mexicans ensured the privileged space of the newly installed Euroamerican center. Because Mexican Americans, out of necessity, were willing to work at the lowest wage level in the mining and agriculture industry, they were able to consolidate the power and wealth of the Euroamericans. The luxury houses of Los Angeles, San Antonio, and Santa Fe were built at considerable cost so as to distance their privileged space from the menace of *el barrio*, while simultaneously capitalizing on the poverty of this marginalized space.

By the beginning of the twentieth century, the United States had created a need for cheap labor throughout the Midwest. The reserve army of Mexican laborers moved to manufacturing centers where they and their children faced forced assimilation (e.g., punishment for speaking Spanish), while a Hispanic middle class began to emerge. Yet, with the coming of the Great Depression of the 1930s, the Euroamerican majority increasingly viewed these "aliens" as taking away jobs from "real" Americans, resulting in the mass deportation of many Latinx to Mexico. An estimated four hundred thousand to 1.8 million persons of Mexican descent were transported to Mexico forcibly, including native-born Mexican Americans who were citizens of the United States.[18] In the twenty-first century, there is still demand for cheap labor from those who will do the work that others will not do, whether they are Mexican Americans, undocumented Mexican immigrant laborers, or undocumented laborers from other parts of Latin America.

To be seen as an alien means a person is always a foreigner even though that person is born within the boundaries of the United States. Yet being an alien has little to do with where one is born and where one migrates. Instead, it has everything to do with how one looks or sounds. Any Latinx person whose appearance demonstrates the physical mestizaje or mulatez of their roots or who speaks with a "funny accent" is automatically seen as an alien.

---

[18] Francisco Balderrama and Raymond Rodríguez, *Decade of Betrayal: Mexican Repatriation in the 1930s*, rev. ed. (Albuquerque: University of New Mexico Press, 2006); Deborah Cohen, *Braceros: Migrant Citizens and Transnational Subjects in the Postwar United States and Mexico* (Chapel Hill: University of North Carolina Press, 2011); Mireya Loza, *Defiant Braceros: How Migrant Workers Fought for Racial, Sexual, and Political Freedom* (Chapel Hill: University of North Carolina Press, 2016). See also Daniel Ramírez, *Migrating Faith: Pentecostalism in the United States and Mexico in the Twentieth Century* (Chapel Hill: University of North Carolina Press, 2015).

Outsiders

Not all Latinx peoples living in the United States are exiles from Latin America (whether political, economic, religious, or a combination thereof), and neither are all Latinxs in the United States aliens in the way the term is usually understood as immigrants. Nevertheless, a third group of Latinx shares the experiences of marginalization with Latinx exiles and aliens. For a significant and growing percentage of Latinx people, their only concept of "home" has been the United States, yet within this home they far too often are consigned to live in ambiguity. Outsiders are those Latinx born within the United States, and therefore having U.S. citizenship, and who nevertheless still are rejected as not being "true" Americans because of their Latin American roots and in many cases because of how they are perceived in the racialized binary context of the United States as nonwhite other. And so, yet again, groups and individual Latinx people have negative constructions and representations of their identities and communities imposed upon them. While outsiders can be found among the children of refugees and immigrants from all Latinx groups, Puerto Ricans from both the island and the mainland typify Latinx outsiders.

Puerto Rico was conquered by the United States through the Spanish-American War in 1898. The initial years of North American hegemony were characterized by colonial attempts to "Americanize" and "civilize" this population. In the popular imagination in the United States, "Porto Rico" was seen as a backward place in need of civilization and uplift, which the North Americans would bring. Instead, as a colonial possession of the United States, Puerto Rico experienced economic exploitation and cultural oppression. Conveniently for the United States in 1917, all Puerto Ricans were granted U.S. citizenship, which also made Puerto Rican men eligible to serve in the U.S. Army in World War I.[19] Puerto Ricans as U.S. citizens were allowed to travel from the island to the mainland as easily as one would travel from state to state. Technically not considered immigration of foreign aliens, this mobility was rather the movement of U.S. citizens within the United States. But even as U.S. citizens on mainland soil, Puerto Ricans were treated as unwelcomed outsiders.

Three major migrations of Puerto Ricans have occurred since 1898, contributing to a major Puerto Rican diaspora population. Members of the first wave of the Puerto Rican diaspora (1900–1945) are referred

---

[19] Eric Daniel Barreto, "Puerto Ricans," in *Hispanic American Religious Cultures*, vol. 2, ed. Miguel A. De La Torre (Santa Barbara, CA: ABC-CLIO, 2009), 471.

to as "pioneers"; the second wave, after World War II (1946–1964), is known as the "Great Puerto Rican Migration"; and the third wave (1965–onward) is characterized by a pattern of ongoing migration and return, sometimes called "revolving-door migration." In that sense, the back-and-forth movements of U.S.-citizen Puerto Ricans prefigured the transnational movements of other populations in the late twentieth- and early twenty-first centuries that the advances in technology and transportation made possible, which in turn were responses to the demands of global capitalism.

Originally, the Puerto Rican diaspora population was centered in the northeastern United States, with New York City the major place of residence, but currently it is more dispersed, with increasing numbers of Puerto Ricans found in Illinois, New Jersey, Florida, and Pennsylvania. The majority of Puerto Ricans live outside New York City and exhibit significantly different characteristics from those of New York City Puerto Ricans, sometimes referred to as Nuyoricans, although not all diaspora Puerto Ricans are Nuyoricans. Puerto Ricans have settled across the entire United States.

Puerto Rican pentecostal theologian Samuel Solivan has used the term "citizen-exiles" to describe the existential situation of Puerto Ricans as outsiders. Although Puerto Ricans have been citizens of the United States since 1917, in practice their reality has been that of second-class citizens.[20] Solivan is among many who identify aspects of Puerto Rican displacement and ambiguous social location in the popular and moving Puerto Rican folksong "En Mi Viejo San Juan" ("In My Old San Juan"). Composed in 1943, first recorded by El Trio Vegabajeno in 1946 and covered by many artists over the decades, "En Mi Viejo San Juan" speaks to many aspects of Puerto Rican conditions across the generations. These few lines demonstrate the poignancy of the song:

Una tarde me fuí
hacia a extraña nación
Pues lo quiso el destino
Pero mi corazón
Se quedo frente al mar
En mi viejo San Juan

One afternoon I departed
toward a strange nation

---

[20] See Samuel Solivan, *The Spirit, Pathos, and Liberation: Toward an Hispanic Pentecostal Theology* (Sheffield: Sheffield Academic Press, 1998), 138–39.

because destiny wanted it so.
But my heart remained
facing the sea,
in my old San Juan.

Even for Puerto Ricans who have never lived on or perhaps not even visited the island, a strong connection remains.

This connection between island Puerto Ricans and diaspora Puerto Ricans became stronger when Puerto Rico was first hit by Hurricane Irma on September 6, 2017, and then devastated by Hurricane María on September 20, 2017, one of the deadliest natural disasters in the history of the United States. The tepid response of the Trump administration to the plight of U.S. citizens demonstrated how the president saw Puerto Ricans not as U.S. citizens but as undesirable outsiders trying to cheat the federal government. Thousands lost their lives due to the inept government response to Hurricane María. The combined catastrophes of Puerto Rico's debt crisis, the devastation of Hurricane María and the related humanitarian crisis, halfhearted federal relief response, commonwealth government corruption, the disdain and insults of political elites, and a surge in police violence against the Puerto Rican people resulted in large-scale public protests and increased solidarity among all Puerto Ricans in the struggle for life. Political anthropologist Yarimar Bonilla contends, "The insistence that we must pay attention to Puerto Ricans because they're United States citizens is troubling. It's not because they're U.S. citizens that we should pay attention; it's because they're experiencing a humanitarian crisis. Creating this distinction between citizens and noncitizens in the Caribbean, and between citizens and noncitizens in the United States is really problematic as a moment when noncitizens are under attack."[21] This insight clarifies one of the problems with being designated an outsider: it is also an attack on and denial of one's basic humanity.

Sadly, another aspect of the outsider experience is the constant threat and reality of rejection by other Latinx when one might have expected acceptance and solidarity. Far too often, later-generation Latinx are treated poorly by others within Latinx communities, particularly regarding the level of competence with the Spanish language. The late Tejana singer Selena was extremely popular in Spanish-language settings and on the verge of a breakthrough into mainstream fame at the time of her

---

[21] Yarimar Bonilla and Naomi Klein, "The Trauma Doctrine" in *Aftershocks of Disaster: Puerto Rico before and after the Storm*, ed. Yarimar Bonilla and Marisol LeBrón (Chicago: Haymarket Books, 2019).

death. She had built her career with Tejano audiences singing in Spanish, yet few people knew at the time that she was not bilingual herself. A more recent example is around the use of Spanish among Democratic candidates for the presidency of the United States during the 2020 presidential election. Anglo Beto O'Rourke of Texas, a former member of the House of Representatives, was praised for his use of Spanish, while Latino Julián Castro was criticized for his Spanish being inadequate. Castro openly admits that he does not speak Spanish fluently. A former mayor of San Antonio, Texas, and U.S. Secretary of Housing and Urban Development, Castro has been criticized and sometimes ridiculed for his facility in Spanish, to the point where some view him as less than Latino and as an outsider to the U.S. Latinx experience. However, the opposite is true in that Castro's experience is very common among Latinx peoples. Castro describes his parents as the victims of internalized oppression to make sure their children spoke English well and could succeed in an English-dominant world.

The dominant U.S. culture continues to see Latinx groups as exiles, aliens, and outsiders, regardless of their historical connection to U.S. lands. To be a Latino/a within the United States is never to belong, unless the person can pass for a Euroamerican. This deep sense of otherness informs how Latinx theological perspectives are developed. In fact, these social locations serve as the starting point for most Latinx in their quest for understanding the Deity. To ignore these spaces runs the risk of never fully comprehending Latinx theologies.

Communities and Places

The physical space where many Latinx people reside, called in some contexts *el barrio*, has an influence on how Latinx develop their theological perspectives. Pew Research Center population projections in 2017 estimated the Hispanic/Latinx population at 58,838,000. Table 2.1 lists the fifteen largest U.S. Hispanic/Latinx groups by origin, based on self-described race or ethnicity. This growing Latinx population is concentrated primarily in the urban centers of the United States, although it is dispersed across all fifty states, partly as the result of waves of immigrations from Central and South America since the early 1970s.[22]

---

[22] Ruth Enid Zambrana, *Latinos in American Society: Families and Communities in Transition* (Ithaca, NY: Cornell University Press, 2011), 19–21.

Table 2.1. *Hispanic origin profiles, 2017*

U.S. Hispanic Population: 58,838,000	
The 15 Largest U.S. Hispanic Groups by Origin	
(based on self-described race or ethnicity)	
Mexicans	36,634,000
Puerto Ricans	5,614,000
Salvadorans	2,307,000
Cubans	2,298,000
Dominicans	2,067,000
Guatemalans	1,444,000
Colombians	1,246,000
Hondurans	940,000
Spaniards	810,000
Ecuadorians	738,000
Peruvians	679,000
Nicaraguans	484,000
Venezuelans	421,000
Argentines	278,000
Panamanians	210,000

Source: Pew Research Center tabulations of the 2017 American Community Survey (1 percent IPUMS).

Other significant facts about U.S. Latinx population, according to the Pew Research Center, are that the vast majority of Latinxs are U.S. citizens; immigrants are a declining share of the Latinx population, but a growing share of Latinx immigrants are longtime U.S. residents. Among Latinx groups, Venezuelans, Dominicans, and Guatemalans have seen the fastest population growth since the 2010 U.S. Census. Also, the number of Latinx who speak English proficiently has increased significantly. In 2017, 70 percent of Latino/as ages five and older spoke English proficiently, up from 65 percent in 2010, with Spaniards (93 percent), Panamanians (87 percent), and Puerto Ricans (83 percent) having the highest percentages of English proficiency; interestingly, the percentage of Mexicans who speak English proficiently (71 percent) is similar to that of the overall Latinx population. Even among those groups with lower percentages of English proficiency—for example, Hondurans (48 percent), Guatemalans (48 percent), and Salvadorans (53 percent)—there is still significant facility in English. All of this contradicts a narrative of Latinx refusing to speak English.

They are often simultaneously young, poor, and highly segregated. The reasons underlying these basic features reflect national trends affecting the several component groups of the Latinx community and the bleak economic path it faces. Saying the Latinx *comunidad* is mostly urban communicates another obvious, but usually unstated, aspect of that reality—namely, not all Latinx live in urban barrios. Latinx are found in cities, rural settings, suburban bedroom communities, and the new exurban settings. Many others are seasonal farm workers in places that do not realize there is a rural Latino/a presence, such as Wisconsin, Ohio, and Michigan. Others work in meatpacking plants in Kansas, service industries in Boston, or poultry processing facilities in Georgia; some are professionals in Los Angeles. This far-flung community faces difficult day-to-day economic realities, with little, save their own resilience, to draw on to change the position of that community in the overall structure of society.

Living in suburbs, rural areas, small towns, and cities, Latinx peoples have developed various expressions of theologies of place. Harold Recinos's barrio theology, for example, affirms "that Jesus can be found at the center of social reality."[23] A theology of place such as barrio theology affirms the worth of the *comunidad* to God and God's abiding presence in Christ in the day-to-day economic realities—realities defined by Latinx who are marginalized, poor, and undereducated. Forty-three percent of Latinx live in majority-Latinx neighborhoods, making it difficult to ignore the economic link to spatial segregation. As Hispanic immigration increased during the last thirty to forty years of the previous century, there has been a 32 percent "residential separation of high-income Americans" from all other Americans, thus draining capital and investment from Latinx and other neighborhoods of color.[24]

At the same time there is at least partial recognition that Latinx churches in the barrio are in a period of transition. Daniel A. Rodriguez notes, "Older barrios in cities like Chicago, Dallas, Los Angeles, Houston, Miami, New York, Philadelphia, and San Antonio, once dominated by foreign-born Spanish-speaking *mexicanos*, *cubanos*, and *puertorique-ños*, are now dominated by their native-born children and grandchildren. Even more significantly, a growing number of U.S.-born Latinos are not only English dominant, but they do not speak Spanish at all!"[25] This pro-

---

[23] Harold J. Recinos, *Who Comes in the Name of the Lord? Jesus at the Margins* (Nashville: Abingdon Press, 1997), 38.

[24] Paul Taylor and Richard Morin, *Americans Say They Like Diverse Communities; Election, Census Trends Suggest Otherwise* (Washington, DC: Pew Research Center, 2008), 9.

[25] Daniel A. Rodriguez, *A Future for the Latino Church: Models for Multilin-*

vides opportunities to rethink the nature of Latinx barrio communities and to reimagine various types of barrio theologies.

Even Latinx barrios in generational transition, as well as other areas of Latinx settlement, create an environment in which the vast majority of the Latinx community experiences residential segregation, employment discrimination, and political isolation. Nonetheless, elements of the Latinx community have realized the power of the vote. Urban Latinx are clustered in eleven key states that make up 217 out of the 270 electoral votes needed for the presidency. With the 2000 and 2016 presidential elections being decided by the electoral college rather than the popular vote, the distribution of Latinx is of prime political importance.

Latinx are learning that the best defenses against xenophobic laws are U.S. citizenship and the right to vote. Population projections from the U.S. Census Bureau estimate that by 2020 the total U.S. Latinx population will be 20 percent, reaching 52 percent in New Mexico, 44 percent in both California and Texas, 36 percent in Arizona, and 33 percent in Nevada. Even states as dissimilar as Georgia, Hawaii, and North Carolina each are estimated to have 11 percent Latinx population in 2020. Is it any wonder presidential contenders repeatedly made campaign stops in California, Texas, Florida, Arizona, and New Mexico, greeting their audiences in Spanish? Yet, in spite of the potential opportunity to succeed, Latinx are constantly threatened by institutionalized racism. Even though Latinx yearly pump billions into the U.S. economy, 40 percent of their children still live in poverty, the highest rate ever recorded in the United States. Because their children live in poverty, Latinx now constitute an undereducated class that will soon mature into an underskilled workforce.

People of color are relegated to inner-city poverty and are segregated from the middle class, making it difficult for them to break through barriers that foster and maintain their poverty. Last to be hired, they are also among the first to lose their jobs during downsizing, as was the case during the 2008 Great Recession. In 2009, Latinx unemployment rates were at 11.4 percent (African American unemployment rates were at 13.3 percent), compared to whites at 7.9 percent.[26] In August 2019, unemployment among Hispanic or Latinx workers was 4.2 percent, the lowest in years, but at the same time, Hispanic/Latinx men earn about 75 percent of what white workers do. Latina women fared worse, mak-

---

gual, Multigenerational Hispanic Congregations (Downers Grove, IL: InterVarsity Press, 2011), 16.

[26] These rates were worse for workers between twenty and twenty-four years old. Blacks were at 23 percent, Latinx were at 16 percent, and whites were at 12.5 percent.

ing only fifty-three cents on the dollar.[27] The 2018 *Beyond Wages* report stated, "More than three million family households in the United States are headed by Latinas, and 34 percent of these households live below the poverty level, compared to 12.3 percent of all U.S. households. This means that more than one million Latina-headed family households live in poverty."[28] For every one hundred new children who slipped into poverty during the previous year, seventy-one were Latinx.[29]

Latinx groups have the lowest levels of educational achievement of any ethnic group. Their children are more likely to drop out of school. According to the Census Bureau, the majority of Latinx (more than 51 percent) drop out of high school, while 78 percent of non-Hispanics graduate. Dilapidated school buildings and insufficient budgets for books contribute to this rate of attrition. In fact, even before a Latinx child attends their first day of school, they often are culturally predetermined to fail. Because of the social conditions, their educational pathways are limited, college is unattainable for most, and for those who go to college, many are ill-prepared; fewer than 10 percent expect to graduate, and only half of the 4 percent of all Latinx persons who enter graduate school finish.[30]

Race, Ethnicity, and Culture

Latinx communities (*comunidad*) are characterized by mestizaje and mulatez, both terms used to acknowledge and affirm the multicultural and multiracial heritages of various Latinx peoples. Elias Ortega-Aponte notes, "On the positive side, interest in the discussion of mulatez opens space to uncover how Africanized worldviews and forms of expressions can be included in U.S. Latino/a religious discourse from which they are often missing. . . . On the negative side, including mulatez in the U.S. Latino/a religious discourse presents the problem of deciding what aspects of African culture will be included in theological reflection."[31]

---

[27] UnidosUS and National Partnership for Women & Family, *Beyond Wages: Effects of the Latina Wage Gap* (Washington, DC: National Partnership for Women & Family, November 2018), 1.

[28] Ibid., 2.

[29] William H. Frey, "The New Republic: Minorities Hit with Poverty Increase," NPR News, September 14, 2009, www.npr.org; Valerie Strauss, "Public Education's Biggest Problem Gets Worse," *Washington Post*, September 14, 2011.

[30] Ruth Enid Zambrana, *Latinos in American Society: Families and Communities in Transition* (Ithaca, NY: Cornell University Press, 2011), 80–82.

[31] Elias Ortega-Aponte, "Mulatez," in De La Torre, *Hispanic American Religious Cultures*, 1:390.

But even when one wants to affirm the multicultural identities of Latinx peoples and be inclusive in the construction of Latinx theological discourses, caution should be exercised. Jorge Aquino observes, "In Latin@ theology, *mestizaje* begins as a critical, anti-racist analytic, but takes a subtle, ideological U-turn, becoming the all-but-transparent identity discourse of a whitened theological *conjunto* that does too little to promote the entrée of Latin America's truly despised cultures: the African and the Amerindian."[32]

Latinx in the United States live in a binary racial culture that classifies individuals as either white or nonwhite. Because Latinx are a multiracial *comunidad*, the dominant culture sees all Latinx as nonwhite. Regardless of how Latinx may construct racial categories within their own communities, the dominant culture's racism relegates all Latinx to the category of "people of color." Their color is not determined solely by skin pigmentation; rather, they are also considered to be "of color" due to sound. In many cases, language or even the assumptions about the language spoken become another way for imposed identification and categorization. Their accents and Spanish-sounding surnames determine their race, their "color," and hence their marginality. Yet, "honorary whiteness" or at least temporary, situational whiteness may await those who have a lighter skin pigmentation, acquire economic or cultural capital, and speak English without a Spanish accent.

Racial designations in the United States are more descriptive of the social constructions of the dominant society than a set of characteristics. Sociologists Michael Omi and Howard Winant describe as follows aspects of the power relations that result in racial categories in the United States:

> The definitions of specific categories are framed and contested from "above" and "below." The social identities of marginalized and subordinate groups, for example, are both imposed from above by dominant social groups and/or state institutions, and constituted from below by these groups themselves as expressions of self-identification and resistance to dominant forms of categorization.[33]

---

[32] Jorge A. Aquino, "*Mestizaje*: The Latina/o Religious Imagery in the North American Racial Crucible," in *The Wiley Blackwell Companion to Latino/a Theology*, ed. Orlando O. Espín (Malden, MA: Wiley Blackwell, 2015), 303.

[33] Michael Omi and Howard Winant, *Racial Formation in the United States*, 3rd ed. (New York: Routledge, 2015), 106.

Speaking from a theological context, Elizondo arrives at a similar position:

> White Western supremacy permeates our way of life to such a degree that even good persons act in racist ways without even realizing that they are being racist. That is the tragedy of the social blindness of North American society. Racism and ethnocentrism are interwoven in literature, entertainment, institutions, marriage relations, finances, and even religious symbolism. This racist culture continues to bombard the non-Western and nonwhite with the message that they are nonhuman. This is not said in so many words, but the message is loud and clear through all the media of communication.[34]

The naming process itself displays the power of cultural codes. Part of the power of naming is that it disguises the nature of the social classes present in U.S. society. A name can foster false consciousness. If a person launches a concerted effort to tell people that they are something other than what they perceive themselves to be, a group's commonsense understanding of reality can become supplanted by someone else's understandings through coercion, deceit, or a combination of the two. When individuals and groups subscribe to a definition of "self" constructed by someone else, they can fall into the trap of domination. But unless the cultural codes are known, the trap remains unseen, although clearly felt. Many Latinx people feel the pressure to ignore known cultural pasts and to accept a new interpretive designation (i.e., dominant cultural myth) in the United States.

Machismo

Another cultural root that influences Latinx theology is the phenomena of gender relationships, specifically machismo. Although the term is used synonymously with "sexism," it originally referred to a celebration of conventional masculinities. Neither solely associated with the oppression of women nor solely used in a pejorative sense, the term "machismo" described the values associated with being a man, a *macho*. Similarly, the celebration of female attributes is known as *hembrismo*. A popular Latinx saying is, "Soy tan hembra como tú macho" (I am as much woman as you are man). Although sexism exists in both the

---

[34] Virgilio P. Elizondo, *Galilean Journey: The Mexican-American Promise*, 2nd ed. (Maryknoll, NY: Orbis Books, 2000), 111.

Hispanic and Euroamerican cultures, when Euroamericans use the term "machismo," even though a comparable English term exists, it implies Latinos are somehow more sexist than Euroamericans, hence absolving the Euroamerican culture of its own misogynist structures and attitudes. Although manifested differently, Euroamericans and Latinxs are both equally oppressive toward women.

Many Latinx men—as the products of two distinct patriarchal societies—are conditioned to be sexist. For Latinos, to be a man, a *macho*, implies both domination and protection for those under them, specifically the females in the family. The macho worldview, like ancient honor-shame paradigms, creates a dichotomy in which men operate within the public sphere—that is, the overall community—while women are relegated to the private sphere, specifically, the home. The family's honor is augmented by the ability of the *macho* to provide for the family. The wife who works becomes a public testament then to the *macho*'s inability to be a good provider. While family honor is achieved by the *macho*, shame can come to the family via the women. In the mind of the *macho*, the possible sexual infidelity of the women in his household makes his honor susceptible, thus their banishment to the home. By confining women to the private sphere, the *macho* protects "his" women from their supposed sexual urges. Yet, the *macho*'s own sexual urges require no protection. In fact, his actions of infidelity only enhance his machismo. While some might argue that such honor-shame attitudes are receding, others claim they are simply being manifested in different ways. For example, the woman may work outside the home, but she is still mainly responsible for maintaining the home. And of course, this heteronormative construct ignores the development among some Latinx of nonbinary identities, relationships, or both.

The *machos'* responsibility, their burden, is to educate those below their "superior" standards. Because of the privilege that comes with the male gender, Latinos are complicit with the sexist and heteronormative social structures of both the dominant Euroamerican culture and their own Latinx cultures, a complicity motivated by personal advantage. The sexist attitudes toward women are not simply a belief in the superiority of men; rather, Latinos are able to exploit the power that comes with maleness to profit from customs, traditions, and laws designed to limit certain activities of Latinas while not limiting them for Latinos. All things being equal, Latinos prevail over Latinas in the marketplace, in the church, in the *comunidad*, and within the family structure.

Latinas contend that their struggle against sexism is a response to the machismo existing within the Latino community and the racial, ethnic, and class prejudice existing within the Euroamerican feminist community, which ignores the fundamental ways that white women benefit from the oppression of women of color. Latinas attempt to find liberation as members of Latinx communities that struggle to obliterate all institutions and communal structures contributing to the poverty and suffering of the entire *comunidad*, a poverty and suffering that lead to systematic death within the Latinx community. The goal of most Latinas is not to equate liberation with Euroamerican middle-class males, but to create new social structures in which all—regardless of gender identification, or lack thereof—can find the fullness of life and liberation within a justice-based community.

Multiple Heritages and Cultural Influences on Theology

Latinx theologies reflect the cultural milieu, and therefore it is important to comprehend how social locations shape Latinx community-based theologies. While such broad generalizations obviously do not apply to every single U.S. Latinx person, they do, however, provide an accurate view into the lives and struggles of many Latinx.

As we have seen, the Latinx *comunidad* shares multiple heritages. Not only is the U.S. Latinx community multicultural, it is an intercultural reality. Common among diverse Latinx heritages is their religiosity and spirituality as an important component of their daily lives, although a great deal of diversity exists in particular expressions. The central role that Western Christendom (as distinct from Western Christianity) via Iberia played in Latin America influenced Latinx customs, idioms, and traditions of religiosity. Catholic theologian Virgilio Elizondo best expresses this thought in his foreword to Protestant theologian Justo González's significant and foundational book *Mañana: Christian Theology from a Hispanic Perspective:*

> Let me be very clear—I do not want to say that every Hispanic has to remain a member of the Roman Catholic Church in order to be Hispanic, but I am saying that when a Hispanic ceases to be catholic (to participate in the religious-cultural expressions of our people), he or she ceases to be a Hispanic. But it should be equally clear that the most cherished religious-cultural expressions of the people are certainly practiced in some Roman Catholic Churches while despised in others, yet they are not the sole property of the Roman Catholic Church. . . . We can go to any church we choose to go to, but we should not be asked to change our name and destroy our identity in order to be accepted. Being reborn in Christ certainly transforms us from within, but it does not destroy us. We do not cease being Black, Chicano, Cuban-exile, or Puerto

Rican, nor do we cease liking *tamales* or *pastelitos*, *cumbias* or *polkitas*, nor do we forget our history or the road we traveled, or give up the treasures of our heritage.[35]

Consequently, *la comunidad* can be understood partly as a religious community due to the cultural influence of Catholicism within specific Latin American contexts. This development was constantly in conversation with indigenous Indian and African cultures. The shared cultural roots produced distinctive theological concerns. One focus is the need to convince Latinx aliens, exiles, or outsiders that they have personal dignity because they are created in the divine image.

While the majority of Latinxs either actively identify or are affiliated with Catholicism, it would be erroneous to see all Latinxs in the United States as Catholics. In fact, a Protestant presence, although not large, existed in sixteenth-century Spain. Many *conversos* embraced the new teachings of the Reformation, but the efforts of the Spanish Inquisition either eradicated them or forced them into exile. Some of these exiles made their way to the so-called New World in the regions of European colonization. In the border regions of the English colonies, contact with the border regions of New Spain, later Mexico, took place. It is possible to trace a Latinx Protestant community in the United States to at least the mid-nineteenth century. The nineteenth century also witnessed the growth of Protestantism in Latin America, with an exponential increase occurring in the twentieth century. A number of these Latin American Protestants, especially members of pentecostal churches, made their way to the United States. Recent decades have seen an increasing number of Latinx Catholics join Protestant denominations. The Pew Research Center reported in 2014 that almost one-third of Latinx (32 percent) had switched from the religion in which they were raised and that 13 percent of Latinx raised Catholic had become Protestant.[36] However, a Latinx who is a first- or fourth-generation Protestant still shares cultural roots of the *comunidad* with Catholicism.

Popular Religiosity and Spirituality

A rich complexity of shared cultural roots exists both within and beyond the recognized boundaries of Christianity; this is sometimes referred to as "popular religion" or "lived religion." More specifically,

---

[35] Virgilio P. Elizondo, "Foreword," in Justo L. González, *Mañana: Christian Theology from a Hispanic Perspective* (Nashville: Abingdon Press, 1990), 17.

[36] Pew Research Center, "The Shifting Religious Identity of Latinos in the United States," May 7, 2014, 9–11.

Rebecca M. Berrú-Davis defines Latinx popular Catholicism as "an expression of Catholicism that emerges from the needs, desires, and hopes of the Latino/a community. It arises from the community. Thus, the word 'popular' denotes 'of the people.'"[37] Elsewhere Edwin Aponte discusses the nature of Latinx popular spirituality, religiosity, and theology, one of the characteristics of which is its desire for identity and theological reasons to "very intentionally avoid religious practices that seem too Catholic."[38] Typically Latinx Protestant popular religiosity can be seen through linguistic and word-centered expressions such as testimonies, daily devotions, preaching, and other types of word proclamation, including communal worship.[39]

Many indigenous Native American and African traditions continue to influence community life. Among these are different types of spiritism, or African diaspora traditions such as *Vodou*, Santería, *Umbanda*, and *Candomblé*. Some of these practices lived underground due to centuries of racism and oppression, making it necessary to maintain an outward mask of Catholicism. This influence can also be viewed as a mask or as an expression of popular religiosity or, as some argue, a direct continuity with pre-Columbian beliefs and practices. Part of all these diverse shared roots is that a cultural mestizaje is drawn upon, one in which the supernatural influences everyday life. That Latinx spiritual worldviews impact everyday realities emphasizes the importance of home devotional practices, like home altars, prayers to saints, or *promesas* (vows). A detailed analysis of Latinx popular religiosity appears in chapter 5; for now, we briefly survey Latinx spirituality and worship.

The shared cultural roots of different traditions point to an important aspect of the various manifestations of Latinx cultures, namely, popular religion / devotional piety / spirituality. These spiritual expressions are situated dynamically in grassroots religious beliefs and practices of the everyday. Popular religiosity is a focus point for individual and communal feelings and actions for daily sustenance, meaning-making, and survival through religious symbols and actions that create order in the world and provide a concrete point of contact with the Divine.

Latinx popular religiosity has widespread appeal, appearing in formal and informal settings and exhibiting the affective dimensions of devotion and spirituality. Examples of popular religion in Latinx contexts include the *via crucis* (way of the cross), *quinceañeras* (fifteenth birthday celebra-

---

[37] Rebecca M. Berrú-Davis, "Theologizing Popular Catholicism," in Espín, *Wiley Blackwell Companion to Latino/a Theology*, 387.

[38] Edwin David Aponte, "Theologizing Popular Protestantism," in Espín, *Wiley Blackwell Companion to Latino/a Theology*, 408.

[39] Ibid., 408–9.

tion, comparable to a "sweet sixteen" or a debutante party), home altars and *ofrendas*, daily devotions, *coritos* (choruses) and *estribillos* (literally "refrains," another term used for choruses), prayer meetings, *testimonios* (testimonies), *vigilias* (vigils), Bible study groups, and *posadas* (processions). Latinx popular religion includes cultural elements of faith but is much more than a mere recovery of cultural roots; it is both a source of theology as well as the expression of Latinx theological interpretations, a creative way of being, a means of cultural self-identification for survival, and a uniting force for the *comunidad*.

Among Protestant and Catholic Latinxs, popular religiosity is widespread and adaptable, often unbothered by official religious boundaries. Occasionally this has led to informal as well as formal ecumenical dialogue and cooperation on possible common sources of spirituality, including European religiosity, Native American spiritualities, and African worldviews, as well as how Latinx negotiate their multicultural and multiracial heritage. Among Latinx Christians, these practices and discourses of religiosity and spirituality have become pivotal to their faith and have been incorporated as part of informal and formal liturgical experiences.

Reflections on Worship and Liturgy

Elements of Christian worship present in Latinx worship include an emphasis on the importance of a believing community coming together to praise God, who calls them into community. Known for his contributions to the early development of a theology of and for U.S. Latinx, Allan Figueroa Deck states that Latinx Roman Catholic religiosity "is permeated with a symbolic, sacramental imagination that continues its influence even as these people migrate and experience 'the acids of modernity.'"[40] Likewise, Latinx Protestant worship is also richly imaginative and far from monolithic.

Latinx Christian communities express their individual and corporate relationship with God in various types of corporate worship. While a great deal of variety exists in the theological approaches employed by different Latinx congregations, for theological reasons some things are held in common, such as beliefs about worship and actual worship practices, even across Catholic/Protestant boundaries. A common characteristic that many Latinx theological interpreters have cited is Latinx worship as sacred fiesta. Depending on the particular Latinx context,

---

[40] Allan Figueroa Deck, "Hispanic Catholic Prayer and Worship," in *¡Alabadle! Hispanic Christian Worship*, ed. Justo L. González (Nashville: Abingdon Press, 1996), 30.

in some Latinx Protestant settings this might include an informal time of greeting and assembly, enthusiastic singing, freely expressed praise, a confession of sin, and the confession of faith in the One who forgives sin. Sacred fiesta occurs in community where baptism and the Santa Cena (Holy Communion), the two common ordinances or sacraments, are celebrated. Of course, the two distinct designations point to significant theological understandings about baptism and the Lord's Supper.

Another common Latinx theological interpretation is what Latinx Catholics deem to be the three most important features of worship: *misa* (Mass), *mesa* (table), and *musa* (muse, i.e., the arts). Also present in Latinx Protestant contexts, these features are part of the *culto*, or worship service. In the Protestant *culto*, as in the Catholic *misa*, a reaffirmation of community and identity occurs. Elizabeth Conde-Frazier observes this among Latinx Protestants:

> The *culto*, or worship, is the celebration of the victory of the cross. It is the "fiesta" expression of our spirituality, and music and testimonies reflect this. The *culto* has been described by Hispanic theologians as the place of dialogue between persons and God. This dialogue takes place through verbal and symbolic expressions. It has also been called the *locus theologicus* of the Hispanic community. The preaching, hymns, testimonies, and prayers all express parts of our theology. Worship is our place for using the spiritual tools for struggle and survival as a community.[41]

Conde-Frazier's observation about Latinx Protestants emphasizes the critical reflective aspect of Latinx worship as expressed in the communal celebration of sacred fiesta, which to the uninformed outsider may seem like unsophisticated frenzy. Indeed, *"fiesta"* can be translated as "party." Again the interpretation of worship as celebration in both Latinx Protestant and Catholic contexts is not a remote, formalized drama that is watched, but rather a more intimate event in which all are invited to participate. Eminent Latinx historian and theologian Justo González, like Conde-Frazier, develops the interpretation of Latinx worship as fiesta and observes,

> It is a celebration of the mighty deeds of God. It is a get-together of the family of God. It is important to remember this in order

---

[41] Elizabeth Conde-Frazier, "Hispanic Protestant Spirituality," in *Teología en Conjunto: A Collaborative Hispanic Protestant Theology*, ed. José David Rodríguez and Loida I. Martell-Otero (Louisville, KY: Westminster John Knox Press, 1997), 137.

to understand some of the features of our worship that sometime disconcert or even upset those of the dominant culture. First of all, because worship is a fiesta rather than a performance, it may be planned, but not rehearsed. Oftentimes, Hispanic worship may seem chaotic. . . . But in most cases the difference between our worship and that of the dominant culture is that we think in terms of planning a party more than rehearsing a performance.[42]

Although the specific liturgical manifestations are different, the impulse of celebration is held by many interpreters of Latinx Christianity as a common and shared characteristic. For such interpreters the language of fiesta, or "party," is a natural and expressive way to speak of the joyful understanding that both Latinx Protestant and Roman Catholic Christians as communities have of its present and eschatological (or future) connection with God and its celebration of that connection. But there may be greater complexity at work. The specific phrases "sacred fiesta" and "sacred party" are suggested by historian Daniel Ramírez: "The more problematic thing is the English rendering of *fiesta* as 'party.' It is that, but much more. Celebration also fails to do justice to the term. It is communal, and can have both sacred and profane elements to it."[43] This view of the term "fiesta" shows the usefulness of the concept of contextual ritualization. For some members of the dominant culture, both inside and outside the church, viewing worship as fiesta, as party, is inappropriate and even offensive. The contrast in perspectives is another illustration of the nature of Latinx Christian communities to create their own alternative public spaces for God-talk and their related practices and actions.

At the same time, anyone exploring Latinx theologies, especially if they are serious about deferring to the actual discourses, actions, and interpretations of Latinx people and communities, does well to heed the caution of researchers who question the extensive reduction of Latinx spirituality and worship to fiesta as a one-size-fits-all designation and description. Mark T. Mulder, Aida I. Ramos, and Gerardo Martí name as the greatest challenge in exploring Latinx Protestantism the omnipresence of a type of "ethnoracial essentialization." They write, "In our narrative, we discussed the vague assessments that confidently assert Latino

---

[42] Justo L. González, "Hispanic Worship: An Introduction," in González, *¡Alabadle!*, 20–21.

[43] Daniel Ramírez, correspondence with Edwin David Aponte, December 16, 1997, based on Catherine Bell's concept of contextual ritualization. See Catherine M. Bell, *Ritual Theory, Ritual Practice* (New York: Oxford University Press, 1999).

Protestants have 'worship services with a Latino flavor' or characterized by 'the spirit of fiesta.' Such tautological and racialized stereotypical statements have no analytical value. They fail to describe—less explain—any concrete dynamics or mechanisms operating in these churches."[44] This calls for greater attention and study of Latinx worship in all its diverse expressions.

Religious Beliefs in Practice

Is it appropriate to speak of a common Latinx communal cultural ethos, given the breadth of difference that exists among the various groups subsumed under the Latinx-Hispanic/Latino-Latina/o-Latin@-Latinoa labels? Is it appropriate to ask, how does a shared Latinx community ethos shape what is theologically important to Latinx peoples? Latinx cultural contexts contribute to the popular religiosity of Latinx, specifically in the manifestation of Latinx spirituality and worship. Likewise, Latinx social location informs what the various and diverse manifestations of Latinx *comunidad* deem to be important. Before concentrating on the contributions made by Latinx to specific theological concepts (the task of the next chapter), we turn our attention toward two areas where a shared Latinx community ethos shapes what becomes important to Latinx peoples, specifically the concepts of family and justice.

Significance of Familia

As discussed, a central aspect of U.S. Latinx Christianity is the important role of *comunidad*. This sense of community has corporate expressions in the lives of its members, particularly in popular religiosity. In a North American context, where hyperindividualism is on the rise, a countervailing impulse in *comunidad* among U.S. Latinx exists. Even within the diversity of national origins, races, language facilities, denominations, and classes, the omnipresence of the notion and experience of community is a unifying factor and source for ministry, engagement with the dominant Euroamerican culture, and theology.

One common feature found within Hispanic communities is the importance of *familia* (family), which is closely tied to the concept of *comunidad*. Some consider the family to be the basic and perhaps most important social institution in the different Latinx cultures. A shared aspect of the concept of *familia* is that it encompasses a broadly extended

---

[44] Mark T. Mulder, Aida I. Ramos, and Gerardo Martí, *Latino Protestants in America: Growing and Diverse* (Lanham, MD: Rowman and Littlefield, 2017), 139–40.

network of relatives and fictive kinships. Even when Latinx persons are not literal blood relations, they often re-create family through the *compadrazgo* system. Among Latinx Catholics and some Latinx Protestants who practice infant baptism, the sponsoring godparents (*padrino, madrina*) become "coparents" (compadres, comadres) and enter into lifelong relationships not only with the child but also with the family. Indeed, the hope is that the compadres and comadres (literally "co-father" and "co-mother") would become part of an extended family (if they were not already part of it), nurturing the child and being reliable companions to the parents, as well as assuming parental responsibility should the parents die.

Within Latinx Protestant circles that adhere to other understandings of baptism, members of the congregation refer to each other as *hermano* (brother) and *hermana* (sister). Congregations as communities of re-created families provide support, stability, and hope in settings where people are confronted by a host of challenges and difficulties. Whether in Catholic or Protestant settings, many Latinx in the United States participate in some re-creation of family as a means to maintain community.

In U.S. Latinx communities, the sense of family and kinship can cross racial, ethnic, and national categories that might have been impenetrable barriers in Latin America. In that sense, Hispanic family relational networks become additional indicators of the distinctiveness of Latino/a communities in the United States, as well as showing continuities with Latin America. Through family and the re-creation of family, larger Latinx communities are built and maintained.

Particularity and Latinx Theologies

Connections exists between Latinx people's social location and how those cultural roots significantly affect their resulting theology. To explore Latinx theology without considering these cultural roots runs the risk of creating a theology disconnected from the daily human struggle of disenfranchised groups who look for solutions to their oppression as well as meaning and purpose in life. Latinx theological perspectives do not exist within a vacuum but rather come forth as the consequences of the social space Hispanics are usually relegated to occupy. In fact, the practice and articulation of all theologies, not just Latinx, are mainly influenced by the social and cultural location from which they arise.

Latinx theologies are community-based. Usually, Eurocentric theologies do not recognize their own cultural and contextual boundedness and therefore claim some sort of objectivity, which divorces their theological perspectives from their social location, which in turn leads to a rejection of community-based Latinx theologies as unsophisticated, underdeveloped, and illegitimate. Latinx theologies, on the other hand, openly admit their connections to the communities from which they arose. The task next in chapter 3 is to examine some basic theological concepts from Latinx social, cultural, and religious perspectives.

3

Theoretical and Theological Perspectives

Latinx theological thought, religious practices, and spirituality have always been an integral part of the wider U.S. Latinx community. On the other hand, the formal theological articulations of what we have been calling "Latinx theologies" are a more recent phenomenon appearing in the last part of the twentieth century, when Latinx scholars, theologians, and practitioners began to unapologetically and assertively enter the overall theological discourse from the perspective of their own sociocultural locations. Their contributions are central in understanding spiritual movements within U.S. culture, particularly since the United States is being redefined by the growing Latinx presence. Although they are constructed and practiced from multiple Latinx contexts, Latinx theologies are not solely for Latinx peoples but rather are theological discourses important for other expressions of Christian thought and practice more generally, as well as for better understanding the increasingly diverse U.S. religious landscape.

In the previous chapter we started with the traditional basic definition of "theology" as the study of God, emphasizing the social locations of those who are doing the studying. What is being called "collective Latinx theology," but really are multiple theologies, are distinct understandings that emerge from various Latinx social and cultural contexts. But actually, the same can be said about the development and articulation of all Christian theologies. Theologian Orlando Espín describes what ought to be obvious but far too often is forgotten—namely that theologians are as contextualized as all other human beings. Consequently, their theological constructs (because they are constructs of humans) will always be inescapably contextual, perspectival, historically and culturally bound, and expressive of asymmetric power relations. Whether theologians acknowledge it or not, their theologies are produced and shaped in a complex

77

web of contexts. That is why their work is not necessarily relevant in sociocultural and historical contexts outside their own.[1]

Such an understanding is useful for discussion of Latinx theologies, especially as they set out for themselves the goals to be relevant and connected to the daily lives of Latinx communities. This focus is especially important in articulating how Latinx understand the presence of God, and the ways that Latinxs make meaning in the midst of everyday life. While, of course Latinx can be found within multiple and different faith traditions, or no faith tradition, the focus of this chapter is on Christian Latinx-based theology. While there is no monolithic theological perspective (which is why we speak of Latinx theologies, in the plural), some common theological themes do resonate with many Latinx Christians. Before turning toward some of these shared Latinx religious and theological perspectives found among many scholars, clergy, congregations, and individual Latinx persons, it is helpful to discuss further what we mean by the term "theology."

For Latinx Christian faith communities, theology becomes the verbal expressions of faith as practiced, believed, articulated, and celebrated by Latinx people. It moves beyond the Eurocentric Enlightenment project that attempts to rationally understand God and communicate this rationality to unbelievers so that they too can believe. Although critical rational appraisals of theology are important and should not be underestimated, for Latinxs, theology is more than dogmas or faith formulas—it is the daily articulation of life in community where it is known that God and the divine activity move and participate within history to save, liberate, and reconcile. In effect, theology becomes the reflection of God's praxis in the world, God's activity in bringing about liberation from both corporate and individual sins. Doing theology is participating in the loving actions of God, best illustrated and embodied in the figure of Jesus the Christ. From the particular U.S. social locations of Latinx peoples, struggling to overcome racial/ethnic discrimination as well as class oppression, theology becomes a religious construction of and for faith communities responding to overt and subtle forms of repression. In short, Latinx theology is the Latinx voice of faith trying to understand the transcendence within the immanence of Latinx existential contexts.

Another clarification is in order in describing the nature of Latinx theologies. It would be an error to assume that Latinx theological thought derives exclusively and completely from Latin American liberation theologies. Certainly, there are similarities and points of contact between them—for example, language, overriding concern for justice, liberation

---

[1] Orlando O. Espín, *Idol and Grace: On Traditioning and Subversive Hope* (Maryknoll, NY: Orbis Books, 2014), 39.

of the oppressed, and interpreting the gospel through the lived experience of the people. Nevertheless, different geographical locations along with their dissimilar contexts created very distinct contextual theological expressions. Latinx theologies differ by focusing more on the cultural, social, political, and economic issues touching U.S. Latinx communities. Unfortunately, well-meaning theologians—possibly influenced by dominant Euroamerican theological paradigms and uninformed about the U.S. Latinx population or Latinx theological thought, but nonetheless wanting to appear sensitive and inclusive—look to Latin American liberation theologians to be the voice for U.S. Latinx theology. In fact, both authors have seen Latin American liberation theology and Latinx theology lumped together in courses and texts as if they are one and the same, which is not a good representation of either.

What, then, are the distinct theological themes of Latinxs existing on the margins of the United States at the very same time that the Latinx population is growing? What contributions do Latinx peoples make to overall theological discourses? This chapter presents a brief systematic approach to theological concepts developed by Latinxs since at least the 1970s with the modest goal of highlighting some of the more significant Latinx theological perspectives.

Methodology

How do we "know" what is "truth"? Epistemology is a term that describes the process of discovering how knowing occurs and taking into consideration its validity, limitations, and relationship to truth. For many theologians, "epistemology" is the relationship between the believer's knowledge of God and the revelation of the Deity. Even if it is held that all knowledge about God is derived from Scripture, the church, tradition, or the spiritual experience of an individual (i.e., conversion), the process of interpreting these authorities is the function of epistemology. Simply stated, epistemology attempts to understand the process by which self-revelatory knowledge about God is derived. For the theologian, the function of theology is the unveiling of an understanding of God through established sources of authority.

Traditionally, Eurocentric Christian epistemology has been based on the following elements:

- Divine revelation as found in the Scriptures
- The authority of the institutional church (especially for Roman Catholics, but certainly some Latinx Protestants also have hierarchal authoritative structures) operating under the guidance of the Holy Spirit

- The life, death, and resurrection of Jesus Christ
- A "scientific" methodology that uses human reason as the bases for any truth
- The unique inner feeling of a conversion experience (especially for evangelicals)

Typically, an attempt is made to arrive at truth—that is, orthodoxy (literally "correct doctrine")—through one or a combination of the above listed sources of authority.

U.S. Latinxs have made significant contributions to the field of epistemology.[2] Influenced by Latin American liberation theologians, many Latinx maintain that "knowing" truth is insufficient and that so-called objective concepts of knowledge are problematic. The purpose of theology is praxis, the *doing* of theology, also known as "orthopraxis" (literally "correct action"). Latinxs strive to ascertain meaning for their existence by being faithful to God's calling in God's overall objective of redeeming creation. Praxis as a starting point is found in the location, time, and experience of particular people, especially those living under oppression. The main purpose of doing theology, or orthopraxis, is to change the structures causing such oppression in order to liberate those who exist under these injustices.

Latinx theological perspectives are directly connected to Latinx social contexts. To do theology from those particular contexts is to participate in a process that gives voice to ones who usually are voiceless, a process where those on the margins as a *comunidad* articulate God's salvific plan. Latinx theologians are committed to having their theological perspectives—their knowing—be influenced by the community of believers. This methodology that seeks theological truth is an ongoing process called *teología de conjunto*—a theology constructed in a shared way with a commitment to unity and communion. Loida I. Martell-Otero, Zaida Maldonado Pérez, and Elizabeth Conde-Frazier describe *teología de conjunto* as "a collaborative approach to theological reflection; an understanding that theology should be done in

---

[2] See Mayra Rivera, *The Touch of Transcendence: A Postcolonial Theology of God* (Louisville, KY: Westminster John Knox Press, 2007); Santiago Slobodsky, *Decolonial Judaism: Triumphal Failures of Barbaric Thinking* (New York: Palgrave Macmillan, 2014). See also Eduardo Medieta, "The Ethics of (Not) Knowing: Take Care of Ethics and Knowledge Will Come of Its Own Accord," in *Decolonizing Epistemologies: Latina/o Theology and Philosophy*, ed. Ada María Isasi-Díaz and Eduardo Mendieta (New York: Fordham University Press, 2012), 246–64.

and among community, particularly among diverse voices."[3] At its best, in *teología de conjunto* the community of believers works collectively in seeking and expressing theological precepts. Edwin David Aponte reminds us that one of the consequences of grouping together the diversity of Latinx peoples as if they were homogeneous is the discovery of what it means to be a community that simultaneously is "imagined and real, imposed and embraced." This *teología de conjunto* attempts to articulate the theological dimension of a "diverse and constantly developing life together" within the United States.[4]

Teología de conjunto analyzes the reality of the everyday experience of Latinx people reflects on what the good news of biblical text has to say about this reality, implements praxis that can bring about a more just change, and evaluates the results of these praxes to ascertain if new actions are required. With this collaborative methodology, Latinx theology moves the discourse away from the hyperindividualism that undergirds how theology normatively is conducted and the abstract theological theories normative to Eurocentric religious thought. Latinx religious scholars commit to a collaborative *teología de conjunto* conducted within, by, and for the overall community, working as organic intellectuals in which there is a relationship between praxis (action), theory, and an ongoing process of evaluative reflection.

Latinx Christian theologies are based on a praxis-centered theology of *acompañmiento*, that is, of accompaniment with Latinx people. As Roberto Goizueta reminds us,

> To "opt for the poor" is thus to place ourselves *there*, to *accompany* the poor person in his or her life, death, and struggle for survival. . . . Such a theology would, in turn, underscore four dimensions of the option for the poor: 1) the affective dimension, as enfleshed in particular relationships; 2) the spatial, geographical dimension, as represented by the unity of home and city; 3) the dimension of interiority, as reflected in the theologian's own, personal appropriation of the option for the poor; and 4) the spiritual dimension, as incarnated in the faith of the poor, which transgresses all spatial, geographic barriers.[5]

---

[3] Loida I. Martell-Otero, Zaida Maldonado Pérez, and Elizabeth Conde-Frazier, *Latina Evangélicas: A Theological Survey from the Margins* (Eugene, OR: Cascade Books, 2013), 142.

[4] Edwin David Aponte, "Introduction: Theological and Cultural Competence *en Conjunto*," in *Handbook of Latina/o Theologies*, ed. Edwin David Aponte and Miguel A. De La Torre (Cleveland: Chalice Press, 2006), 2–3.

[5] Roberto S. Goizueta, *Caminemos con Jesús: Toward a Hispanic/Latino*

The God understood by Latinxs became human, enfleshing Godself, then and now, in the everyday lives and experiences of the marginalized. Theologian Luis Pedraja describes further Latinx understandings of the incarnation, saying, "Latino/a Christologies draw parallels between the Hispanic experience and Jesus, making it possible to identify with Jesus as one who understands and, to some extent, validates the Latina/o borderland experience and marginalization."[6] For Latinxs, the salvific nature of God is experienced in the daily struggles of and for humanity. It is through *acompañamiento* that a preferential option is made for the oppressed, becoming the praxis of being present alongside disenfranchised Latinx.

For Latinx peoples praxis occurs when reflection is brought to bear upon action. For many Latinxs, relevant theological thought is inductive, where orthodoxy flows from orthopraxis. Theology becomes a second step to action, thus articulating a praxis-based theology that reflects the struggles of U.S. Latinx peoples. Theologian, practitioner, and activist Fernando Cascante-Gómez asserts,

> Hispanic theologies are, for the most part, praxis-based theologies. This praxis aims at being both pastoral and prophetic. It is *pastoral* because it is a praxis that seeks to empower and liberate the Latino/a people to face and transform the realities that oppressed them. It is *prophetic* because it is a praxis that seeks to engage the dominant theological and cultural paradigms that maintain and promote those oppressive realities.[7]

Many Latinx scholars would argue that only through justice-based praxis whose goal is social transformation can individuals come closer to understanding God and God's will.

Also important to Latinx theological approaches to the epistemological project is the concept of *lo cotidiano* (the everyday, the ordinary), probably the most important contribution Hispanics have made to the academic discourse. What we know about theology is based on the daily experiences and existence of Latinx, focusing on the everyday struggles and joys that accompany life. Centering *lo cotidiano* shifts the discussion toward the real flesh-and-blood dilemmas that marginalized Latinx communities face. Focusing on the daily existence of Latinxs critically

---

Theology of Accompaniment (Maryknoll, NY: Orbis Books, 1995), 192.

[6] Luis G. Pedraja, "Christology," in *Hispanic American Religious Culture*, vol. 2, ed. Miguel A. De La Torre (Santa Barbara, CA: ABC-CLIO, 2009), 596.

[7] Fernando A. Cascante-Gómez, "Orthopraxis," in De La Torre, *Hispanic American Religious Culture*, 2:697–98.

analyzes the good and bad that occurs, which in turn shapes and forms the construction of Latinx theological thought. Moreover, *lo cotidiano* can become the catalyst for structural changes, serving as the foundation upon which all liberative praxis can be determined and implemented. It is *lo cotidiano* that creates for Latinx an "epistemological privilege," a privilege based on their ability to know how to live and survive in both the center and periphery of society.

This theology arises from the borders—that is, not only geographic borderlands but also from that in-between space that separates privilege from paucity, power from disenfranchisement, whiteness from "colored," wholeness from brokenness. Living on the borders within the United States, Latinx find themselves disjointed both from the culture of their heritage and the culture in which they reside, outsiders and foreigners to each. Theology, among Latinxs, is mainly done from this in-between space called *nepantla*, a Nahuatl term that connotes the middle.[8] To exist in *nepantla* means neither denying the indigenous customs and traditions of Hispanics, nor the new religions and concepts brought about by cultural conflicts. The Latinx mestizaje, birthed from the pain and anguish of continuous conquest, contributes to this notion of *nepantla*. From this social location of having one foot in two worlds, Latinx attempt to understand the movement of God.

Latinx Readings of the Bible

If epistemology describes the process of discovering truth, then what are the sources that influence said truth? For many Latinx Christians the Bible is paramount in the formation of truth for their faith communities. The process of reading and understanding a historically distant text is a process known as "hermeneutics." Biblical hermeneutics includes the analysis, interpretation, explanation, textuality, language, and historicity of the Bible. One goal of biblical hermeneutics is to provide a sound response that can guide humanity toward understanding the biblical text. Francisco Lozada Jr. describes the work of Latina/o biblical interpretation as a process in which "the interpreter encounters or engages the text's meaning in relation to his or her (their) community's own interest."[9]

---

[8] For what have become classic explorations of *nepantla*, see Gloria Anzaldúa, *Borderlands / La Frontera: The New Mestiza*, 4th ed. (San Francisco: Aunt Lute Books, 2012); and Pat Mora, *Nepantla: Essays from the Land in the Middle* (Albuquerque: University of New Mexico Press, 1993).

[9] Francisco Lozada Jr., *Toward a Latino/a Biblical Interpretation* (Atlanta: SBL Press, 2017), 11.

Challenges

Every reader's interpretation of a text is based on what they bring to the reading, including gender, social-economic location, sexual identity, and race. Justo González, in his book *Santa Biblia: The Bible through Hispanic Eyes*, advocates methodically reading the Bible through Latinx perspectives. By consciously claiming a Latinx identity, González looks to the text from within Latinx contexts of struggle in order to learn what God wants Latinx people and the world to be. Yet which Hispanic eyes should be used? Are Salvadoran, Puerto Rican, Peruvian, Dominican, and Mexican eyes all identical? Are the eyes of the Latinx rich the same as the eyes of the Latinx poor? Since the experiences of Hispanics are different, all Latinx eyes are not the same. According to González, Latinxs read the Bible from multiple places of marginality, poverty, mestizaje/mulatez, exile, experiences of oppression, and solidarity.[10]

While González is correct that the vast majority of U.S. Latinxs live under such conditions, it also is true that the vast majority do not read the Bible at all. And many who do, read it through a methodology of popularization in which biblical stories at times are merged with family and folk wisdom and stories from other religious traditions, as providing a lesson that teaches Latinx peoples how to live and survive. This type of reading is another way Latinxs represent how the text is understood in their daily lives. Many Latinxs do not necessarily read the biblical text but rather express their deeply held religiosity through customs and traditions. This approach yields popularized versions of the biblical stories, combining at times indigenous or African traditions for the purpose of stressing a spiritual point. Additionally, some Latinx in their daily lives employ a combination of approaches, that is, using both a methodology of popularization and indeed reading the Bible within the particular Latinx contexts. This brings an additional level of complexity to reading the Bible through Hispanic eyes. An example of this type of grassroots mixed methodology is described by David Sánchez as he correlates the East Los Angeles murals of the Virgin of Guadalupe with the book of Revelation.[11]

Jean-Pierre Ruiz describes that when biblical interpretation is done in Latinx contexts with an intentional focus on the significance and particularity of those Latinx settings, then it is characterized by

---

[10] Justo L. González, *Santa Biblia: The Bible through Hispanic Eyes* (Nashville: Abingdon Press, 1996), 19, 28–29.

[11] David A. Sánchez, *From Patmos to the Barrio: Subverting Imperial Myths* (Minneapolis: Fortress Press, 2008).

- Collaboration: "that the work of biblical interpretation and the work of theology is less about *me* than it is about *us*."
- Connection: "it takes lived daily experience, la *vida cotidiana*, as a primary point of reference."
- Commitment: "in which the interpretive task is driven, animated, and nourished by the ethical imperative to side with those brothers and sisters in the human family who have been shoved to the very edges of society, often to the very edge of survival."[12]

Those threefold characteristics that Ruiz articulates also assume what Francisco Garcia-Treto calls "a community of interpretation," from particular contexts where Scripture is read *en conjunto*, in light of and in service to the ecumenical Latinx community.[13]

Another challenge to reading the biblical text through Hispanic eyes is that an emphasis on a collective Latinx reading may deflect from Latinx particularities and mask intra-Latinx repression. Ada María Isasi-Díaz raises the valid concern of how Latinxs in positions of power have used Jesus to marginalize Latina women. For example, those who speak from the pulpit demand obedience (particularly from women toward men) in the application of Scripture, when in fact they are only presenting their own interpretation of Scripture as biblically authoritative.[14] For this reason, Miguel A. De La Torre insists that the biblical text is to be read from the margins—that is, from the perspective of the disenfranchised and dispossessed—using John 10:10 ("I come that they may have life, and have it abundantly") as the primary lens for interpretation. Simply stated, if a textual interpretation prevents the experience of abundant life by any segment of the population—or worse, if it brings death—then said interpretation is antigospel and anti-Christ. Biblical interpretations closer to the meaning of the text are those that enhance and expand the abundant life for all of God's creation.[15]

---

[12] Jean-Pierre Ruiz, "The Bible and Latino/a Theology," in *The Wiley Blackwell Companion to Latino/a Theology*, ed. Orlando O. Espín (Malden, MA: Wiley Blackwell, 2015), 116–17.

[13] Francisco Garcia-Treto, "Reading the Hyphens: An Emerging Biblical Hermeneutics for Latino/Hispanic U.S. Protestants," in *Protestantes/Protestants: Hispanic Christianity within Traditions*, ed. David Maldonado Jr. (Nashville: Abingdon Press, 1999), 161, 164.

14 Ada María Isasi-Díaz, *En la Lucha / In the Struggle: Elaborating a Mujerista Theology*, rev. ed. (Minneapolis: Fortress Press, 2004), 62, 69, 160.

[15] Miguel A. De La Torre, *Reading the Bible from the Margins* (Maryknoll, NY: Orbis Books, 2002), 52.

Latinx readings of the Bible pursue various liberative interpretations that serve as sources for praxis, including rereading biblical texts in ways that unmask how the text is not as necessarily liberating as we would hope. In this regard, Fernando F. Segovia is among the principal architects of postcolonial biblical criticism, which asks how the Bible has been used to enforce and reinforce colonial structures. Reading the Bible with postcolonial Latinx eyes questions the relationship between the Bible, colonialism, and theology from the social location of margins, in the hope of moving toward a liberation rooted in challenging the self-serving assumptions of colonizers.[16]

Latinx religion scholars insist that the biblical text (or any other holy script for that matter) should be read from the Latinx social locations as a second act to justice-based praxis. Again, Jean-Pierre Ruiz observes, "Postcolonial biblical interpretation, for its part, foregrounds the place of Christian discourses in the construction and legitimation of Western colonial-imperial expansion in Africa, Asia, and the Americas."[17] Emphasizing the importance of social location, Ahida Calderón Pilarski summarizes her understanding of being "a Latina biblical critic" doing the work of interpretation as meaning

> to take, through a process of conscientization, a well-informed and well-engaged stance in the process of inquiry. This particular stance should be informed by at least four distinct but intersecting perspectives: ethnicity, gender, hermeneutics, and faith. This intersection, as a standpoint, situates me together with the larger community of Latina intellectuals, and it is from this locus that I speak as a biblical critic.[18]

Readings, including postcolonial readings, from particular Latinx places require a turning toward a search within Latinx communities for an understanding of the text. In that regard, biblical scholars Efraín

---

[16] Fernando F. Segovia, *Decolonizing Biblical Studies: A View from the Margins* (Maryknoll, NY: Orbis Books, 2000), ix–xi. For more regarding the importance of social location and biblical interpretation, see also Randall C. Bailey, Tat-siong Benny Liew, and Fernando F. Segovia, eds., *They Were All Together in One Place? Toward Minority Biblical Criticism* (Atlanta: Society of Biblical Literature, 2009).

[17] Jean-Pierre Ruiz, *Reading from the Edges: The Bible and People on the Move* (Maryknoll, NY: Orbis Books, 2011), 135.

[18] Ahida Calderón Pilarski, "A Latina Biblical Critic and Intellectual: At the Intersection of Ethnicity, Gender, Hermeneutics, and Faith," in *Latino/a Biblical Hermeneutics: Problematics, Objectives, Strategies*, ed. Francisco Lozada Jr. and Fernando F. Segovia (Atlanta: SBL Press, 2014), 247.

Agosto and Jacqueline M. Hidalgo also emphasize "the importance of place," observing that

> Because the United States is a settler colonial state, the various peoples who have migrated here or who were forcibly brought to these shores have had to grapple with either making home or surviving in this new land. Meanwhile Native populations were forced to transform their religious relationships with the landscape, and settler colonists forced many Native populations to migrate to regions of this continent far from ancestral homelands. Even as dominant Euro-diasporic settler colonists sacralized their homemaking processes in this hemisphere, minoritized communities in particular have turned to religion as they struggled to make home.[19]

Coming from the places of minoritized religious communities in the United States to read the biblical text as a Latinx is to read it identifying with a profound sense of "otherness"; as a legitimization of alternative perspectives, which cross traditionally dominant boundaries and social categories; and as a subversive text that radically challenges what the dominant culture has labeled normative truths.

If reading the text implies implementation, then Latinxs are in a unique position to hear God's word in the context of their own sufferings, making their oppressed existence part of the text's interpretation. This subversive reading of the text uses what is known as the "hermeneutical privilege of the oppressed," who have learned how to function without power in a realm constructed by those with privilege, knowing more about the overall U.S. culture than those with power, who only know their own protected space. This does not confer truth exclusively on those who are oppressed. It only states that they are in a better position to understand the biblical call for justice than those who deceive themselves into thinking that justice already exists.

Reading in the Languages of the People

Often the dominant culture sees a Latinx person and presumes they are able to communicate in Spanish, but this assumption can be erroneous. Some Latinx only speak English, others only speak Spanish or Portuguese,

---

[19] Efraín Agosto and Jacqueline M. Hidalgo, "Introduction: Reading the Bible and Latinx Migrations / The Bible as Text(s) of Migration," in *Latinxs, the Bible, and Migration*, ed. Efraín Agosto and Jacqueline M. Hidalgo (New York: Palgrave Macmillan, 2018), 9.

and some are bilingual and bicultural, or perhaps even multilingual and multicultural, whereas still others speak Spanglish or Espanglish, switching between languages and cultural boundaries depending on contexts, needs, and desires.[20]

Carmen Nanko-Fernández suggests, "The significance of language in the navigation of boundaries and in the negotiation of identities within and across generations emerges as a legitimate and necessary locus for theological reflection."[21] Moreover, Latina/os who are able to converse in Spanish are not necessarily literate. Yet, for those who do read the Bible in Spanish, they discover a text that provides theological interpretations different from those who read the same passages in English. Reading the Bible in Spanish affects how Latinxs discern the Divine, influencing their theological perspectives.

Differences in theological interpretations can arise based on which language is used, as three examples show. First, the English word "love" is used to characterize how we feel toward diverse objects, persons, and experiences. By using the same word to describe how we feel toward family and pizza, the word "love" loses some of its intimacy and significance. In Spanish, a distinction is made. *Te amo* (I love you) is only reserved for spouses, partners, or lovers. *Te quiero* (literally, I want you) is used to connote love toward family and friends. *Me gusta* (I like it) usually refers to pizza, hiking, and other things or experiences we like. When referring to the love of God in Spanish, the more intimate term *te amo* is used.

Another example is the English word "you," which can be translated into Spanish as either *tú* or *usted*. *Tú* is an informal pronoun used when addressing one's equals, those who are friends, coworkers, or co-laborers. *Usted*, on the other hand, is a formal pronoun used when addressing those who occupy a higher station in life, for example, one's boss, teachers, political leaders, or elders. When referring to God, the informal *tú* is used, not the formal *usted*. God is recognized as one who is in solidarity with Latinxs as family, hence the informal familiar pronoun is employed.[22]

Finally, Pedraja contrasts the first verse of the Gospel of John and the way it is usually translated into English, "In the beginning was the Word,

---

[20] For more on Spanglish, see Ilan Stavans, *Spanglish: The Making of a New American Language* (New York: HarperCollins, 2003).

[21] Carmen Nanko-Fernández, *Theologizing en Espanglish: Context, Community, and Ministry* (Maryknoll, NY: Orbis Books, 2010), 62.

[22] For another example of the contextual nature of interpretation, see the multilingual examination of Mark 8:27–30 by Neomi De Anda, "Jesus the Christ," in Espín, *Wiley Blackwell Companion to Latino/a Theology*, 163–66.

and the Word was with God, and the Word was God" (John 1:1), with the Spanish version, "*En el principio era el Verbo . . .*" (In the beginning was the Verb). In Spanish, Jesus is not the Word, rather he is the Verb, God's living and active Verb. God as noun makes the Divine static. As a verb, an action Word, God's incarnation in flesh continues as a praxis, an action, within the human experience. Rather than reflecting on a noun as the basis for theology, Hispanics write and talk about *doing* theology.[23]

The Centrality of Justice

To know God is to do justice (Jer 22:15–16). The central tenet of any Latinx theology is praxis, doing the deeds of justice, yet the word "justice" is itself in need of liberation. "Seeking justice" has become a worn-out expression constructed in response to the actions of the dominant culture over against the actions of disenfranchised communities. One person's justice has become the other person's tyranny. Sometimes when the word "justice" is used, what is really being sought is "revenge." We are then left asking, whose justice do we seek?

Along with *agape*, unconditional love, justice is an important component of Christianity. For Latinx Christians, it is perhaps the most important component. Justice based on love toward one's neighbor reflects one's love for and by God. Yet the concept of justice can be lost in the ambiguous term "righteousness" when a biblical text is read in English. Latinxs who read the biblical text in Spanish use the word *justicia*, which is translated as "justice" rather than "righteous."

When English-speakers read "righteous," Latinxs read "just." The dictionary defines "righteous" as "morally right or justifiable, acting in an upright, moral way."[24] That definition implies an action that can be performed privately. However, justice can only be exercised in community, never in isolation, for the concrete reality of sin is always manifested in relation to others. Likewise, justice can only manifest itself in relation to Others. Stranded on a deserted island, an individual can be righteous by remaining conscientious and God-fearing in thought. Justice, on the other hand, can never be practiced on a deserted island because justice needs others to whom justice can be administered. If there is no community, there can be no justice since it is, by definition, a public manifestation of God's acting grace in the lives of Latinx peoples.

By using the words *justo* and *justicia*, the Spanish translation reinforces communalism as opposed to individualism. For example, the Epis-

---

[23] Luis G. Pedraja, *Jesus Is My Uncle: Christology from a Hispanic Perspective* (Nashville: Abingdon Press, 1999), 47–48, 85.

[24] *The Random House Dictionary*, s.v. "righteous."

tle of James 5:16 tells us that "the prayer of the righteous is powerful and effective," that is, one who is pious, whose relationship with God is based on an individual conversion, has their prayers answered. One Spanish version tells us, "La oración eficaz del justo tiene mucha fuerza." It is the prayer of the just one (the one doing justice within the community in obedience to God) that has much power. In English, the Gospel of Matthew 5:6 quotes Jesus as saying, "Blessed are those who hunger and thirst for righteousness, for they will be filled." In other words, those who hunger for moral purity and thirst for chastity will be rewarded. In Spanish, "Bienaventurados los que tienen hambre y sed de justicia, porque ellos serán saciados." Those who hunger for justice to be done to all members of the community, especially to the disenfranchised, and who thirst for justice against all oppressors—these are the ones whom God will fully satisfy.

The Gospel of Luke tells us in English about the centurion who witnessed Christ's crucifixion by saying, "Certainly this man was righteous" (23:47). Christ was the unsoiled innocent lamb who died for our sins. In Spanish, this same centurion says, "Realmente, este hombre era justo." Christ was a just person who died an unjust death. The advice given to Timothy in English reads, "The law is laid down not for the righteous but for the lawless and disobedient, for the ungodly and sinful, for the unholy and profane" (1 Tim 1:9). In Spanish, this advice reads, "La ley no fue puesta para el justo, sino para los trangresores e insumisos, para los impíos e pecadores." While English-language readers are assured that the law does not apply to them because by faith in Christ they have been justified and is not ungodly, sinful, unholy, or profane, the Spanish reader understands that the individual practicing justice does not need the law, for the law is already internal and their actions are only an outward expression of their inward conversion. And for those who are living in a Spanglish world, theological interpretation takes on additional complexity and richness.

Through justice we are able to dismantle the social structures erected and normalized by the dominant culture. When we espouse justice as a universal ideal, we can demand dignity. An "option for the poor" characterizes Latinx theologies, not because the marginalized are inherently more holy than the dominant classes, but simply because they lack the elite's power and privilege. Justice demands the oppressor's repentance for benefitting from social structures that provide them with privilege at the expense of the marginalized. If there is no repentance, then there is no salvation, no liberation, no reconciliation, and accordingly, no justice.[25]

---

[25] Ethicist Ismael Garcia argues that, for many Latinx, conversations concern-

Doing Ethics

The struggle for humanity and dignity is the starting point for any type of a Latinx-based ethical framework. Ethicist Miguel A. De La Torre argues for an "indecent" approach to ethics. De La Torre believes the global success of neoliberalism makes any hope of liberation from oppressive economic systems unrealistic. The marginalized occupy the liminal space between the crucifixion of Friday and the resurrection of Sunday. To occupy Holy Saturday is a hopeless space where all that is known is the brutality and violence of Friday. Sunday remains uncertain, too far away to just wait. To live in the space of Holy Saturday is to embrace the hopelessness of the moment.[26] Those with middle-class privilege are too much in a rush to get to Sunday. To be hopeless is not to give into fatalism. The oppressed have no choice but to continue fighting for the basic necessities, regardless of whether they are going to win or not. And here is the true liberative ethical question: Do we fight for justice because we know we will win, or do we fight for justice, regardless of the outcome, for the sake of justice alone? As a means of defining the faith we claim?

What then becomes a response to neoliberalism? De La Torre developed what he calls an ethics *para joder* (an ethics that screws with). When the oppressive structures cannot be overturned, the only ethical response is to screw with the structures, to create disorder and chaos. This is an ethics that employs the trickster image to upset the normative law and order of those in power who require stability to maintain their privileged position.[27]

Latinx theological thought focuses on *doing* theology with responses in deeds, in actions, and in praxis, rather than arguing over abstract theological frameworks. Doing theology is more than individual piety or virtue, but rather action that leads to salvation and liberation for both the oppressed and their oppressors. Influenced by Latin American liberationists, many U.S. Latinx do theology based on the Roman Catholic social teaching model of *seeing–judging–acting*,[28] which De La Torre

---

ing justice usually explore the dominant motifs of economic, cultural, and political justice. These motifs are further expanded by paying close attention to power and decision making, cultural identity, and the social division of labor. See Ismael Garcia, "Justice," in *Hispanic American Religious Cultures*, vol. 1, ed. Miguel A. De La Torre (Santa Barbara, CA: ABC-CLIO, 2009), 318–23.

[26] Miguel A. De La Torre, *Latina/o Social Ethics: Moving beyond Eurocentric Moral Thinking* (Waco, TX: Baylor University Press, 2010), 92–93.

[27] Ibid., 93–105.

[28] See the Vatican documents *Gaudium et spes* and *Octogesima adveniens*.

expands to a five-step hermeneutical circle for ethics. Society cannot be transformed apart from first doing social analysis.

The hermeneutical circle begins in the first step with observation to understand why the present moral dilemma exists, and to consider seriously the historical situation responsible for the present oppressive circumstances under which Latinxs are forced to live. Understanding the Latinx social location requires exploring why, how, and when the present oppressive structures were created, maintained, normalized, and legitimized. The second step, reflection, seeks to understand how social structures contribute to and maintain the oppression of Latinx peoples. The third step, prayer, attempts to understand what should be the responsibility of Latinxs of faith. Prayer establishes *comunidad*, where the stories of Latinxs are critically listened to and where there is a commitment to work in solidarity for full liberation. The fourth step, action, becomes a response based on what Christians claim to believe. The fifth and final step is assessment. An opportunity is created to examine the results of praxis and change them accordingly if they did not lead the people closer to justice.[29]

On Being Humans

Anthropology refers to the study of humans. Depending on the nature of the discussion, "anthropology" can refer to a field of social-scientific study of humanity and human societies, or it can refer to theological study focused on humanity in relationship to God. Christian theological anthropology stresses the origins of humans as products of God's creativity. Developing theological anthropology further, Orlando Espín talks about the relationship between *humanitas* and identity: "By *humanitas*, I mean that which we share and recognize in persons and communities— that is, that living, historical, complex reality that allows us to speak of 'humanity.' . . . *Humanitas*, therefore, implies identity: our own and that of others. *Humanitas*, furthermore, can be best recognized interculturally in others."[30]

While they may draw upon the social science of anthropology, most Christian theologians engaging in theological anthropology study beliefs about the nature of humans in relation to the Divine. Such beliefs usually include the creation story, specifically the origin of humanity in God, and the fall. A recurring motif within Christian anthropology is

---

[29] Miguel A. De La Torre, *Doing Christian Ethics from the Margins*, 2nd ed. (Maryknoll, NY: Orbis Books, 2014), 47–56.

[30] Orlando O. Espín, *Grace and Humanness: Theological Reflections Because of Culture* (Maryknoll, NY: Orbis Books, 2007), 52–53.

the healing of humanity, known as "salvation," from the consequences of the fall. Regardless of whether the scholar accepts or rejects the creation story of Genesis as historically accurate, the essence of the story is that creation's source is God. As such, humans bear the image of God (the *imago Dei*), but due to the fall, sin entered humanity, alienating humans from God due to the latter's transgression. Yet, even while humans remain in need of redemption, the promise of a new humanity exists. The focus of this new humanity is Christ, as the second Adam (Rom 5:12–21), who is the completion of all humanity. Obviously, not all Latinx accept the concept of the fall nor the product of original sin as its consequence. The theological proposition that all humans carry the original sin of Adam that alienates God from humans has been rejected by some Latinx scholars, including Miguel A. De La Torre in his commentary on Genesis.[31]

Many Latinx theologians have stressed aspects of the creation story, specifically the means by which God brings forth a new humanity. The good news, according to Latinx theologians, is that the biblical narrative proclaims a God who reveals Godself from within disenfranchised communities. Historically God has chosen the disenfranchised as agents of God's new creation. The stone rejected by the builders becomes the keystone of God's creation (Mt 21:42). God did not make God's will known to the court of Pharaoh but instead to their slaves, the Hebrews, to reveal God's movement in history. It was not Rome, the most powerful city of the known world, where God chose to perform the miracle of the incarnation, nor was it Jerusalem, the center of Yahweh worship; rather, it was impoverished Galilee where God chose to first proclaim the message of the Gospels. Nazareth was so insignificant to the religious life of Judaism that the Hebrew Bible never mentions it. If it were not for Jesus being a Nazarene, Galilee may have been just another unknown and unimportant region of the world.

Jesus's contemporaries had a low opinion of Galilee. According to John 7:52–53, when the multitudes discovered Jesus's origins they exclaimed, "Surely you are not also from Galilee, are you? Search and you will see that no prophet is to arise from Galilee." John 1:46 also gives us the example of Nathanael, one of Jesus's future disciples, who, upon learning Jesus was from Nazareth, showed his bias by saying, "Can anything good come out of Nazareth?" It would be as if Jesus would be born today in the barrios of the Bronx, East Los Angeles, or Miami's *sagüesera*, rather than from the "good" neighborhoods with their ornate

---

[31] Miguel A. De La Torre, *Genesis: Belief: A Theological Commentary on the Bible* (Louisville, KY: Westminster John Knox Press, 2011), 70–80.

sanctuaries. To carry out God's salvific plan, God chooses a stone from the margins that the dominant culture has rejected.

Latinx theologians are quick to point out that those marginalized in Jesus's time, contrary to cultural expectations, occupied the privileged position of being the first to hear the good news—not because they were holier, nor more faithful to God, but because God chooses sides. God makes an option for those who exist under the weight of oppression. Jesus willingly assumes the role of the ultra-disenfranchised. The radical nature of the incarnation for Latinx peoples is not that God became human, but that God assumed the condition of a slave. In Paul's letter to the Philippians (2:6), he says of Christ, "Who, though he was in the form of God, did not regard equality with God as something to be exploited but emptied himself taking the form of a slave." Why is it important to see Jesus and construct theology through the lens of the disenfranchised? By making the disenfranchised recipients of the good news, Jesus emphasized the political edge of his message (Lk 4:18–19).

Latinxs expect the Divine to work God's ways through today's marginalized communities. Because of the disenfranchised space designated for Latinx, they hold the sacred responsibility to proclaim the good news to all, specifically to the centers of power and privilege. This is not an attempt to romanticize their marginalization, but instead it is an attempt to formulate a theological response to their social location. Latinx theologies do not call people to resign themselves to their economic conditions while hopefully awaiting their reward in the hereafter; rather they seek the elimination of the sin of injustice in the present. Latinx theology is a call to participate in a consciousness-raising experience so that Latinx peoples can transcend their objectification by the dominant culture and establish their humanity.

Theological Topics

Before turning our attention to specific theological topics, one final point needs to be made about the methodology employed in the development of Latinx theological perspectives. In emphasizing the differences existing between Euroamerican and Latinx theological views, it is important to remember that Euroamerican theological views and the theological traditions of the church are not identical. It would be erroneous to conclude that any reaction against Euroamerican theological perspectives is automatically a reaction against the historical tradition of the church (in any of its several streams). Latinx perspectives are not necessarily against the historical tradition of the church; rather, it is against those perspectives that have dominated the theological discourse while marginalizing important teachings of the faith tradition. By listening to the theological voices of historically marginalized groups, the discourse becomes revitalized by bringing to the forefront valuable concepts of the faith tradition that have been systematically ignored because they challenge the power and privilege of those setting the theological agenda. Hence, in this section we begin to reflect upon some of the many specific Christian theological topics.

Sin

Sin, for Christians, opposes God's benevolent purposes for creation and is responsible for the enslavement of the human race and the corruption of God's created order. The liberation found in Christ is displaced by the individual's transgressions and/or the sins of those with power and privilege. The essence of sin is idolatry, striving to supplant the Creator with something or someone else. This displacement can be voluntary, as when individuals exchange the glory of God for money. However, God can also be deposed involuntarily, as in the case of structural mechanisms that foster the subjugation of many to the privileged few. The consequences of sin are alienation from God, God's community, God's creation, and God's will for each person.

Many Euroamerican Christians often look to the cross as the remedy for sin. Salvation is found in Christ's death, a substitute for the sinner to appease an angry God. Latinx, while understanding the cosmic importance of Jesus's death, also focus on his life, which becomes an avenue for Latinxs to overcome their own alienation. For many Euroamerican Christians, Jesus's death saves, while for Latinxs, Jesus's life, suffering, and resurrection also become the center of his salvific plan. The connection with Jesus's suffering on the cross is present in the devotions of the Penitentes of northern New Mexico during Holy Week.[32] The suffering

---

[32] Penitentes are a confraternity or brotherhood of devout Hispano Catholic men in New Mexico (the term "Hispano" is a self-designation by many New Mexico Latinx). The brotherhood traces its roots back to the Spanish colonial period. While drawing on a stream of popular religiosity in northern New Mexico, the Penitentes formally emerged as a distinct group in the nineteenth century. They annually commemorate the sufferings and death of Jesus Christ during Holy Week. Their use of self-flagellation during devotions was opposed by the institutional Roman Catholic Church. These Penitentes demonstrate a strong sense of religious autonomy, particularly as expressed in their initiative and creativity to structure their expressions of faith in the face of the occasional neglect or opposition from the church. See also Michael P. Carroll, *The Penitente Brotherhood: Patriarchy and Hispano-Catholicism in New Mexico* (Baltimore, MD: Johns Hopkins University Press, 2002).

of Christ is also depicted in the dramatic re-creation of the passion during the Holy Week celebrations, such as at San Fernando Cathedral in San Antonio, Texas; or the *Via Crucis* in Chicago's Pilsen neighborhood; or Guadalupan processions in New York City.[33]

But, lest we become too focused on Jesus's death on the cross, it should be remembered that particular Latinx Christian communities end Holy Week with a grand celebration of the resurrection of Jesus. For many Latinx Christians, the crucifixion has less to do with an atonement from sin and more to do with solidarity. Jesus, like so many Latinx people today who are crucified on the crosses of unjust immigration policies, neoliberalism, ethnic discrimination, and brutality at the hand of law enforcement, also died unjustly at the hands of religious and political leaders. The Latino Jesús accompanied the marginalized and disenfranchised by sharing in their same fate. Latinxs have a God who also knows what it means to be unjustly crucified, thus providing hope for resurrection from the present injustices.

Within the North American ethos, influenced by hyperindividualism, sin is often regarded as a private matter. "Jesus," many Protestant evangelists would tell us, "has a plan for our *individual* lives, only if we repent from *our* sins, and accept him as our *personal* Savior." Yet, while Latinxs understand the importance of confessing and repenting of sins committed by the individual, there also exists a recognition that while sin may be individually committed, it is never personal. Regardless as to how private we may wish to keep sin, it always affects others because we are communal creatures. Hence, Latinxs who accept the concept of sin maintain that sin has both an individual and communal dimension.

Sin is inherent within social structures. "Sin," according to Ismael Garcia, "manifests itself within social practices, including the accepted laws and moral regulations that allow some to live and prosper at the expense of others."[34] David Traverso Galarza reminds us that "sin is a reality, a force that delivers death and destruction to countless num-

---

[33] See Virgilio P. Elizondo and Timothy M. Matovina, *San Fernando Cathedral: Soul of the City* (Maryknoll, NY: Orbis Books, 1998); Timothy Matovina, *Guadalupe and Her Faithful: Latino Catholics in San Antonio, from Colonial Origins to the Present* (Baltimore, MD: Johns Hopkins University Press, 2005); Karen Mary Davolos, "'The Real Way of Praying': The Via Crucis, Mexicano Sacred Space, and the Architecture of Domination," in *Horizons of the Sacred: Mexican Traditions in U.S. Catholicism*, ed. Timothy Matovina and Gary Riebe-Estrella (Ithaca, NY: Cornell University Press, 2002), 47; Ayshia Gálvez, *Guadalupe in New York: Devotion and the Struggle for Citizenship Rights among Mexican Immigrants* (New York: New York University Press, 2009), 107–39.

[34] Ismael García, *Dignidad: Ethics through Hispanic Eyes* (Nashville: Abingdon Press, 1997), 137.

bers of persons and communities daily." For Traverso Galarza and many other Latinx, sin is "social, institutional, structural, systemic as well as personal."[35] Hence, Jesus's purpose was not solely to save individuals from their sins, but also, and just as importantly, to save the community from the sins of its social structures.

Oppression related to race, class, gender, and sexual identity normatively transcends the individual's personal bias by becoming the collective bias of society. These biases, in turn, are institutionalized by the society, specifically in the government, the marketplace, and the church. Latino/as who face discriminatory practices often realize that the source of this form of violence is not necessarily found in an individual within an organization; rather, the organization is constructed to protect the privileged space of the dominant culture at the expense of the disenfranchised. Therefore, individual repentance is insufficient to change or challenge the status quo. Institutions also must repent by unmasking their normative procedures.

For many Latinxs, life exists under institutionalized violence, that is, under the consequences of oppression operative within social structures. Those structures, the antithesis of Jesus's life-giving mission, bring figurative and literal death to Latinx. Those who are victimized by institutionalized violence are usually seen by the dominant culture as being responsible for their own suffering. One reason Latinx people are poor, according to many in the dominant culture, is that they are lazy (refusing to implement the Protestant work ethic), ignorant (preferring to live in the mire of the barrio), or violent (responsible for many of our cities' crimes). Absent from the discourse is any examination of the structures of society that have intentionally created an army of low-skilled laborers for the profit of commerce, of those who benefit from it, or of their complicity with the plight of the poor.

Yet it would be erroneous to assume that Latinx people are the only victims of the dominant culture's corporate sins. Euroamericans who ignore their complicity with structural sins are also trapped and negatively affected by the existing relationship between those with privilege and those who are disenfranchised. Those whom social structures privilege are forced to live according to their assigned community roles, roles created at the expense of people of color. Hence, Latinx theologies call for the liberation/salvation of those who suffer under the burden of corporate sin, as well as those who benefit because of it.

---

[35] David Traverso Galarza, "Sin: A Hispanic Perspective," in *Teología en Conjunto: A Collaborative Hispanic Protestant Theology*, ed. by José David Rodríguez and Loida I. Martell-Otero (Louisville, KY: Westminster John Knox Press, 1997), 119.

Christology

On which Christ should Latinx Christians anchor their theology? Is it the Christ constructed and created in the image of Euroamericans? The Euroamerican Christ is problematic because Jesus historically has been used (or muted) to divinely justify societal actions detrimental to Latinx's well-being. The Euroamerican Jesus is the Christ that inspired the quasireligious ideology of Manifest Destiny, leading the United States in its military conquest of northern Mexico, thus impeding the ability of that nation to build wealth while simultaneously disenfranchising those over whom the border crossed. The Euroamerican Jesus is the Christ who remained silent during the implementation of gunboat diplomacy that denied Latin American nations their sovereignty and provided U.S. corporations the freedom and protection to extract cheap labor and natural resources. The Euroamerican Jesus is the Christ of present-day politicians whose main purpose is the maintenance of U.S. global hegemony. Latinx should remain suspicious of the Euroamerican Christ because of its complicity with empire. As long as Latinx people bow their knees to a Christ who is silent about what it means to live at the margins of Euroamerican power and privilege, as long as this Christ refuses to motivate speaking out about the marginalization faced throughout the barrios of this nation, as long as this Christ does not elicit solidarity with the thousands who die in the Sonoran desert of Arizona because of unjust immigration laws, then those Latinxs insisting on worshiping the Christ that looks and acts like the dominant culture would in fact be worshiping the symbolic cause of their oppression.

Some Latinx theological thought attempts to sever the link between oppressive power and disenfranchisement, between privilege and marginality. One strategy employed by Miguel A. De La Torre, in his book *The Politics of Jesús*, recognizes Jesus as ontologically Latinx by insisting on literally doing "Christology with an accent—and not just over the *u*." Only a Latinx Jesús, not a white Jesus, can save Latinx peoples.[36] This Latinx Christ is informed by the historical identification of Jesus with those who suffer under oppression. Christ's "Latinoness" is not due to some simplistic attempt to be politically correct, nor to some psychological need existing among Latinx to see the Divine through their own cultural symbols. Jesus is Latinx because the biblical witness of God is of one who takes sides with the least among us against those who oppress them.

Harold J. Recinos argues that reflecting on Jesus from Latinx perspectives shows that "the study of Latino/a Christology enables U.S. Chris-

---

[36] Miguel A. De La Torre, *The Politics of Jesús: A Hispanic Political Theology* (New York: Rowman and Littlefield, 2015), 13.

tians to more accurately understand the different dimensions of their Christian reality."[37] Consequently, for many Latinx people only a Latinx Christ can liberate Latinxs. Whatever Christ means to Latinx people, he must be understood within sociohistorical and ecopolitical contexts of the Latinx faith communities that are responding to the biblical message of liberation. For numerous Latinxs, however, Christ is defined or understood foremost as a liberator. From the underside of U.S. culture, where Latinx people are forced to suffer, a quest for a Hispanic Christ becomes a quest for liberation from ethnic discrimination. Whoever this Jesus is, Latinxs see him through their own eyes as being quite different than how Euroamericans see Jesus.

For many Latinx, Jesus has the following characteristics:

- Jesus is born homeless (Lk 2:7). The Bible tells us that although divine, he became human, assuming the condition of a slave (Phil 2:6–8).
- Jesus is born into poverty (Lk 2:22–24) and willingly assumed the role of the ultra-disenfranchised, being born into, living in, and dying in poverty.
- Jesus is an undocumented immigrant (Mt 2:14). Over two thousand years ago the Holy Family arrived in Egypt as political refugees, migrants fleeing the tyrannical regime of Herod.
- Jesus dwelled among us (Jn 1:14). God does not stand aloof from the experiences or sufferings of human experiences; instead God enfleshes Godself in the concrete events of human history.
- Jesus lived a life of poverty (Lk 9:58), wandering throughout Judea without money in his purse and relying on the charity of others (Lk 8:1–3), having no place to lay his head.
- Jesus comes from the barrios (Jn 1:46). Recall that when the multitudes discovered Jesus's origins, they exclaimed, "Are you not also from Galilee? Search the Scriptures and see that no prophet out of Galilee has been raised" (Jn 7:52–53).
- Jesus was perceived to be a mestizo—of mixed race (Jn 8:41). Jesus was not simply a Jew, he was a Galilean Jew, marginalized, as Virgilio Elizondo reminds us, from the center of Jewish life and society.[38]
- Jesus is tempted with possessions, power, and privilege (Mt 4:1–11).

---

[37] Harold J. Recinos, "Introduction," in *Jesus in the Hispanic Community: Images of Christ from Theology to Popular Religion*, ed. Harold J. Recinos and Hugo Magallanes (Louisville, KY: Westminster John Knox Press, 2009), xxi.

[38] Virgilio P. Elizondo, *Galilean Journey: The Mexican-American Promise*, 2nd ed. (Maryknoll, NY: Orbis Books, 2000), 49–53.

- Jesus is willing to learn from the margins (Mt 15:21–28). After calling a Canaanite woman a dog, succumbing to the prevailing xenophobia of his day, Jesus realized faith was not contingent upon a person's (Jewish) ethnicity.
- Jesus calls the privileged to change (Mk 10:17–31). He does not invite the rich young ruler to simply repent of his sins, but rather Jesus tells him to sell all and distribute the proceeds to the poor.

The gospel message of liberation from oppressive societal structures resonates with Latinxs who discover that those marginalized in Jesus's time occupied the privileged position of being the first to hear the good news. God makes a preferential option for those who exist under the weight of oppression. The radical nature of the incarnation is not that God became human, but that God assumed the condition of one of *los humildes* (the humbled). If God was to reincarnate today, God would come to us in the form of those most despised by the culture, those most humbled. No doubt God would incarnate Godself as an undocumented immigrant, for they are the ones who are hungry, thirsty, naked, foreign, ill, and if caught crossing, imprisoned.

Salvation

For all Christians, the gospel message is a message of salvation (although admittedly there are different concepts of salvation). Soteriology is precisely the theological attempt to understand how an individual and communities obtain salvation. If a typical Protestant believer (in a broadly evangelical or theologically conservative tradition) was asked how to obtain salvation, they would likely recite John 3:16. For many, the entire message and purpose of the Bible can be reduced to this verse: "For God so loved the world, that he gave his only Son, so that everyone who believes in him may not perish but have eternal life."[39]

While most Latinxs do not deny the importance of John 3:16, Luke 4:18–19 also plays a major if not more important role in their understanding of salvation. This passage recounts Jesus's first proclamation in the Gospel of Luke concerning his mission. On the Sabbath he attended the synagogue, opened the scroll to the book of Isaiah, and used a passage to describe his earthly commission: "The Spirit of the Lord is upon me, because he has anointed me to bring the gospel news to the poor.

---

[39] Such soteriological understanding is not prevalent among mainline Protestant traditions. U.S. Protestantism is diverse, reflecting myriad theological perceptions on how salvation occurs. Also see the discussion in the introduction for more about U.S. mainline Protestantism.

He has sent me to proclaim release to the captives and recovery of sight to the blind, to let the oppressed go free, to preach the year of the Lord's favor." So angered were those who heard this message that they sought to kill him.

Many Latinx Christians see a Jesus who links salvation with a praxis of liberation. Salvation is the bringing of life—abundant life (Jn 10:10)—to where death reigns along with the injustices and oppression that lead to death. These Latinx remember the words of Jesus, as recorded by Luke, who said "every tree therefore that does not bear good fruit is cut down and thrown into the fire" (Lk 3:9). Such an understanding of salvation subverts the dominant culture's reduction of the salvific act to the recitation of a proclamation of belief. Influenced by Martin Luther, Euroamericans, specifically Protestants, insist that salvation can never be earned, but rather is a gift from God: we are saved through God's grace, not by works. Although Latinxs agree that salvation begins as a love praxis from God, they insist such praxis is an outward expression of an inward conversion. This praxis demands justice for the disenfranchised.

Jesus tells his followers through the parable of the Sheep and the Goats as recorded in Matthew 25:31–46 how salvation will be dispensed. In this story the saved and the unsaved are divided by what they did or failed to do for the hungry, the thirsty, the naked, the foreigner, the infirm, and the incarcerated. Salvation was not determined by one's belief in doctrine (orthodoxy) or one's church affiliation, but rather by what one did (orthopraxis) or did not do to "one of the least of these." For Latinxs, salvation is linked with the treatment of those who are oppressed. Ignoring the plight of the disenfranchised is to ignore Christ's message of salvation, a message synonymous with liberation. To be saved is to be liberated from the sins of the individual through the acceptance of a new life in Christ; to be liberated from the oppressive economic, political, and social conditions that constitute corporate sin; and to take control of one's own destiny. In the deepest sense possible, liberation is salvation.

Ecclesiology: A *Familia* of Believers

Ecclesiology is the study of how the church understands its own existence and its faithfulness to its historical development. Across Christian traditions there is agreement that the church can be understood as a community of the faithful impacted by the life, death, and resurrection of Jesus Christ. Beyond this formal understanding, Latinxs are aware that, within their context, Roman Catholics and Protestants have had different trajectories in their formal ecclesiology. This is naturally the case, as Latinx theologies seek to be articulated from within the contexts of specific U.S. Latinx communities. However, one cultural commonality that seems to affect all Latinx understandings of ecclesiology is the concept of *familia* (family).

For many Latinx Christians, *familia*, as we briefly discussed in the last chapter, is the archetype of the church and also an important aspect of Latinx cultures. This seems to be the case even when individual family dynamics and relationships may be challenging, difficult, or sometimes nonexistent. The dominant concept of the nucleus or immediate family—composed of father, mother, and 2.4 children—is too narrow to fit the U.S. Latinx realities. *Familia* embraces a broader extended family: cousins, uncles, parents, grandmothers, nephews, and siblings living either together or in close proximity. *Familia* is not limited to blood ties and can include those brought in. The concept of *padrinos/madrinas* (godparents) binds different clans together. Compadres (co-parents) are united at the baptismal sacrament of the child, assuming joint responsibility for that child's welfare and creating new family bonds. Originally, this was a Catholic concept but it has transcended religious borders as Protestants who insist on "believer's baptism"—the baptism of adults—have baby dedication services with the equivalent of *padrinos* and *madrinas* serving as witnesses.

Through the extended family and the binding together of different families through the social institution of compadres/comadres, Latinxs enlarge and strengthen the social institution of *familia*, offering a healing alternative to insidious individualism. Compassion, a will to sacrifice, and an ability to sustain each other are crucial elements in a healthy *familia*. They serve as a counterbalance to a survival-of-the-fittest mentality. Such a cutthroat environment, while sought after in the North American marketplace, still undermines the gospel message of sacrificial love. *Familia*, as an example for churches, becomes a much-needed theological perspective manifested in the terms of endearment used by many Latinx faith communities: *hermano/a* (brother/sister).

Church as a *familia* of believers becomes the basis for how Latinxs understand ecclesiology. Such a church is endowed with the gifts of God's Spirit, which attempts to understand and do the will of God. The importance of the *familia* or *comunidad* of believers in doing theology creates a church-centric understanding of theology that subverts the individualistic theologies. Ada María Isasi-Díaz advocated for an expansive understanding of the *familia* of believers:

> In *mujerista* theology we suggest replacing "kingdom" with "kin-dom." We suggest moving away from a political metaphor

to which we have hardly any way of relating to a more personal metaphor that lies at the core of our daily lives. The idea of kin-dom of God, of the family of God, we suggest, is a much more relevant and effective metaphor today to communicate what Jesus lived and died for. This suggestion of the kin-dom of God in many ways is a response to the ongoing concern for the loss of family values and the loss of even a true sense of family in present-day society. Kin-dom of God as the core metaphor for the goal of Jesus' life will help us reconstitute our sense of family.[40]

One model under which Latinx people attempt to create this church-centric approach to theology is called a *pastoral de conjunto* (collaborative pastoral ministry). The reemergence of the concept of *pastoral de conjunto* originated from pastoral experiments in Latin America in the 1960s and 1970s. The Latin American Roman Catholic bishops, meeting in Puebla in 1979, adopted it as the preferred pastoral strategy to meet the exigencies of evangelization. This strategy calls for full participation by every level of the faith community. The goal, according to the bishops, was for the church to learn "how to analyze reality, how to reflect on this reality from the standpoint of the Gospel, how to choose the most suitable objectives and means, and how to use them in the most sensible way for the work of evangelization."[41]

In the United States, *pastoral de conjunto* came to prominence through the several national meetings of Hispanic/Latino Catholics known as Encuentro Nacional de Pastoral (1972, 1977, 1985, 2000, 2018). Through those meetings, U.S. Latinx Catholics appropriated the concept of *pastoral de conjunto*. According to Ana María Pineda, this collaborative pastoral ministry "invites the people of God to commit themselves actively to continue the work of Jesus by entering into the cultural, religious, and social reality of the people, becoming incarnate in and with the people."[42]

[40] Ada María Isasi-Díaz, "*Identifícate con Nosotras*: A *Mujerista* Christological Understanding," in *Jesus in the Hispanic Community: Images of Christ from Theology to Popular Religion*, ed. Harold J. Recinos and Hugo Magallanes (Louisville, KY: Westminster John Knox Press, 2009), 44. See also Ada María Isasi-Díaz and Yolanda Tarango, *Hispanic Women: Prophetic Voice in the Church* (Minneapolis: Fortress Press, 1992), 116.

[41] CELAM, "Final Document," in *Puebla and Beyond: Documentation and Commentary*, ed. John Eagleson and Philip Scharper (Maryknoll, NY: Orbis Books, 1979), no. 1307.

[42] Ana María Pineda, "Pastoral de Conjunto," in *Mestizo Christianity: Theol-*

U.S. Latinxs are developing a process that attempts to understand the Divine from within social locations, a process that analyzes Latinx realities and is tied to theological perspectives that demand sociopolitical responses to both internal and external oppression. A relationship has developed between oppressed Latinxs and theologians or intellectuals aware of the structural crises that Latinxs face in the United States. *Pastoral de conjunto* connects the pastoral work done by those in pastoral ministry and the academic work of intellectuals with people within local Latinx congregations. These clerics and scholars attempt to learn from the disenfranchised while serving them as organic intellectuals grounded in the social reality of the people and acting in the consciousness-raising process of the faith community.

For Latinx communities these tasks attempt to heal the brokenness of lives. Most Latinx people living in this country are disjointed from the culture of their heritage and the culture in which they reside—outsiders and foreigners to both—all the while creating and living within a distinct third cultural sphere. *Pastoral de conjunto* seeks mending for a broken existence through the rich diversity found among multiracial and multicultural Latinx. A holistic collaborative spirit emerges when Latinxs gather to share the Word of God—their stories of suffering and pilgrimage. *Pastoral de conjunto* is the construction of a collaborative theology and its impact upon the theological reflection of Latinx people who struggle in understanding their faith and vocation as it is contextualized in their lives and struggles.

Evangelism and Evangelization

At first blush, the words "evangelism" and "evangelization" might seem to mean exactly the same thing, but they can have very different nuances, especially when they are contextually used in Protestant and Catholic settings. Although sometimes used interchangeably, "evangelism" is often used in Protestant circles to mean "sharing of the gospel of Jesus Christ through a variety of means," whereas the word "evangelization" is less used by Protestants; most often it is as a synonym for "evangelism."[43] Drawing on Pope Paul VI's *Evangelii Nuntiandi (On Evangelization in the Modern World)*, "evangelization" means "bringing the Good News of Jesus into every human situation and seeking to convert individuals and society by the divine power of the Gospel itself. At its essence are the

---

ogy from the Latino Perspective, ed. Arturo J. Bañuelas (Maryknoll, NY: Orbis Books, 1995), 128.

[43] Donald K. McKim, *Westminster Dictionary of Theological Terms*, 2nd ed. (Louisville, KY: Westminster John Knox Press, 2014), 110.

proclamation of salvation in Jesus Christ and the response of a person in faith, which are both works of the Spirit of God."[44] Both ecclesiastical communions might be comfortable with the definition from the other, but part of the nuance is whether we are coming into initial Christian faith or growing into responsible Christian discipleship.

For the majority of U.S. Latinx Protestants and Latin American Protestants, evangelism is about inviting people into initial Christian faith, no matter what their prior religious roots might have been. Therefore, Juan Francisco Martínez is able to say,

> One of the reasons for the growth of Latina Protestantism, and of Protestantism in Latin America, has been the evangelism born from the commitment of the converted. New converts are most often a result of the preaching of those who do it because it is so important in their own lives. Latino Protestants are much more likely to view (and practice) evangelization as the task of all believers and not as a responsibility of mission experts.[45]

Missiology, the study of missions, articulates the purpose and function of the community of faith. The mission of the church, especially for evangelicals, is the proclamation of the gospel message of salvation that is found in Christ Jesus, that is, evangelism. This Great Commission is based on Mark 16:15–16: "Go into all the world, and proclaim the good news to the whole creation. The one who believes and is baptized will be saved; but the one who does not believe will be condemned." For most evangelicals, Christian discipleship encompasses the responsibility of witnessing the message of salvation to unbelievers so that they too can hear, be converted, and gain eternal life. Many Euroamerican evangelicals understand the Great Commission to be Christ's appointment of the believer to go and convert the world to the message and lordship of Christ. Yet an assumption that most Euroamerican churches make is that because they hold the "truth," and the unbeliever lives in darkness, the unbeliever must change and assimilate to the missionaries' worldview. Unfortunately, in many cases, the missionaries' cultural traditions are confused with the biblical message.

Ironically, *evangélicos* (which within the Latinx contexts also encompasses mainline Protestants and not just evangelicals), who exist on the margins of U.S. religiosity, have historically been pressured to assimilate

---

[44] United States Conference of Catholic Bishops, http://www.usccb.org/beliefs-and-teachings/.

[45] Juan Francisco Martínez, *Los Protestantes: An Introduction to Latino Protestantism in the United States* (Santa Barbara, CA: ABC-CLIO, 2011), 102.

to the Euroamerican evangelical norm. Thus, Latinx *evangélicos* know what it means to be seen as the ones who must convert from understanding the gospel through their own cultural symbols to the usage of the "purer" Euroamerican symbols. This has led to greater sensitivity in understanding missiology. Rather than questioning how the unbeliever must change to become part of the church, we all should be asking how the church must change to welcome the outsider. A careful reading of the early church's mission, as recorded in the book of Acts, revealed that the church did not conceive of its mission on the day of Pentecost, rather, it was an ongoing process. As going about fulfilling its mission of solidarity with Christ, the church discovered how that mission was to be fulfilled. The original church was forced to die to its traditions in order for God's ministry to begin. While there is a difference between *evangélicos* and evangelicals in English, some Latinx *evangélicos* very much align themselves with U.S. evangelicals.

The Spirit

For Christians, human life and the world are sustained by God through the Spirit. The study of the Spirit of God, pneumatology, examines how God's presence is made real within each epoch of human history as well as within specific Christian communities, fulfilled through humans transforming their society in each and every ensuing generation. Life in the Spirit for many Latinx means a greater sense of identity, freedom, and community in which the various callings of women and men find expression, and thereby affirmation and empowerment by God's Spirit. Furthermore, the charismatic revival among different religious traditions has produced among Latinx faithful a liberative theological response to their disenfranchisement. In what has become a classic and foundational study in Latinx theology, *The Liberating Spirit: Towards an Hispanic American Pentecostal Social Ethic*, Eldin Villafañe explains how Latinx pentecostal Christians understand the working of the Holy Spirit. Interpreting Galatians 5:25, Villafañe maintains that to live in the Spirit (a theological self-understanding) is to also walk in the Spirit (an ethical self-understanding). The Spirit's historical project is to participate in the reign of God, that is, a reign concerned with the establishment of justice by restraining evil and fostering conditions for an ethical moral order. Through the power of the Spirit, structures of sin and evil are challenged and confronted as disenfranchised congregations receive charismatic empowerment and the spiritual resources to encounter social struggles.[46]

---

[46] Eldin Villafañe, *The Liberating Spirit: Towards an Hispanic American Pentecostal Social Ethic* (Grand Rapids: Eerdmans, 1993), 195.

In another Latinx theological classic, *The Spirit, Pathos, and Liberation*, Samuel Solivan explores orthopathos as a necessary corrective and balance to orthodoxy and orthopraxis.[47] Soliván accuses North American theological orthodoxy and orthopraxis as having failed in their callings. In naming the need for this corrective, Soliván says, "Those of us who seek to speak on behalf of the sufferer must return to that place of suffering. Our propinquity to suffering informs not only our method, but also our epistemology. *Orthopathos* as an interlocutor seeks to or links us in community with those who suffer."[48]

The almost sacramental emphasis on the Word strongly influences the nature of Latinx Protestant popular religion. Especially in those communities influenced by Pentecostalism, there is a profound emphasis on the Holy Spirit and the experience of the Spirit that shapes the expressions and practices of the faith of the people. Added to this mix of the high authority of the Bible as the Word of God and the importance of a personal experience of God's Spirit is the historical aversion of many Latinx Protestants to overt elements of Latinx popular Catholicism, one of the primary areas of expression of faith in that context. These factors combine to produce different expressions of popular religion by Latinx Protestants, even while some underlying shared characteristics of Protestants and Catholics still can be identified. Pentecostal theologian and pastor Sammy Alfaro explores how *coritos* and *cuentos* (worship choruses / songs and stories) are some of the ways that Latinx pentecostal spirituality is expressed.[49]

Latinxs not only contribute to the understanding of the function of the Spirit but also to the role the Spirit plays within the Trinity. Several Latinx theologians understand the relationship existing within the Trinity, between Father, Son, and Holy Spirit, as the pattern for humanity. Thus, it is not viewed as a cosmic puzzle in need of a solution, but rather as a paragon to be emulated. Father, Son, and Spirit do not exist in a hierarchy; all three share equally in substance, power, and importance. Trinity represents a Godhead whose very existence is that of a sharing Being, coequal in power, awe, and authority.[50] The Triune God provides an economic pattern of sharing for those who claim belief in the doctrine of the Trinity, consequently subverting any eco-

---

[47] Samuel Solivan, *The Spirit, Pathos, and Liberation: Toward an Hispanic Pentecostal Theology* (Sheffield, UK: Sheffield Academic Press, 1998).

[48] Ibid., 37.

[49] Sammy Alfaro, *Divino Compañero: Toward a Hispanic Pentecostal Christology* (Eugene, OR: Pickwick Press, 2012), 143–48.

[50] Justo L. González, *Mañana: Christian Theology from a Hispanic Perspective* (Nashville: Abingdon Press, 1990), 113.

nomic system that requires an undereducated and underskilled army of laborers so that the few can disproportionately horde the majority of the wealth. Speaking from a Roman Catholic location, Gilberto Cavasos-González, OFM, provides a reflection on the nature of the work of the Triune God that many Latinx Christians across denominations could affirm: "Thanks to Jesus, who pours out his Spirit on his faithful, we are temples of God's Holy Spirit and as such we are filled with the presence of the Most Holy Trinity in the core of our *corazón*, our spirit. The Spirit of God *en conjunto* with our spirit moves us to act as Christians in lives of prayer, devotion, ministry, and social action according to Catholic social teaching."[51]

Devotion to Mary and the Challenge of *Marianismo*

The Virgin Mary plays a profound role among Latinx people. European-origin devotional representations of the Virgin Mary found adherents in the Americas, but her manifestations in the Americas often take shape in the form of those oppressed. For example, for Mexicans, Mexican Americans, and other Latinxs, the story of *La Virgen de Guadalupe*, also known as *la morenita* (the little brown lady), defines their understandings of family, community, and daily spirituality.[52] According to tradition, in 1531 on a hill of Tepeyac (then on the outskirts of Mexico City), *La Virgen de Guadalupe* appeared to an indigenous Chichimeca convert named Juan Diego, and within seven years over 8 million indigenous people were baptized into the Catholic Church, leading some to name the Virgin of Guadalupe the "Evangelizer of the Americas."

What *La Virgen de Guadalupe* represents to Mexicans, *La Virgen de Caridad* means to Cubans. According to the traditional Catholic version, around 1610, two native Taíno brothers, Juan and Rodrigo de Hoyos, along with a black slave boy named Juan Moreno, went rowing on Nipe Bay in search of salt. At about five-thirty in the morning, while in their canoe, they came upon a fifteen-inch carved statue of the Virgin Mary,

---

[51] Gilberto Cavasos-González, *Beyond Piety: The Christian Spiritual Life, Justice, and Liberation* (Eugene, OR: Wipf and Stock, 2010), 34.

[52] See María Del Socorro Castañeda-Liles, *Our Lady of Everyday Life: La Virgen de Guadalupe and the Catholic Imagination of Mexican Women in America* (New York: Oxford University Press, 2018); Jeanette Rodriguez, *Our Lady of Guadalupe: Faith and Empowerment among Mexican American Women* (Austin: University of Texas Press, 1994); D. A. Brading, *Mexican Phoenix: Our Lady of Guadalupe, Image and Tradition across Five Centuries* (Cambridge: Cambridge University Press, 2001).

floating on a piece of wood. Miraculously, the statue was dry. At her feet was inscribed, "I am the Virgin of Charity." She was, in effect, *la primera balsera* (the first rafter) to be rescued.

Las *Virgens de Guadalupe* and *de Caridad*, as well as other *virgencitas*, impact and inform how Latinxs do theology, characterizing Latinx hopes and aspirations, regardless of national ethnicity or religious affiliation. For many, these manifestations of the Virgin Mary provide meaning, reconciliation, and a resource for daily life, giving dignity to the oppressed, serving as a symbol of empowerment for the disenfranchised and as a rallying point for political causes. Images of the Virgin have appeared on banners and medallions of national independence movements throughout Latin America. Latinx farmworkers rallied around the banners of *la Virgen de Guadalupe* during the farmworkers' strikes led by César Chavez and Dolores Huerta.[53] Many Latinxs today (including non-Catholics and nonreligious) venerate the *Virgen* associated with their country of origin, mixing religious fervor with nationalistic pride.

Rather than appearing to the religious leaders, these *virgenes* identified with the economic and racial outcasts by appearing to them instead, in the color of oppression. A *virgen* appearing as a woman of color severs the bond between inferiority and nonwhiteness, as she assumes the color and cause of those oppressed, summoning the indigenous witnesses of her appearance to become *compañeros* (companions) with the Divine. Not surprisingly, *la virgen*'s earliest devotees were indigenous and enslaved people. Finally, her gender provides hope to women against machismo by providing a feminine space within the Divine. As the ultimate mother, she represents God's motherly love, a love that calls all of her children to reconcile.

Yet how do Latinx Protestants come to terms with Marianism? Although *las virgencitas* represent one of the most important symbols within Latinx's popular Catholicism, and Mary as the Mother of Jesus is highly respected by *evangélicos*, nevertheless, for many Latinx Protestants, particular devotion to Mary the mother of Jesus is viewed with suspicion as they insist such veneration should be offered solely to God, and also because of Protestant understandings of Christ Jesus as being the sole mediator between God and humanity. In addressing this challenge, Baptist theologian Nora O. Lozano-Díaz states, "If Mexican and Mexican-American Protestant women cannot approach the Lady of

---

[53] Luis D. León, *The Political Spirituality of Cesar Chavez: Crossing Religious Borders* (Oakland: University of California Press, 2015), 2–3; Mario T. García, ed., *The Gospel of César Chávez: My Faith in Action* (Lanham, MD: Sheed and Ward, 2007), 12–18.

Guadalupe as a religious symbol, they can look at her through other liberating efforts approached from cultural and feminist perspectives. These efforts are an attempt to rediscover the Virgin and to rectify the model she presents for women."[54]

Several Latinx Catholic theologians suggest that devotion to *la virgencita* is not necessarily a veneration of the historical Mary of Nazareth, Jesus's mother. Rather, Marianism is a pneumatological issue. In other words, these manifestations of the Virgins in Latin America are seen as acts of the Holy Spirit and not the historical Mary. The encounter between the marginalized people of the land and *la virgencita* is an experience of "God-who-is-for-us." These images become the authentic language by which the Holy Spirit communicates grace to the oppressed—grace to confront the reality of daily oppression and dehumanization.[55]

The *virgencitas* or patron saints throughout Latin America have become bearers of Latino/as' cultural identity, and as such serve as a rich religious source of empowerment. However, for many Latinx Protestants, especially Latinx Pentecostals, these various pneumatological roles are said to be experienced through direct contact with the Holy Spirit. Notwithstanding that difficulty, some U.S. Latinx Protestants, for example, some Episcopalian communities, have adopted perspectives more akin to Latinx Catholics and have openly brought Mary into the devotional life of their congregations.

Some Latinx scholars have been reassessing the role of the Virgin Mary, questioning if *marianismo* is a sexist paradigm that idealizes gender roles that contribute to the social oppression in which Latinas find themselves. Does the idealized image of *la virgen* essentialize so-called female characteristics of passivity, chastity, and self-sacrifice? Is a false dichotomy established for Latinas between *la virgen* and the whore? *Marianismo* claims Latinas are reduced to objects of male gallantry, and even when the male is abusive or callous, Mary serves as the ideal model for silently accepting her fate and suffering. The rise of Latina feminism in the 1970s began to challenge *marianismo*'s emphases on structural patriarchy. *Marianismo* may also contribute to a romanticization of

---

[54] Nora O. Lozano-Díaz, "Ignored Virgin or Unaware Women: A Mexican American Protestant Reflection on the Virgin of Guadalupe," in *A Reader in Latina Feminist Theology: Religion and Justice*, ed. María Pilar Aquino, Daisy L. Machado, and Jeanette Rodríguez (Austin: University of Texas Press, 2002), 212–13.

[55] Orlando O. Espín, "An Exploration into the Theology of Grace and Sin," in *From the Heart of Our People*, ed. Orlando O. Espín and Miguel H. Díaz (Maryknoll, NY: Orbis Books, 1999), 137–41.

women's spirituality. Some argue that *abuelita* theology masks sexism by relegating Latina theological contributions to the kitchen where the *abuelita* belongs. The question this concept raises is, can a young Latina at the university make profound contributions to the theological discourse without having to ever enter the kitchen?

The Last Days

Eschatology is the study of the "last days," exploring the destiny of the whole cosmos. Among theologically conservative Euroamerican Christians, one particular approach is known as "dispensationalism," in which elaborate timelines and charts are created based on so-called hidden biblical clues, which forecast how and when the world will end. While some Latinx Christians also adhere to a dispensational theology and worldview, others look at the liberative meaning of the last days. Luis E. Benavides reminds us that a Latinx-based eschatology "emphatically has the status of a verifiable objective for social justice today, in which hope for the future becomes, retrospectively, hope for the present."[56] Victory is assured to the believer within the defeats and struggles of living in the underside of North American culture. In spite of structural and individual oppression, hope resonates among Latinxs that a day will come when all, as one body, will eat and drink at the table of the Lord, a sacred fiesta celebration that encompasses the eschatological hope of inevitable liberation.

Latinx theologians reiterate the message of Jesus that the kingdom, reign, or, using Isasi-Díaz's inclusive term, "kin-dom" of God is within us. God's establishment of justice is not limited to a transcendent reality, some pie-in-the-sky hope for fairness. Rather, the eschatological hope for a hereafter justice is a directive to be established in the here and now. Jesus's eschatological pronouncements are to be instituted in the present reality. While perfect justice remains the ultimate hope of God's eventual reign, such justice serves as a touchstone for Christian praxis in the quest for God's will, thus encompassing both the last and present days. And while this emphasis on eschatological hope is prominent among many Latinx scholars of Christianity, some, like Miguel A. De La Torre, have rejected salvation history, calling instead for an embrace of hopelessness as the means by which liberative praxis propels toward subversive resistance.[57]

---

[56] Luis E. Benavides, "Eschatology," in De La Torre, *Hispanic American Religious Cultures*, 2:615.

[57] Miguel A. De La Torre, *Embracing Hopelessness* (Minneapolis: Fortress Press, 2017), 149–50.

Agility of Latinx Theologies

Latinx Christian religious thought and its contribution to the overall theological discourse reflect the realities of the social and cultural contexts, but also demonstrate that Latinxs in theology, as in other areas of life, are multilingual, multicultural, multifaceted, and therefore multicompetent. Latinx communities continue to develop, articulate, and cherish theological discourses and perspectives. Latinx theologians and scholars of religion draw upon these community-based theologies as the source of their theological development, while simultaneously mastering theological information from other communal traditions. As U.S. Latinx people increasingly become a larger part of the church, the challenge exists for theologians from other communities to also become theologically multicultural.

So far, we have seen how the social location of Latinxs contributed to the development of Latinx theological concepts and briefly discussed some of those concepts. In the next chapter we begin a closer examination of the historical development of Latinx theologies, the different manifestations that arose within Latinx communities, and some of the different theologians who participated in articulating the diversity found within these agile multicultural and multidimensional theologies.

4

Historia

REFLECTIONS ON LATINX STORIES

A stereotypical falsehood about U.S. Latinx identity, perceived through the imaginations of non-Latinx, vacillates between a dream of an exotic and happy Latin and a nightmare about a dangerous, murdering gang invader. Throughout the history of the United States, a collective identity has been forced upon Latinx peoples. How then do Latinx people recall their history and tell their own stories apart from the clichéd imagery imposed upon them by the gaze of the dominant U.S. culture? Among the first acts of empowerment for any group seeking to liberate themselves from how they are seen by others is the telling of their own stories. Reclaiming Latinx histories challenges the U.S. dominant culture to come to terms with Latinx people as real human beings, rather than distancing Latinxs as a stereotyped footnote to Euroamerican history. It is no secret that the *historia* (history/story) of Latinxs theology and religion has been peripheral to what historian Hjamil Martínez-Vásquez calls the standard narrative or canon of U.S. religious history.[1]

Like any human community, Latinxs have many stories to tell, and of those many stories one shared characteristic is an aversion to any imposed epic story that attempts to collapse the complexity and richness of multiple stories into a simple tale. Many stories make up Latinx theologies. Depending upon where one chooses to begin, a history can be told with a variety of story lines, each with its own legitimacy. It is not that one is wrong or another inauthentic, but rather that many authentic stories run concurrently, with some accounts going in different directions, as well as different versions of the same history.

---

[1] Hjamil A. Martínez-Vásquez, *Made in the Margins: Latina/o Constructions of U.S. Religious History* (Waco, TX: Baylor University Press, 2013), 13–30.

One way of outlining the history of Latinx theologies is by using a genealogical or chronological lineage. This approach makes historical connections between thinkers and concepts, developing a sequence of events. Who is included on such lists, their order of appearance, and the amount of time spent on examining their thoughts may display an inherent subjectivity of the ones designing such lists, in terms of who chooses what to include in the story. Frequently, with this type of genealogical or chronological approach, Latinx theological thought is imagined in terms of generations of thinkers in which many branches of thoughts stem from a single trunk, which also might be seen as the central source or unifying factor. This prompts a concern that such a genealogical narrative may not adequately describe the fluid and sometimes unpredictable movement of theological concepts. The danger exists that neat descriptive categories may be seen as the most important characteristic. Those theologians grouped closest to the roots or trunk—as selected by the designers of the historical schematic—may be perceived to occupy a privileged position and become the focal point for the development and growth of that particular branch. An additional possibility is that such a genealogical list could create a hierarchical structure that imposes limitations on the movement of theological thought as it attempts to regulate connections between thinkers and concepts. While certainly neat, a chronological or genealogical approach does not always allow for the complexities and unpredictability of life.[2]

Given the pitfalls of utilizing a chronological-genealogical tree to tell history, it is appropriate to try an alternative way of conveying the histories of Latinx theologies. Following Gilles Deleuze and Felix Guattari we suggest a storytelling approach that uses the image of historical rhizomes rather than a historical genealogy. Unlike trees with roots and branches suggesting an upward unidirectional flow, rhizomes are a decentered complex of multiple subterranean stems, spreading in various directions, and sometimes overlapping each other. Rather than one central trunk or root of original "truth," billions of roots exist, with none of them being dominant. Rhizomes manifest themselves in surface extensions or unseen underground tubers, where their interconnections compose unregulated networks that seem to randomly connect. While a tree approach stresses an original, foundational beginning that leads linearly to a conclusion, a rhizome model concentrates on surface connections that construct additional understanding and knowledge, and where there is power in link-

---

[2] Miguel A. De La Torre, "Religion and Power in the Study of Hispanic Religions," in *Rethinking Latino(a) Religion and Identity*, ed. Miguel A. De La Torre and Gastón Espinosa (Cleveland: Pilgrim Press, 2006), 286–92.

age at many points. In other words, the story is always developing and thus can never be completely told—and that is alright.[3]

Many historical stories converge in clusters that connect and flow into the reality of Latinx theologies. What flows is one type of impressionistic historical sketch of some of the rhizomes and connections by which Latinx theologies are attached. These clusters include the forerunners of Latinx theologies as well as their present-day manifestations, with a special focus on some of the connections between Catholics, Protestants, Latina women, and certain Latinx organizations. We briefly investigate these clusters and rhizomatic connections, cognizant that this is only one type of history about Latinx theologies and that other narratives can be told. Some of the stories told here are told only in part, and in the telling of the stories we realize that certain matters may have been left out for a variety of reasons, including the fact that we do not know the complete story. There are hints of other tales, details, and *historia* that wait for another day to be told. And of course, some stories about Latinx theologies that may indeed be connected to these stories we do not know yet, but that *historia* needs to be told by someone else.

Forerunners of Latinx Theologies

Although formal articulations of Latinx theologies emerged in the last half of the twentieth century under different names—for example, Hispanic, Latino, Latino/a, Latin@—they did not appear out of thin air, but rather flowed from the theologies and praxis of earlier communities. Latinx perspectives are rooted in acts of resistance to the oppression of colonial Christendom established during the European conquest of the indigenous peoples of the Western Hemisphere. Latinx theologies find roots in the wisdom and ways of enslaved Africans in the Americas, drawing on the popular religiosity that was brought across the Atlantic. And Latinx theologies are connected to the multiple ways that these connections mixed with many others in the Americas.

---

[3] For more about rhizomes and rhizomatic theory, see Gilles Deleuze and Felix Guattari, *A Thousand Plateaus: Capitalism and Schizophrenia*, trans. Brian Massumi (Minneapolis: University of Minnesota Press, 1987), 3–25; Gregg Lambert, *Who's Afraid of Deleuze and Guattari?* (London: Continuum, 2006); and Todd May, *Giles Deleuze: An Introduction* (Cambridge: Cambridge University Press, 2005), 133–34.

El Cura de Taos

Perhaps one of the earliest antecedents of Latinx theologies in the United States can be seen in the work of Father Antonio José Martínez (1793–1867) of Taos, New Mexico. Known as *el cura de Taos*, he was a respected civic and religious leader among the New Mexican clergy and people. Unfortunately, Martínez was not equally well regarded by the French cleric Jean-Baptiste Lamy (1814–1888), who was appointed Roman Catholic vicar, bishop, and later archbishop to Santa Fe in 1851. Prior to the Mexican-American War, the Catholic parishes in what was to become the southwestern United States were under the jurisdiction of the Mexican Catholic Church. As a result of the war and the Treaty of Guadalupe Hidalgo of 1848, the people of the predominately Indo-Hispano-Mexican Catholic parishes of the Provincia de Nuevo México were made U.S. citizens and found themselves under the jurisdiction of the U.S. Catholic Church, with a French bishop (Lamy). Added to this mix were Protestant missionaries sent from the English-speaking part of the United States to evangelize the new Southwest, an area where there had already been a Christian presence since the sixteenth century with the coming of the Spanish missionaries. And despite the attitudes and actions of some of the white Protestant missionaries and their denominations, a number of the New Mexican Hispanos did indeed become Protestant.[4] Some of the resulting tensions can be examined through the conflict that developed between Father Martínez and Bishop Lamy.

The theologically conservative Lamy, who served previously in Ohio and Kentucky, quickly clashed with Father Martínez. Martínez advocated an understanding of Catholic Christianity that allowed for the continued practice of popular religion, a position that Lamy opposed. Additionally, Martínez questioned the directional flow of tithes from his parish toward Lamy's offices, an act Martínez considered immoral because it was tantamount to taking money from the poor and giving it to the rich. Martínez also challenged what he perceived to be prejudicial attitudes and actions of the official church against local Catholics.

Eventually Father Martínez was excommunicated and removed in 1857, although Martínez did not recognize his removal and kept on ministering. The traditional practices of New Mexican Catholics were strongly discouraged by the new clergy—this included the suppression of the Penitente brotherhoods, such as La Fraternidad Piadosa de

---

[4] Arturo Madrid, *In the Country of the Empty Crosses: The Story of a Hispano Protestant Family in Catholic New Mexico* (San Antonio, TX: Trinity University Press, 2012); Randi Jones Walker, *Protestantism in the Sangre de Cristo, 1850–1920* (Albuquerque: University of New Mexico Press, 1991).

Nuestro Padre Jesús Nazareno (Pious Brotherhood of Our Father Jesus the Nazarene), also known as Los Hermanos Penitentes (the Penitent Brothers).[5] Originally Lamy tried to disband the brotherhoods but then attempted to bring them under episcopal authority. These efforts resulted in a greater rift between the official church and local communities of faith. Nonetheless, local New Mexicans' understandings and practices of Christianity persisted.

The Tejano Catholic Community

Another important antecedent of U.S. Latinx theologies is the Tejano Catholic community centered in San Antonio, Texas. The struggle of the Tejano community and its commitment to its own understanding of faith helped prepare the ground for Latinx theologies, both Catholic and Protestant. Even before Mexico became independent of Spain in 1821, the region of northern Mexico known as Tejas (Texas) developed a cultural identity that provided resources to resist assimilation to Euroamerican religion and culture. The role of public celebration and ritual was a key factor in this resistance and maintenance of identity. Although oppression and suppression of local understandings of Christianity came from a variety of sources, elements that preserved and promoted a culturally relevant understanding of Christianity that was Tejano/a in its essence nonetheless persisted. A key part of this development was and is San Fernando Cathedral in San Antonio, established in 1731 as a local parish. San Fernando "is the oldest cathedral sanctuary continuously in use in what is now the continental United States."[6] San Fernando Cathedral was the center of a vibrant faith community across the centuries, even as the community saw the transitions from the political dominions of Spain, Mexico, the Republic of Texas, the United States, the Confederate States, and again the United States.

Even as Euroamericans came to dominate the social and political spheres of San Antonio and south Texas, especially in the nineteenth and first half of the twentieth centuries, alternative understandings of the Christian faith persevered in families and in the barrios, thereby planting seeds that were destined to produce greater fruit at a later time. Historian

---

[5] For more on the Penitentes, see Michael P. Carroll, *The Penitente Brotherhood: Patriarchy and Hispano-Catholicism in New Mexico* (Baltimore, MD: Johns Hopkins University Press, 2002); Alberto López Pulido, *The Sacred World of the Penitentes* (Washington, DC: Smithsonian Institution Press, 2000).

[6] Timothy Matovina, "San Fernando Cathedral," in *Hispanic American Religious Culture*, vol. 1, ed. Miguel A. De La Torre (Santa Barbara, CA: ABC-CLIO, 2009), 102.

Timothy Matovina writes of the development of local initiatives in religious affairs as San Antonio came under different sovereignties. Local traditions and feasts persisted through the years in the city, despite a growing sense of separation from Mexico as Euroamericans moving to Texas surmounted the social structures of power and privilege.[7] Through it all, San Antonio became a center for Hispanic Catholicism.

Moreover, in the nineteenth century another set of Tejano/a Christian stories emerged, those of Tejanos and Tejanas who became Protestant, the results of white Anglo Protestant missionaries from the United States evangelizing in the lands acquired from Mexico.[8] David Maldonado Jr. summarizes two major motivating factors in the spread of Protestant Christianity in the newly acquired Southwest, including Texas. The first was "the belief that the Protestant faith was clearly superior to Catholicism and was more enlightened." The second factor was the "acculturation and Americanization of the Mexican population."[9] But the religious switching of Mexican Americans from Catholicism to various branches of Protestantism in the U.S. Southwest was fraught with challenges and oppressions. Historian Daisy Machado's analysis of the Christian Church (Disciples of Christ) in Texas describes a state of affairs that was repeated across denominations throughout the Southwest:

> The Texas Disciples shared with the other North American settlers the surety that they were *the* new heirs to the promise of Texas. The Mexican Texan was not only of another race (or mixture of races, which was worse), but also Roman Catholic. Given these characteristics, the North American settlers perceived the *Tejanos* as inferior in many ways. And it was accepted by the dominant group that it was because the Mexican-Texan possessed these

---

[7] Timothy M. Matovina, *Tejano Religion and Ethnicity: San Antonio, 1821–1860* (Austin: University of Texas Press, 1995), 39–48; Timothy M. Matovina, *Guadalupe and Her Faithful: Latino Catholics in San Antonio, from Colonial Origins to the Present* (Baltimore, MD: Johns Hopkins University Press, 2005); Moises Sanadoval, *On the Move: A History of the Hispanic Church in the United States*, 2nd ed. (Maryknoll, NY: Orbis Books, 2006), 38–47.

[8] See Paul Barton, *Hispanic Methodist, Presbyterians, and Baptists in Texas* (Austin: University of Texas Press, 2006); Daisy L. Machado, *Of Borders and Margins: Hispanic Disciples in Texas, 1888–1945* (New York: Oxford University Press, 2003); Juan Francisco Martínez, *Sea la Luz: The Making of Mexican Protestantism in the American Southwest, 1829–1900* (Denton: University of North Texas Press, 2006).

[9] David Maldonado Jr., "Protestantism," in *Hispanic American Religious Culture*, vol. 2, ed. Miguel A. De La Torre (Santa Barbara, CA: ABC-CLIO, 2009), 460.

inherent flaws that they had been supplanted by a "new" people who would now dominate the borderlands history. The Mexican-Texan therefore became the displaced Other, strangers in their own land, not landowners but renters or squatters.[10]

As others have observed, Luis D. León's evaluation of Chicano/a/x *evangélico/a/x* also is an appropriate assessment of early Latinx Protestants more broadly: "Chicano *evangélicos* appropriate Protestantism, inflect it and mirror it back, changing the Protestant symbolic of North America, figuring it with distinctively Mexican-American grammars."[11]

Francisco Olazábal

Elsewhere in the borderlands between the United States and Mexico, Mexican-born pentecostal church leader Francisco Olazábal (1886–1937) was preaching the gospel and ministering to Spanish-speaking people.[12] Olazábal was an important pentecostal evangelist who influenced many through his ministry, not only in the U.S.-Mexico borderlands context of revolutionary Mexico but also throughout the United States and Puerto Rico. Raised as a Catholic in Mexico, Olazábal converted in response to itinerant Methodist lay preachers and later studied at the Wesleyan School of Theology in San Luís Potosí, Mexico. After immigrating to the United States in 1911 Olazábal was pastor of a Spanish-speaking Methodist congregation in El Paso, Texas; studied at Moody Bible Institute in Chicago; and then went to Los Angeles, pastoring two Methodist churches in California. In 1916 Olazábal became a Pentecostal and was ordained by the Assemblies of God; he then served in Los Angeles and Texas and had a significant evangelistic and healing ministry. Many called him the "Mexican Billy Sunday." Olazábal also fought against the racism and segregation of the time, which was openly found in churches of all denominations.

---

[10] Machado, *Of Borders and Margins*, 110–11.

[11] Luis D. León, *La Llorona's Children: Religion, Life, and Death in the Mexican Borderlands* (Berkeley: University of California Press, 2004), 235. See also Martínez, *Sea la Luz*, 146–47.

[12] Gastón Espinosa, "Brown Moses: Francisco Olazábal and Mexican American Pentecostal Healing in the Borderlands," in *Mexican American Religions: Spirituality, Activism, and Culture*, ed. Gastón Espinosa and Mario T. García (Durham, NC: Duke University Press, 2008), 263–95; Gastón Espinosa, "*El Azteca*: Francisco Olazabál and Latino Pentecostal Charisma, Power, and Faith Healing in the Borderlands," *Journal of the American Academy of Religion* 67, no. 3 (Fall 1999): 597–616.

After serious difficulties with the Euroamerican-dominated Assemblies of God, Olazábal left the Assemblies because the "gringos have control," and in 1923 established the independent Latin American Council of Christian Churches, an independent Latinx denomination.[13] Olazábal's evangelistic work was widespread and took him across the United States and to Puerto Rico.

Juan L. Lugo

Soon after the turn of the twentieth century, other developments in the political reach of the United States as well as in religious life and theological thought also had profound effects on the later development of Latinx theologies. As a result of the Spanish-American War, the United States expanded its worldwide overseas empire: Guam, the Philippines, and Puerto Rico became U.S. possessions, while Cuba was placed under U.S. protection (gaining independence in 1902).[14] In 1900–1901 Puerto Rican Juan L. Lugo (1890–1984) found himself in the Territory of Hawaii as part of a wave of Puerto Rican migrant laborers following the acquisition of Hawaii and Puerto Rico in 1898. Through this intra-colonial experience in 1913 Lugo was converted to pentecostal Christianity by Azusa Street pentecostal missionaries who stopped in Hawaii on their way to China.[15] Ordained by the Assemblies of God, and after a period of ministry in San Francisco, California, Lugo returned to the city of Ponce in Puerto Rico in 1916, preaching a pentecostal understanding of the gospel. While not the first pentecostal evangelist in Puerto Rico, Lugo's work had a long-lasting impact, as he and his colleagues planted several pentecostal churches in Puerto Rico and in New York City. In 1940 Lugo left the Assemblies of God and worked with Latinx pentecostal organizations. Gastón Espinosa's assessment is that "the Puerto Rican pentecostal movement was almost completely run and developed by natives themselves."[16]

---

[13] Gastón Espinosa, "Francisco Olazabál," in De La Torre, *Hispanic American Religious Culture*, 2:409–10.

[14] Wilfredo Estrada-Adorno, *100 años después: La ruta de pentecostalismo puertorriqueño*, 2nd ed. (Cleveland, TN: Centro Estudios Latinos Publicaciones, 2016), 20; JoAnna Poblete, *Islanders in the Empire: Filipino and Puerto Rican Laborers in Hawai'i* (Urbana: University of Illinois Press, 2014).

[15] Gastón Espinosa, "Juan León Lugo," in De La Torre, *Hispanic American Religious Culture*, 2:430.

[16] Gastón Espinosa, *Latino Pentecostals in America: Faith and Politics in Action* (Cambridge, MA: Harvard University Press, 2014), 194.

The phenomenal growth of Pentecostalism in Puerto Rico and among Puerto Ricans in the diaspora can be traced to Lugo and his coworkers, especially in the early period of 1920–1940. Lugo's influential ministry led to the establishment of Spanish-speaking congregations in Puerto Rico, California, and the northeastern United States. One example of Lugo's influence is La Iglesia de Dios Pentecostal Movimiento Internacional de la Región Este de los Estados Unidos de América (Pentecostal Church of God International Movement of the Eastern Region of the United States), a movement with roots in Puerto Rico that was founded in 1929 in Brooklyn, New York. Through the establishment in 1937 of the Instituto Bíblico Mizpa, Lugo also left his mark on grassroots Latinx theological education, as students came not only from Puerto Rico but from throughout Latin America.[17]

In an example of unpredictable connections, Mexican Francisco Olazábal and Puerto Rican Juan Lugo were both key figures in the establishment of grassroots theologies and institutions among various groups of Latinx early in the twentieth century. Olazábal and Lugo ministered in New York City and at certain times collaborated in their ministries. They also worked together in Texas, California, and Puerto Rico. Such cooperation helped foster a broader Latinx pentecostal understanding that transcended local or regional identities. Early Hispanic/Latinx Pentecostalism exercised a lasting influence on other expressions of Latinx Christianity in the United States.

A Transnational Pentecostalism

Looking again to the U.S.-Mexico borderlands in the early twentieth century we can find another rhizome set of stories. Daniel Ramírez offers accounts of a type of transnational Pentecostalism among Mexican Americans and Mexicans who were marginalized in multiple ways, but who nevertheless persisted in their own sense of calling, ways of making sense of the world, and experiences of vitality in the midst of marginalization, as well as growing in extraordinary ways. In his book *Migrating Faith: Pentecostalism in the United States and Mexico in the Twentieth Century*, Ramírez traces the history of Latinx Pentecostalism in the U.S.-Mexico borderlands from 1906 through the transnational migratory patterns of laborers in which they had social, cultural, and religious space for creativity and innovation, leading to a strong grassroots type of Pentecostalism. Ramírez investigates the multifaceted causes for the

---

[17] See David Ramos Torres, *Historia de la Iglesia de Dios, M.I.: Una Iglesia Ungida para Hacer Misión* (Río Piedras, PR: Editorial Pentecostal, 1993).

substantial increase of Pentecostalism among people of Mexican descent in the twentieth century. He concludes that for a population that moved in both directions across the international border, pentecostal congregations played an important role as "migration trampolines and alternative transnational public squares, erected in the face and wake of xenophobia," and also through worship music constructed in forms accessible to the people, which provided "exciting sonic spheres."[18] In the early twentieth century through grassroots Latinx pentecostal songs, this type of transnational Mexican / Mexican American Pentecostalism "redeemed the fiesta of Mexican and Latino culture."[19] This set of stories from the borderlands also challenges standard narratives both from the dominant center and from dominant groups within the margins, and "challenges us to rethink ahistorical and acultural approaches to Pentecostalism and politics (praxis)."[20]

Rearticulations of Pentecostalism

Some Latinx pentecostal groups have a very negative understanding of particular denominations and of the concept of "denomination" in general. These Latinx Pentecostals, who maintain that the denominations have been unfaithful to the gospel message of Christian unity, try to avoid anything that may give the appearance of replicating denominations. Those decisions do not mean that these groups are all independent congregations that have abandoned all ecclesiastical connections. Very often, these alternative ecclesiastical connections or cooperative affiliations come under the name of *concilio* (council). As Gastón Espinosa notes, the emergence of various *concilios* played a role as "Pentecostal churches and districts went through a number of schisms and fragmented or developed into new independent and indigenous denominations (or concilios—councils), which in turn did the same." He continues, "It is precisely the indigenization, fragmentation, and localized rearticulation of Pentecostalism in the regional vernacular language, culture, and customs of the people that help explain its phenomenal growth."[21]

---

[18] Daniel Ramírez, *Migrating Faith: Pentecostalism in the United States and Mexico in the Twentieth Century* (Chapel Hill: University of North Carolina Press, 2015), 134.

[19] Ibid., 178.

[20] Ibid., 140.

[21] Gastón Espinosa, "Pentecostalism," in De La Torre, *Hispanic American Religious Culture*, 2:428.

Mama Leo and Santos Elizondo

Another individual whose influence exceeded pentecostal circles, both as a noted woman minister and as a precursor to a Latinx theology rooted in the community, is the Reverend Leoncia Rosado Rousseau, better known as Mama Leo (1912–2006). Born in Puerto Rico, Mama Leo was converted and underwent the baptism of the Holy Spirit in 1932. Shortly thereafter, she entered Christian ministry. She moved to New York City in September 1935 together with her husband, the Reverend Francisco Rosado. There they founded and pastored the Iglesia Cristiana Damasco (Damascus Christian Church) in the Bronx. They also were in regular contact with Mexican pentecostal leader Francisco Olazábal. When Francisco Rosado was drafted into the U.S. military during World War II, Mama Leo became sole pastor, probably making her the first Latina pentecostal pastor in New York City.[22] One of the ministries of Iglesia Cristiana Damasco under Mama Leo's leadership was the launching in 1957 of the Damascus Youth Crusade in the Bronx, which worked with drug addicts.[23] One of the converts of that ministry was the Nuyorican former gang member Nicky Cruz, whose story is partly told in David Wilkerson's *The Cross and Switchblade*, but who also wrote himself about his transformation.[24] A significant part of Mama Leo's ministry was to people on the margins of society, including drug addicts and alcoholics, in effect advocating a pentecostal Christian social engagement, an option for the marginalized that was contrary to some narratives of Pentecostalism.[25] As of 2006 the Concilio Iglesia Cristiana Damasco had eight congregations in the eastern United States, along with thirty-nine churches and missions in Ecuador, fourteen in Mexico, and nineteen in the Caribbean and other locations. Mama Leo continued to preach and teach into her nineties.[26]

---

[22] Hjamil A. Martínez-Vázquez, "Mama Leo," in De La Torre, *Hispanic American Religious Culture*, 2:431.

[23] Espinosa, *Latino Pentecostals in America*, 340; Eldín Villafañe, *The Liberating Spirit: Towards an Hispanic American Pentecostal Social Ethic* (Grand Rapids: Eerdmans, 1993), 94–95.

[24] Juan Francisco Martínez, *The Story of Latino Protestants in the United States* (Grand Rapids: Eerdmans, 2018), 107, 131–32; Nicky Cruz, *Run Baby Run: Life-Changing Testimony of a New York Gang Leader*, with Jaime Buckingham, new ed. (Gainesville, FL: Bridge-Logos, 2017); David R. Wilkerson, *The Cross and the Switchblade* (1962; Grand Rapids: Chosen Books, 2008).

[25] See also Elizabeth D. Ríos, "'The Ladies Are Warriors': Latina Pentecostals and Faith-Based Activism in New York City," in *Latino Religions and Civic Activism in the United States*, ed. Gastón Espinosa, Virgilio Elizondo, and Jesse Miranda (New York: Oxford University Press, 2005), 197–217.

[26] María Pérez y González, "Leoncia Rosado Rousseau (Mamá Léo)," in *Latinas*

Mama Leo was not the only Latina woman forerunner of later formulations of Latinx theologies. Latina women in various roles and callings had always been the backbone of Hispanic churches in the United
States. They served as religious workers and were involved in the educational ventures of congregations and parishes. While most Latino Protestant evangelists and pastors were male, their wives were more than
simple companions. They were real partners in the ministry, participating
in preaching and articulating the faith, even though conventions of the
time among most groups would never have publicly recognized what the
women did as preaching. In some Protestant traditions women were recognized as pastors and evangelists in their own right. One such woman
within the Church of the Nazarene was Santos Elizondo. A native of
Mexico, Elizondo was converted in 1905 and soon after entered the ministry. She did evangelistic work in El Paso, Texas, and Juárez, Mexico,
ministering in the borderlands context until her death in 1941. There
Pastor Elizondo—who founded a school, orphanage, and women's society while working as a nurse and midwife—was the focus of opposition
from other Protestant missions, not only over Nazarene doctrine, but
also over the fact that she was a woman in ministry.[27]

NYC: *The Cursillo Movement and* *Baptist Reverend Santiago Soto Fontánez*

For the majority of U.S. Christian history, church hierarchies, including those that were Roman Catholic, Methodist, Baptist, Presbyterian,
and Christian Church (Disciples of Christ), placed certain types of pressure upon Latinx congregations of all denominations to assimilate into
the Euroamerican norm. Running against this denominational push
were countercurrents of local initiatives for understanding and practicing Christianity. In 1939 the Catholic Archdiocese of New York directly
appointed non–Puerto Rican Redemptorist clergy to minister to Puerto
Ricans in East Harlem. Later, in the 1950s, this ministry was expanded
to include diocesan priests who attempted to create unified parishes
instead of the norm of parishes characterized by language and ethnicity.
An Americanist impulse that had been present in the overall U.S. Roman
Catholic Church was again operative, acting on the assumption that
while a parish might have an English-language and a Spanish-language
congregation in the short run, through assimilation the Puerto Rican

---

in the United States: A Historical Encyclopedia, ed. Vicki L. Ruiz and Virginia
Sánchez Korrol, vol. 2 (Bloomington: Indiana University Press, 2006), 644–45.

[27] Rebecca Laird, *Ordained Women in the Church of the Nazarene: The First
Generation* (Kansas City, MO: Nazarene Publishing House, 1993), 53–62.

culture and the use of Spanish would fade away. The basic premise seemed to be that there would be eventual cultural and linguistic conformity to white/Anglo norms. This latter expectation failed to materialize, creating tensions between English-speaking congregations and Spanish-speaking Puerto Ricans.[28]

In New York City, Spanish-speaking congregations did not fade away, partly due to the Cursillo movement, one of the most significant international and ecumenical expressions of grassroots religious understandings and practices.[29] Cursillo de Cristiandad, literally "small or little course in Christianity," is a renewal movement within the Roman Catholic Church that originated in Spain in 1947 with the Christian Action movement, during the fascist dictatorship of Francisco Franco. This three-day retreat eventually first spread to Latin America and then to the United States, where it quickly crossed denominational borders as Protestants attended these retreats to seek deeper spiritual lives. Among Latino/as, specifically Puerto Ricans in New York City, the Cursillo, combined with a creative practice of Hispanic Catholicism, allowed for Spanish-language liturgies and cultivated lay leadership.[30] Gilberto Cavasos-González notes that Cursillo was seen as more than a weekend spiritual retreat, and that "To ensure that this conversation would continue to develop and mature, participants are encouraged to join small communities based on the three pillars of Christian life: prayer, study, action."[31]

Another example of Latinx Christianity emanating from New York City that influenced the emergence of Latinx theologies was the ministry of Baptist Reverend Santiago Soto Fontánez (1904–1985). Reverend Soto Fontánez was the longtime pastor of the Central Baptist Church in Brooklyn. Born in Caguas and raised in Ponce, Puerto Rico, Soto Fontánez earned bachelor's and master's degrees at the University of Puerto Rico and was a professor of literature at Brooklyn College; he also served as a pastor from 1945 to 1960 and from 1966 to 1972. Reflecting on his first pastorate in New York, Soto Fontánez commented,

[28] Ana María Díaz-Stevens, *Oxcart Catholicism on Fifth Avenue: The Impact of the Puerto Rican Migration upon the Archdiocese of New York* (Notre Dame, IN: University of Notre Dame Press, 1993), 98, 103, 108–14.

[29] Kristy Nabhan-Warren, *The Cursillo Movement in America: Catholics, Protestants, and Fourth-Day Spirituality* (Chapel Hill: University of North Carolina Press, 2013).

[30] Díaz-Stevens, *Oxcart Catholicism on Fifth Avenue*, 115; Anthony M. Stevens-Arroyo and Ana María Díaz-Stevens, *Recognizing the Latino Resurgence in U.S. Religion: The Emmaus Paradigm* (Boulder, CO: Westview Press, 1998), 133–35.

[31] Gilberto Cavasos-González, "Cursillo," in De La Torre, *Hispanic American Religious Culture*, 1:97.

"We started with eighteen people and no money. By the time I left the church in 1960 we had property of $150,000 and a budget of about $30,000 a year. And they were able to call a pastor full time and pay him a decent salary and it has continued to be so."[32] Emphasizing an understanding and practice of the Christian faith that were relevant to the social context of the community, he influenced generations of laity and clergy in his ministry.

Latin American Bible Institute (LABI)

Another forerunner of Latinx theologies is the Latin American Bible Institute (LABI), a distinguished Latinx organization in California. Bible institutes, *instituto*, are theological schools that arise from Latinx communities and provide an education that is focused on knowledge of the Bible and the practice of contextual ministry. *Institutos* are not constrained by the educational standards of regional accrediting bodies that approve postsecondary colleges and universities. As a pentecostal school, LABI, through its own educational ministry as well as through the ministries of those who studied there, has had an international impact that shows many connections with stories and *historias* that can be told. Usually the instructors are those who themselves are engaged in ministry. LABI was one of the early Latinx Bible institutes and was still in operation in the early twenty-first century.

In the early twentieth century Alice E. Luce, after a time of Spanish-language ministry in Texas, went to minister to migrant Mexicans in Los Angeles, which in turn led to her establishing the LABI in 1926, now located in La Puente, California. LABI educated and trained generations of Latinx pastors, missionaries, and other types of ministers. Elizabeth Conde-Frazier notes that, in its early years, LABI offered onsite and correspondence courses, and a three-year ordination track as well as a two-year missionary track, along with transfer agreements for bachelor's-degree schools. "It has a bilingual curriculum and reaches up to four generations of Latino/a leaders."[33] LABI itself now offers associate and bachelor's degrees. The majority of LABI faculty and staff are Latinx. The school is approved by the state of California; is endorsed

[32] Santiago Soto Fontánez, interview by John D. Vazquez, September 18, 1974, Project records, 1976.001.020, transcript, Puerto Rican Oral History, Brooklyn Historical Society, Brooklyn, New York.

[33] Elizabeth Conde-Frazier, "Bible Institutes," in De La Torre, *Hispanic American Religious Culture*, 1:73. See also Elizabeth Conde-Frazier, *Hispanic Bible Institutes: A Community of Theological Construction* (Scranton, PA: University of Scranton Press, 2005).

by the Alliance of Christian Higher Education of the General Council of the Assemblies of God, as well as the Southern Pacific District of the Assemblies of God; and is a 2019 candidate for accreditation with the Association for Biblical Higher Education (ABHE).

Impact on Later Articulations of Latinx Theologies

Of course, throughout the twentieth century the various manifestations of U.S. Latinx Christianity—especially in their national origin or ethnic communities and within their particular congregational, ecclesiastical, and educational contexts—expressed their distinct theological positions and understandings. However, focused formal articulations of Latinx theologies did not emerge until the 1960s. These accounts indicate the presence of themes that would eventually be articulated and developed. In many locations and at different times, the various Latinx communities were active and creative in their own understandings of Christianity amid very distinct (and often difficult) contexts. Although many of these Latinx expressions of Christianity were disregarded, ignored, or held in low esteem as theologically deficient, even by their own denominations, these negative responses do not indicate a lack of theological and pastoral reflection before the 1960s. In fact, these very negative attitudes from the larger Euroamerican denominations toward those who were theoretically part of the same communion or tradition helped create the tension that contributed to the emergence and articulation of distinct Latinx theologies. In the face of numerous difficulties, Latinx Christians in the United States were able to achieve internal coherence, liberative agency and activity, and growth of their communities. Moreover, Latinxs articulated and cultivated understandings of Christian life and ministry that were sensitive to their communities' needs.

Emergence of Hispanic Theology

In their scholarship on U.S. Latino/a religious realities, Ana María Díaz-Stevens and Anthony Stevens-Arroyo speak of a Latinx religious resurgence that started after 1967. Their research focuses mainly on Latinx Roman Catholicism; however, this religious resurgence was much bigger and also included Latinx Protestantism. Sociologists of religion Díaz-Stevens and Stevens-Arroyo note that while there had always been a Hispanic/Latinx presence in the United States, especially after 1848, it was not until the mid-twentieth century that certain events converged to mark the beginning of new forms of Latinx religious life, expressions, and engagement with the wider society.

Noteworthy characteristics of this religious renaissance include its national scope; efforts toward broader coalitions; creation of sophisticated organizations; and styles of leadership that were collegial and collaborative, connected to local communities, and engaged with contemporary social and political realities. Díaz-Stevens and Stevens-Arroyo also perceived several consequences of this Latinx religious resurgence. These included implicit and explicit challenges to church establishments that maintained unsympathetic attitudes and approaches to Latinx Christian ministries. Additionally, the Latinx religious resurgence was characterized by the pivotal emergence of grassroots groups. These Latinx groups developed religious and theological thoughts that were more contextual to urban life. Moreover, the resurgence facilitated the reality of an (at least) situational and provisional pan-ethnic Latinx commonality across church barriers, and it also advocated a wider role for women in church leadership and ministry.[34]

For most of the nineteenth and twentieth centuries, efforts in Hispanic/Latinx ministry initiated by many denominational hierarchies were characterized by paternalism and efforts focused on assimilationism. However, with the social changes and upheavals of the 1960s, including the civil rights movement and a new sense of La Raza (the Race or the People), came a shift toward a more formal articulation of Hispanic/Latinx theology in the years 1966–1972. The mid-1960s was an era of social, political, and cultural ferment; during this time Mexican American labor leaders César Chávez (1927–1993), Delores Huerta (b. 1930) organized what would become the United Farm Workers' labor union. In 1965 Chávez, Huerta, Richard Chavez, and others organized the Delano grape strike, with a nationwide boycott of California grapes whose goal was obtaining fair labor contracts for agricultural workers. The year 1967 brought riots in Spanish Harlem in New York City; the rise of the Young Lords; the takeover of a county courthouse in Tierra Amarilla, New Mexico; the appearance of the poem "I Am Joaquín / Yo Soy Joaquín" by Chicano Rudolfo "Corky" Gonzáles; and the rise of the Chicano/Chicana movement, all major cultural landmarks in the conscientization or critical consciousness of the various Latinx communities. Also in the mid-1960s, Chicano/a/x and Puerto Rican activism emerged.[35] These and other events point to

---

[34] Stevens-Arroyo and Díaz-Stevens, *Recognizing the Latino Resurgence in U.S. Religion*, 124–25, 149.

[35] Rudolfo "Corky" Gonzáles, *Message to Atzlán: Selected Writings of Rudolfo "Corky" Gonzáles*, ed. Antonio Esquibel (Houston: Arte Público Press, 2001); Juan Gómez-Quiñones and Irene Vásquez, *Making Atzlán: Ideology and Culture of the Chicana and Chicano Movement, 1966–1977* (Albuquerque: Uni-

a significant shift in Latinx consciousness, which in turn affected religious understandings and actions.

Roman Catholics

During the 1960s a younger generation of Hispanic/Latinx pastoral leaders, women religious, educators, and laity sought to make connections between their faith, culture, traditions, and their times. Early efforts toward forming theological responses to the particular Latinx conditions included the work of two early Roman Catholic organizations: PADRES (Padres Asociados para Derechos Religiosos, Educacionales y Sociales [Priests for Religious, Educational, and Social Rights]) and Las Hermanas.[36] Founded in 1970 PADRES was initially a Mexican American /Chicano organization of Roman Catholic clergy advocating a more intentional effort to address the ministry needs of the Chicano/a community. PADRES advocated "recommendations for social justice action [and] promoted education in church leadership skills."[37] PADRES later broadened its Latino/a membership to include non-Chicanos. As an organization, PADRES completed its work in 1989.

In 1971 the organization Las Hermanas (The Sisters) was founded by fifty mostly Latina nuns and religious women, and in 1972 was formally chartered with four goals: "(1) to activate leadership among themselves and the laity; (2) to effect social change; (3) to contribute to the cultural renewal of La Raza; and (4) to educate Anglo-dominant congregations on the needs of Spanish-speaking communities."[38] Although the initial leadership consisted of Mexican American religious women, membership from the start was open to all Latina women in religious orders, and later to laywomen. In one of its founding documents Las Hermanas declared that

---

versity of New Mexico Press, 2014); Sonia Song-Ha Lee, *Building a Latino Civil Rights Movement: Puerto Ricans, African Americans, and the Pursuit of Racial Justice in New York City* (Chapel Hill: University of North Carolina Press, 2014); Derrel Enck-Wanzer, ed., *The Young Lords: A Reader* (New York: New York University Press, 2010).

[36] Richard Edward Martínez, *PADRES: The National Chicano Priest Movement* (Austin: University of Texas Press, 2005); Lara Medina, *Las Hermanas: Chicana/Latina Religious-Political Activism in the U.S. Catholic Church* (Philadelphia: Temple University Press, 2004).

[37] Anthony Stevens-Arroyo, "PADRES," in De La Torre, *Hispanic American Religious Culture*, 1:109.

[38] Neomi De Anda, "Las Hermanas," in De La Torre, *Hispanic American Religious Culture*, 1:107.

Hermanas is an organization that wants to keep itself aware of the suffering of our Hispano people. By reason of our heritage, and in response to the mind of Vatican II and the encyclical *Populorum Progressio*, we feel obliged to be faithful to the Christian message of hopeful creation for a Christian humanism within the context and culture of the Hispano community.[39]

Lara Medina notes that with its commitment to social change, renewal, and consciousness-raising education in the church, Las Hermanas fought against sexism in the church and advocated for childcare, the rights of farmworkers, and women's ordination.[40] By 1991 the membership of Las Hermanas had reached about a thousand.[41] Las Hermanas participated in establishing the Mexican American Cultural Center in San Antonio, Texas (see below), and members of Las Hermanas directly contributed to the development of Latinx theology.

Another important series of events for Latinx theologies in the United States came in the national conferences of Hispanic lay and religious leaders held under the name of Encuentro Nacional Hispano de Pastoral (National Hispanic Pastoral Encounter). Sponsored by the U.S. Conference of Catholic Bishops (USCCB), the Encuentros focused on "developing pastoral leadership and collaboration between the Hispanic faithful and U.S. bishops. The collaborative discussions from the *Encuentros* would be the source for the bishops' 'National Pastoral Plan for Hispanic Ministry' in 1987."[42] Each of the Encuentros Nacional Hispano de Pastoral that have been held—in 1972, 1977, 1985, 2000, and 2018—were major efforts to address the Latinx cultural and pastoral realities that confront the U.S. Roman Catholic Church in its ministry to the Latinx population. Also, in 2006 the Primer Encuentro Nacional Hispano de Pastoral Juvenil (First Hispanic Youth National Encuentro) was held to listen to the voices of Hispanic/Latino youth and to identify effective ways to address their hopes and needs.

Luis A. Tampe examined the first three Encuentros Nacional Hispano de Pastoral (1972–1985), which were characterized partially by grassroots participation and by the involvement and response of U.S. bishops. Tampe also identified several themes that surfaced from those three Encuentros:

[39] Sister Maria Iglesias and Sister María Luz Hernández, "Hermanas," in *Prophets Denied Honor: An Anthology of the Hispano Church of the United States*, ed. Anthony M. Stevens-Arroyo (Maryknoll, NY: Orbis Books, 1980), 141.

[40] Medina, *Las Hermanas*, 4, 231, 373.

[41] Ibid., 123–24.

[42] Oswald John Nira, "United States Conference of Catholic Bishops," in De La Torre, *Hispanic American Religious Culture*, 1:111.

- Commitment to evangelization, missionary work, justice, and community
- Promotion of ecclesial co-responsibility, dialogue, and synodality (i.e., the involvement of the local church through deliberative bodies in the governance of the universal church) through a *pastoral de conjunto*
- Concern for the ecclesial formation of Hispanics as well as for the family, the poor, young people, and women[43]

The Encuentro 2000 (IV Encuentro) had the theme "Many Faces in God's House, Unity in Diversity." Carmen Nanko-Fernández gives an assessment of a noticeable shift in the nature of the gatherings with Encuentro 2000:

> There had been a degree of ownership by Hispanic Catholics of the Encuentro name and process that was nurtured over three national meetings from 1972 to 1985. Encuentro was a way of meeting, developed with Catholic Latin@s, that promoted agency, favored consultation, and served as a means to involve the grassroots in the ecclesial decisions that affected la comunidad. While the initial idea of a more inclusive Encuentro recognizing the variety of cultures in the U.S. church was said to have come from the Hispanic Affairs Committee, there was a sense, on the part of some, that the name, process, and players had been coopted. The positive spin on Encuentro 2000 was that it reflected the hospitality of the new plurality in recognizing "the many faces in God's house." The reality was that this invitation had come from the bishops of the United States, and the faces of those with the power to extend the invitation did not (and do not) reflect this rising majority.[44]

Encuentro V in 2018 focused on the theme of "Missionary Disciples: Witnesses of God's Love." The Encuentros also have had an impact far beyond Roman Catholic circles.

An important contemporary (and historical) center for Hispanic/Latinx Catholic theology and ministry is in San Antonio, Texas, which moved from being a center of Tejano religion toward providing broader

---

[43] Luis A. Tampe, "Encuentro Nacional Hispano de Pastoral (1972–1985): A Historical and Ecclesiological Analysis" (STD dissertation, Catholic University of America, 2014).

[44] Carmen Nanko-Fernández, *Theologizing en Espanglish: Context Community, and Ministry* (Maryknoll, NY: Orbis Books, 2010), 7–8.

leadership in the overall Latinx church. By 1970 Patricio Flores became the Catholic auxiliary bishop of San Antonio. From 1983 to 1995 Virgilio Elizondo (1935–2016) served in his hometown as rector at San Fernando Cathedral, where his pastoral ministry and his writings were in conversation with the rich resources of Tejano/a and, more broadly, Mexican American religiosity and spirituality. Through his fifteen books and over one hundred scholarly essays and popular articles, Elizondo explored the themes of mestizaje, Jesus coming from the margins and periphery of life, and devotion to and the role of the Virgin of Guadalupe. In many circles Elizondo is "acclaimed as the founder of U.S. Latino theologies."[45]

Under the authority of the Archdiocese of San Antonio, Elizondo, along with other Mexican American Catholic clergy and laity—including members of Las Hermanas, PADRES, and the Texas Catholic Conference—founded the Mexican American Cultural Center (MACC) in 1972 to focus on the spiritual, temporal, and educational needs of the Mexican American Catholic community in the United States.[46] Elizondo served as MACC's founding president from 1972 to 1987. MACC offered culturally focused studies in Hispanic pastoral ministry, language studies, and research. In 2008 MACC became the Mexican American Catholic College, which continued to provide a bilingual education in Hispanic and pastoral ministry.

Elizondo advocated a culturally relevant Catholicism that sought to bring the good news to all situations of life. In his 1983 book *Galilean Journey* (revised edition in 2000), Elizondo connects the shared Hispanic identity of mestizaje with the marginality of first-century Christianity.[47] Central to this approach is mining the theological and cultural riches found in popular religiosity, especially the devotion to the Virgin of Guadalupe. Elizondo developed a connection between mestizaje and popular religiosity and combined this theological perspective with his ministry as rector at San Fernando Cathedral and his work at MACC, as well as in his writings and teachings, to forge pastoral and religious leadership that empowered Hispanic ministry.

Jesuit priest and theologian Allan Figueroa Deck (b. 1945) explored the role of liturgy in Mexican American culture in his early written

---

[45] Timothy Matovina, "Virgilio Elizondo," in De La Torre, *Hispanic American Religious Culture*, 2:659.

[46] Medina, *Las Hermanas*, 70.

[47] Virgilio Elizondo, *Galilean Journey: The Mexican-American Promise*, 2nd ed. (1983; Maryknoll, NY: Orbis Books, 2000). The first edition of *Galilean Journey* drew upon Elizondo's 1978 doctoral dissertation *Mestissage, violence culturelle, announce de l'évangele* from Instiut Catholique in Paris.

works. Deck later published the influential *The Second Wave* in 1989, in which he explored the implications of a "new wave" of Catholic immigrants from Latin America. He believes a new pastoral approach was necessary for Latinx, one that would take seriously the North American contexts of U.S. Latinx and avoid both a replication of earlier assimilation-type models and methods or an unmodified adoption of Latin American initiatives.[48] At the time of this writing, Deck serves as Distinguished Scholar in Pastoral Theology and Latino Studies and lecturer in the Departments of Theological Studies and Chicano/Latino/a Studies at Loyola Marymount University in Los Angeles, California.

A connected development in Latinx/Hispanic theology was the founding in 1988 of the Academy of Catholic Hispanic Theologians of the United States (ACHTUS). ACHTUS is a Roman Catholic "association of scholars dedicated to promoting research and critical theological reflection within the context of U.S. Hispanic Experience." In summarizing the origins of ACHTUS, Deck notes that as early as 1945 Archbishop Robert Lucey of San Antonio, Texas, and other Roman Catholic leaders encouraged greater understanding about the Hispanic population in the United States. Following Vatican II (1962–1965) and the Second Conference of Latin American Bishops in Medellín, Colombia, in 1968, there was growing awareness of connections between socioeconomic, political, and cultural realities and doing justice with an emphasis on God's preferential option for the poor through a praxis-based theology. Building upon those developments, in 1985 Deck and Arturo Bañuelas envisioned a theological academy that would speak to the pastoral and ecclesial needs of U.S. Catholic Hispanics. Then in January 1988 Deck and Bañuelas met with theologians María Pilar Aquino, Virgilio Elizondo, Orlando Espín, Roberto Goizueta, Roger Luna, and C. Gilbert Romero and founded ACHTUS, with the first gathering taking place in June 1989.

ACHTUS names as its purposes:

1. accompany the Hispanic communities of the United States, helping to critically discern the movement of the Spirit in their historical journey;

---

[48] Allan Figueroa Deck, "Liturgy and Mexican American Culture," *Modern Liturgy* 3, no. 7 (1976): 24–26; Allan Figeroa Deck, *The Second Wave: Hispanic Ministry and the Evangelization of Culture* (New York: Paulist Press, 1989). See also Jay P. Dolan and Allan Figueroa Deck, eds., *Hispanic Catholic Culture in the U.S.: Issues and Concerns* (Notre Dame, IN: University of Notre Dame Press, 1994); Allan Figueroa Deck, Yolanda Tarango, and Timothy M. Matovina, eds., *Perspectivas: Hispanic Ministry* (Kansas City, KS: Sheed and Ward, 1995).

2. thematize the faith experience of the people within their historical, socio-economic, political and cultural contexts;
3. encourage interdisciplinary scholarly collaboration;
4. create resources, instruments, and a professional network to develop a U.S. Hispanic *teología de conjunto*;
5. support Hispanics currently engaged in theological research and studies;
6. develop a scholarship fund to promote the theological education of Hispanics in general and of Hispanic women and Hispanic blacks in particular.[49]

An important dimension of the work of ACHTUS is publication of the peer-reviewed *Journal of Hispanic/Latino Theology (JHLT)*, which first appeared in 1993. *JHLT* describes its focus as publishing "Latinx Christian scholarship in systematic, pastoral and practical theology, scriptures, ethics, religious history, and U.S. Latinx cultures." Like many academic journals, the *Journal of Hispanic/Latino Theology* has shifted to be an online periodical.

Protestants

Among Latinx Protestants, the Cuban-born United Methodist minister, historian, theologian, and educator Justo L. González (b. 1937) is internationally well known, especially in Latin America and in the U.S. Latinx community. González is a leader in the development of Hispanic theology, and his 1969 book, *The Development of Christianity in Latin America*, is an early example of how he ties his work in Christian history and theology to important concerns of U.S. Latinx theology.[50] González regularly publishes in both English and Spanish, and a good number of his many publications that have explored dimensions of Hispanic/Latinx theology have become foundational texts, including *Mañana: Christian Theology from a Hispanic Perspective*; *Santa Biblia: The Bible through Hispanic Eyes*; the edited anthology *¡Alabadle! Hispanic Christian Worship*; and *Púlpito: An Introduction to Hispanic Preaching*, coauthored with Pablo Jiménez.[51]

---

[49] "A Brief Story about the Founding of ACTHUS," ACTHUS, http://www.achtus.us/history/.

[50] Justo L. González, *The Development of Christianity in Latin America* (Grand Rapids: Eerdmans, 1969).

[51] See Justo L. González, *Mañana: Christian Theology from a Hispanic Perspective* (Nashville: Abingdon Press, 1990); González, *Santa Biblia: The Bible through Hispanic Eyes* (Nashville: Abingdon Press, 1996); Justo L. González, ed.,

González also was the founding editor of *Apuntes Reflexiones Teológicas desde Contexto Hispano-Latino*, an ecumenical journal of Latinx theology that first appeared in 1981 and is published by the Hispanic/Latin@ Ministries Program of Perkins School of Theology at Southern Methodist University. *Apuntes* was the first regularly published theological journal that addressed Latinx religious contexts. Articles in *Apuntes* discuss theological, pastoral, and cultural concerns and are printed either in English with a Spanish summary or in Spanish with an English summary. Latinx Catholics, mainline Protestants, evangelicals, Pentecostals, and Charismatics all publish in *Apuntes*, making it an important forum for a developing *teología en conjunto*, a vehicle for the public discussion of Latinx theology, and an entry into a type of de facto Latinx ecumenism or interdenominational conversation.

Orlando E. Costas (1941–1987) was an influential theologian, pastor, scholar, and leader at all levels of the Latinx Christian life, from the grassroots faith communities where he did work as a pastor and missionary, to the academy as a professor, administrator, mentor, and seminary academic dean, showing his holistic service to both church and academy as a theologian. Costas had clergy standing in both the American Baptist Churches and the United Church of Christ. As a scholar, Costas was formally a missiologist, but the interdisciplinary range of his interests and the issues he addressed were quite expansive—and therein lies part of his significance in the development of Latinx theology. Costas was a Puerto Rican Protestant born in Yauco, Puerto Rico, who had migrated to the mainland United States.

Costas served as a minister and missionary in Latin America, where he encountered liberation theology and brought it into dialogue with North American evangelical theology, resulting in his own development of a type of Latinx theology. Later Costas was a pastor to a Baptist congregation in Milwaukee, Wisconsin. Through his ministry experiences and writings, Costas crafted his own understanding of the nature of the Latinx church and its mission. Always connected to but also critical of his evangelical heritage, Costas remained ecumenical in his work and his outlook. Costas published a number of works in English and Spanish. Two of his first books in English (already having been published in Spanish in 1971 and 1973, respectively) were *The Church and Its Mission* in 1974 and *The Integrity of Mission* in 1979, making Costas one of the earliest Hispanic/Latinx theologians in print in the United States.[52]

¡*Alabadle! Hispanic Christian Worship* (Nashville: Abingdon Press, 1996); Justo L. González and Pablo Jiménez, *Púlpito: An Introduction to Hispanic Preaching* (Nashville: Abingdon Press, 2005).

[52] Orlando E. Costas, *The Church and Its Mission: A Shattering Critique from*

Costas also explored the marginality of Jesus and the nature of Christian calling in his 1982 book, *Christ outside the Gate: Mission beyond Christendom.* Reflecting on the meaning of Hebrews 13:12, "Therefore Jesus also suffered outside the city gate in order to sanctify the people by his own blood," Costas wrote,

> Salvation is to be focused on that person who has assumed the perpetual identity of the outsider. We can know Jesus only as the crucified Son of God suffering and dying for the world amid the outcasts and rejects. Since Jesus died outside the gate, mission has become the crossing of the walls and gates of our secured and comfortable compounds, the continuous movement toward him to bear "the abuse he endured" for the world. It is only in this continuous movement toward his cross, in our identification with him and his cause, in our participation in his suffering death outside and for outsiders that we can be authentic witnesses of God's saving grace. Only thus can we lift him up and enable women and men to be drawn to him (Jn. 12:32).[53]

After being the first director of the Hispanic Program at Eastern Baptist Theological Seminary in Philadelphia, Costas was named academic dean at Andover Newton Theological School, a position he held until his untimely death in 1987. Costas continues to have a tremendous influence upon Latinx Protestant pastors, teachers, and activists through his direct contact with people, the countless connection of others who never knew him, and those impacted through his writings. While many examples of his reach can be cited, among the most significant is the expanding work of Esperanza USA, more widely known simply as Esperanza, based in Philadelphia, Pennsylvania, under the leadership of Luis Cortés Jr. and Danny Cortés. Esperanza is a major faith-based organization providing services to the Latinx community and is responsible for founding Esperanza College and for hosting the National Hispanic Prayer Breakfast and Conference.

Latina Women

From the very beginning of the emergence of Latinx theologies, Latina women have played significant leadership roles in its growth, as we have noted with individuals including the Reverend Leoncia Rosado (Mama

---

the Third World (Wheaton, IL: Tyndale, 1974); Orlando E. Costas, *The Integrity of Mission* (San Francisco: Harper and Row, 1979).

[53] Orlando E. Costas, *Christ outside the Gate: Mission beyond Christendom* (Maryknoll, NY: Orbis Books, 1982), 192.

Leo) and Santos Elizondo. Historically, sexism—regardless of race or ethnicity—has always been a social construction that assumed men to be inherently superior to females, with the very structures by which society and the church function arranged to perpetuate this assumption. Operating from this premise, some Christian traditions teach that God made "man" in God's own image while the woman is a deficient copy, made in the image of man, thus giving men divine authority to rule over women. As an elite group, men insist on their superiority and justify their right to dominate and domesticate those they consider to be inferior, often to enhance their own social standings. Laws, traditions, and church doctrines, established mostly by men, reinforce these societal assumptions about the nature of gender in order to establish a power structure that becomes normative and legitimate in the minds and hearts of the community, including women abused by the system. In fact, many of these women learn to perceive reality through the eyes of men (a type of false consciousness) and at times become the most vocal defenders of the status quo, thereby internalizing their oppression. Yet, despite these oppressive contexts, many Latin American and Latina women in the United States have developed alternative understandings and strategies of survival that coexist covertly with dominant paternalistic and patriarchal interpretations.

The sexism faced by Latinas is not relegated solely to history. Latina women still contend with situations of oppression and discrimination. If women are employed to do the same jobs as men, it is usually for less pay. However, the absence of fair wages is only part of the oppression; the limitation on the types of work available to Latina women is another part. Latina women must deal with the internal sexism of the community as manifested in machismo and the external sexism of the dominant white culture. Increasingly Latina women are heads of households and, with their children, are more likely to be living in poverty. Yet these spiritual, familial, and community leaders are quite literally the backbone of the Latinx church. Their daily reality requires Latinx theologies to address fully their needs in the future and includes a thorough investigation into how the Latina perspective affects every aspect of theological discourses.

Although Latinas are often silenced, their voices and actions constitute an invaluable contribution to Latinx theologies. While it ought to be obvious that the U.S. Latinx *comunidad* contains a majority of women who, both today and throughout history, provide leadership in all areas of life, this fact is only infrequently recognized by official leadership structures or within the institutional church. Latinas in the United States must contend with deep-rooted paternalistic and sexist ascriptions, from their Latinx cultures, their communities of origin, and the dominant U.S. American culture, from within and outside of the church. To listen to the voices of Latinx women is to hear a concern for issues and actions that affect the daily existence of the entire *comunidad*, especially the lives of women. Latina feminist theologies seek to correct the harm done by androcentric (male-centered) approaches and theories that in the past and present ignore women. As Gloria Inés Loya has stated, Latina women are frequently the *pasionarias* and *pastoras*—the spiritually passionate and pastoral leaders of Hispanic communities.[54] Whether they are given official titles or not, Latina women are engaged in ministries within the context of the struggle for survival.

Although Latina feminist theologies have been critical of North American feminist theologies, especially in the area of race and class analysis, they still share some general characteristics. Both types of theologies are primarily concerned with a genuine respect for the personhood and well-being of all women, an emphasis on social location, an unmasking of the traditional understandings of humanity, and a valuing of women's experience as a source and lens for the critique and construction of theologies. In addition, U.S. Latina feminist theologies enable Latina women to understand multiple oppressive structures, identify their preferred future, and confront internalized oppression. Furthermore, Latina feminist theologies identify the importance of female leadership, even in the midst of oppression, in maintaining the health and life of the *comunidad*.

Elements of what later developed into *mujerista* theology can be discerned as early as 1977.[55] By 1988, together with Yolanda Tarango, Ada María Isasi-Díaz published *Hispanic Women: Prophetic Voice of the Church*. In this book, the authors sought to represent the beliefs and understandings of the women they interviewed.[56] They advocated for the usage of the term *mujerista* (from the Spanish word for "woman," *mujer*)

---

[54] Gloria Inés Loya, "The Hispanic Woman: Pasionaria and Pastora of the Hispanic Community," in *Frontiers of Hispanic Theology in the United States*, ed. Allan Figueroa Deck (Maryknoll, NY: Orbis Books, 1992), 124–33.

[55] "Differences, difficulties—they do not divide us. The celebration of the Eucharist makes visible, surfaces what unites us—our value system: friendship, importance of family, sincerity, spontaneity, hospitality, openness, accepting others and, above all, our faith—our common belief. Yes, we are brought together by our faith, a faith we live as we struggle to understand it and which we understand as we live it" (Ada María Isasi-Díaz, "The People of God on the Move—Chronicle of a History," in Stevens-Arroyo, *Prophets Denied Honor*, 332).

[56] Ada María Isasi-Díaz and Yolanda Tarango, *Hispanic Women: Prophetic Voice of the Church / Mujer Hispana: Voz Profética en la Iglesia* (San Francisco: Harper and Row, 1988).

to name the theological reflection conducted by Latinas who found the term "feminist" alienating. The term *mujerista* was originally coined in Peru in the 1970s to name the movement and ideology of a radical feminist group.[57] Using this term within the U.S. context, Isasi-Díaz, a Cuban and one of the earliest developers of Hispanic/Latinx theology in the United States, advocated a methodology focused on the stories of women to analyze their reality, develop new expressions of worship, and seek means for empowerment. She writes,

> A *mujerista* is a Hispanic woman who struggles to liberate herself not as an individual but as a member of a Hispanic community. She is one who builds bridges among Hispanics instead of falling into sectarianism and using divisive tactics. A *mujerista* understands that her task is to gather the hopes and expectations of the people about justice and peace to work, not for equality within oppressive structures, but for liberation. A *mujerista* is called to gestate new women and new men—Hispanics who are willing to work for the common good, knowing that such work requires us to denounce all destructive sense of self-abnegation. A *mujerista* is a Latina who makes a preferential option for herself and her Hispanic sisters, understanding that our struggle for liberation has to take into consideration how racism/ethnic prejudice, economic oppression, and sexism work together and reinforce each other.[58]

Isasi-Díaz states that "*feminista hispanas* have been consistently marginalized within the Euro-American feminist community because of our critique of its ethnic/racial prejudice and its lack of class analysis."[59] *Mujerista* theology is a particular way of identifying and examining Latina understandings of faith and its function in the struggle for life and liberation. It is an intentionally different theological perspective that seeks new approaches to the issues of sexism, ethnic prejudice, and economic oppression. *Mujerista* theology identifies Latinas' explanations of their lives and faith and how the two are connected in the struggle for liberation. Isasi-Díaz explains,

> Because of the centrality of religion in the day-to-day life of Hispanic women, our understanding of the divine, and about ultimate

---

[57] Gary Dorrien, *Social Ethics in the Making: Interpreting an American Tradition* (Oxford: John Wiley & Sons, 2008), 648.

[58] Ada María Isasi-Díaz, *En la Lucha / In the Struggle: Elaborating a Mujerista Theology*, rev. ed. (Minneapolis: Fortress Press, 2004), 23.

[59] Ibid.

meaning, plays a very important role in the process of giving significance to and valuing our experience. It is imperative for us,
therefore, to comprehend better how religious understandings and
practices impact our lives. In order to do this, we need to start
from what we know, ourselves, our everyday surroundings and
experiences.[60]

Such an emphasis becomes a means of empowerment for Latina women.
While originating in the Latina social-religious reality, it is concerned not
just with Latina women but with the well-being of the entire *comunidad*.

While some Latinas refer to themselves as *mujeristas*, some Latina
women prefer the term "Latina feminist."[61] In explaining the nature of
Latina feminism and feminist theology, Theresa Torres writes, "Latina
feminism and Latina feminist theology do have similarities of approach
with feminism, but the assumption that no differences exist among them
is the reason that Latina feminists and theologians strongly explain their
position and challenge Euro-American feminists."[62] A major developer
and pioneer of a Latina feminist theology is María Pilar Aquino. Like
Isasi-Díaz, Aquino is critical both of Latin American liberation theology for its male-centeredness and of North American feminism for
not addressing issues of race and class. However, she distinguishes her
approach from *mujerista* theology, believing that *mujerista* theology's
attempt to set itself up as the opposition to a Eurocentric feminism that
ignored the Latina voice is simply too narrow. Aquino bluntly writes,
"The main reason we have chosen deliberately not to call ourselves
mujeristas, as Ada María Isasi-Díaz does in her theological perspective,
is that there are no *mujeristas* sociopolitical and ecclesial subjects or
movements in the United States or in Latin America."[63]

For Aquino, *mujerista* theology overgeneralizes the complexities
of feminist thought by creating a homogeneous identity for Latina
women that many Euroamerican feminists, ignorant of the complexi-

---

[60] Ada María Isasi-Díaz, "Mujerista Theology's Method: A Liberative Praxis,
a Way of Life," *Listening* 27, no. 1 (1992): 49.

[61] For another example of a self-identified *mujerista*, see Alicia Vargas,
"Through Mujerista Eyes: Stories of Incarnate Redemption," in *Transformative
Lutheran Theologies: Feminist, Womanist, and Mujerista Perspectives*, ed. Mary
J. Streufert (Minneapolis: Fortress Press, 2019), 99–106.

[62] Theresa L. Torres, "Feminism," in De La Torre, *Hispanic American Religious Culture*, 1:260.

[63] María Pilar Aquino, "Latina Feminist Theology: Central Features," in *A
Reader in Latina Feminist Theology: Religion and Justice*, ed. María Pilar Aquino,
Daisy L. Machado, and Jeanette Rodríguez (Austin: University of Texas Press,
2001), 138.

ties within the Latina theological discourse, perpetuate as myth. Many Euroamerican feminists see *mujerista* theology as the sole expression for all U.S. Latinas. This becomes obvious when well-meaning Euroamerican feminists tack on the term "*mujerista*" after the phase "feminist, womanist, and" without any real understanding of the Latina theological conversation.[64]

Aquino argues for a more pluralistic approach and emphasizes the importance of the sociocultural context of Latinas, particularly the multilayered oppression in which "theological reflection must take into account their multiple interests as believers, as poor, and as women, together with their religious and cultural values."[65] In the midst of manifold oppression, Latina women live holistically, with their Christian faith permeating all aspects of life. A realistic understanding of contexts, in which women are the primary actors for putting the gospel into practice, is an important ingredient in determining liberating practices for the present and the future. Since an important aspect of the context is the historical setting, Aquino states,

> For us indigenous women, *mestizas,* or Afro-Caribbean women, it is radically impossible to disregard the fact that we sprang from a conquered and colonized continent. Our ways of looking at life, understanding our own existence, and interpreting our faith-experience are all indelibly marked by this fact, regardless of whether it results in the perpetuation of an oppressive reality or brings forth emancipating experiences.[66]

With this recognition, Aquino calls for Latina American feminist approaches that are engaged in a search for women's autonomy and human integrity within their particular social and historical contexts. Aquino sees women as both the subjects and the objects of a theological enterprise of hope and emancipatory praxis that addresses the sociocultural and socioeconomic realities of Latinx in the United States and Latin America. As Latinas and Latin American women do theology, they bring their unique points of view as they continue to participate in the *comunidad.*

---

[64] Ibid., 139.

[65] María Pilar Aquino, "Perspectives on a Latina's Feminist Liberation Theology," in Deck, *Frontiers of Hispanic Theology in the United States,* 36.

[66] María Pilar Aquino, "The Collective 'Dis-covery' of Our Own Power: Latina American Feminist Theology," in *Hispanic/Latino Theology: Challenge and Promise,* ed. Ada María Isasi-Díaz and Fernando F. Segovia (Minneapolis: Fortress Press, 1996), 240.

Nancy Pineda-Madrid helpfully notes that, when considering these two approaches, "Neither of these terms when used alone—mujerista theology and Latina feminist theology—can accurately represent the writings of all Latina theologians committed to feminism."[67] With that in mind, another perspective in Latina feminist discourse to consider is Latina *evangélica* theology, done from the perspective of Latina Protestants who are integral to grassroots churches and communities. Important to Latina *evangélica* theology is the concept known as *abuelita* (little or dear grandmother [the diminutive in Spanish often being an indicator of deep affection and connection]) theology, also known as "kitchen theology." This is a contextually distinct Protestant theology inherited from the wise women of the community who transmit spiritual beliefs and practices to the next generation through the women of the household, thus suggesting a matriarchal core. They are concerned with constructing theological models that contribute to the transformation of their communities by focusing on the liberation of Latinas. They operate within a tension that affirms life-giving aspects of *evangélica* thought while providing a prophetic critique of the tradition that contributes to the oppression of women in particular, and the marginalization of the community in general.[68]

Another important voice in the development of Latina feminist theology in particular and Hispanic theology as a whole is Ana María Pineda, who was born in El Salvador and migrated to the United States. Pineda is a member of the Sisters of Mercy order, worked in the earlier Encuentros, and for a number of years was the director of the Hispanic Ministries Program at the Catholic Theological Union in Chicago, before moving to Santa Clara University in California. Writing from the theological perspective of pastoral work, Pineda explores the connections between identity, culture, and faith. Additionally, in her theological work, Pineda draws on the religious and theological depth of the Latinx communities in a way that speaks to the wider Christian church. One example of her ability to make connections is how Pineda explores a theology of welcome

[67] Nancy Pineda-Madrid, "Feminist Theory and Latina Feminist/Mujerista Theologizing," in *The Wiley Blackwell Companion to Latino/a Theology*, ed. Orlando O. Espín (Malden, MA: Wiley Blackwell, 2015), 350. See also Nancy Pineda-Madrid, "Latina Theology," in *Liberation Theologies in the United States: An Introduction*, ed. Stacey M. Floyd-Thomas and Anthony B. Pinn (New York: New York University Press, 2010), 61–85; Ana María Pineda, "Hospitality," in *Practicing Our Faith: A Way of Life for a Searching People*, ed. Dorothy C. Bass (San Francisco: JosseyBass, 1997).

[68] Loida I. Martell-Otero, Zaida Maldonado Perez, and Elizabeth Conde-Frazier, *Latina Evangélicas: A Theological Survey from the Margins* (Eugene, OR: Wipf and Stock, 2013), 1–6.

that is practiced within Hispanic communities, such as in the ritual of Las Posadas. Pineda states that through this annual Advent ritual, which re-creates the story of Mary and Joseph searching for a place for Jesus to be born, Latinxs "ritually participate in being rejected and being welcomed, in slamming the door on the needy and opening it wide. They are in this way renewed in the Christian practice of hospitality, the practice of providing a space where the stranger is taken in and known as one who bears gifts."[69] In this way, persons who may themselves be strangers in the United States act out their popular religion with a deep awareness of the Christian faith's call for hospitality.

While numerous approaches taken by Latina theologians have found expression in *mujerista* and Latina feminist theologies, the differences that exist are partly a result of different perspectives and methodologies brought to the study of Latinas in their communities. Each approach, as well as other Latina theological projects, addresses the roles that gender, race, ethnicity, and class play in the lives of their communities, as well as in the formal articulation of systematic theologies. However, the issues facing Latina women are so pressing and the stakes so high that differences in approaches may be an indication of the complexity of the struggle for the greater common good of Latina women in particular, and the U.S. Latinx community as a whole.

Latinx Theological Work *en Conjunto*

Like the rest of Christian theology, Latinx theologies can be studied by historically tracing the development of perspectives and traditions of theological interpretation. Nevertheless, due to the multiple connections and influences within Hispanic theologies, it is not yet clear if one can speak of definite schools of thought. Indeed, one of the hallmarks of Latino/a theologies is a certain type of ecumenical awareness and solidarity that crosses traditional denominational and interpretive boundaries. Reflecting an intentional effort to do theology together as the whole household of God in Christ, this new ecumenism of Latinx theologies emerged in the late 1960s and the early 1970s, cognizant of the mixed histories of the U.S. National Council of Churches and the World Council of Churches, and similar associations. A grassroots ecumenism of Latinx theologies—or perhaps better, Latinx theological *conjunto*—developed along alternative paths with a profound sense of the various Latinx communities to which many Latinx theologians and scholars of religion felt an ongoing responsibility and commitment.

---

[69] Pineda, "Hospitality," 31.

One place where Latinx theological work *en conjunto* is most apparent is within organizations that have taken on roles as de facto Latinx collaborative institutions and efforts. Justo González played a leading role in these efforts, including the Hispanic Summer Program, the Hispanic Theological Initiative, and the Associación para la Educación Teológica Hispana (AETH). Two of these, the Hispanic Summer Program (HSP) and the Hispanic Theological Initiative (HTI), have their roots in an earlier organization then known as the Fund for Theological Education (FTE, now the Forum for Theological Exploration). The HSP and the HTI are different in their missions, but closely connected, particularly through an overlap of constituencies.

The HSP started in 1989 as an annual, two-week Hispanic seminary program managed by the FTE. The Hispanic Summer Program "provided an ecumenical program of seminary-level courses taught by Latina faculty" that focuses on the specific needs of the Latino community."[70] In November 1993 the Pew Charitable Trusts, a major underwriter of the prior incarnation of the Hispanic Doctoral Fellowships offered through the FTE, as well as being the managing agency for the HSP, began to contemplate a change in the funding priorities, prompting a reevaluation of the structure and the funding of the HSP. With the Pew Trusts' grant funding to the FTE coming to an end, González took the initiative and leadership, inviting accredited seminaries and schools of theology within the Association of Theological Schools to enter into a new type of partnership as a consortium of support for the continuation of the HSP. At the reorganization meeting of the "new" HSP held at Princeton Theological Seminary in June 1995, the attending seminary representatives committed to this new initiative in collaborative ecumenical Latinx graduate education in theology and religion with approximately forty sponsoring institutions.

While conceptually rooted in the HSP, the Hispanic Theological Initiative (HTI) is a distinct program that provides grants and mentoring for Latinx pursuing degrees in theology and religious studies, with the hope that many HTI grantees would become faculty in theological education institutions in North America. Established in 1996 the HTI also initially was funded by the Pew Charitable Trusts with the goal of increasing the number of Latinx faculty in North American seminaries, schools of theology, and universities by funding early-career Latinx scholars at various stages of their doctoral work. Through bringing together Latinx scholars of diverse backgrounds and different ecclesiastical traditions, both the HSP and HTI foster professional and relational Latinx understanding,

---

[70] Martínez, *The Story of Latino Protestants in the United States*, 154.

collaboration, and solidarity—and, like rhizomes, both organizations connect in multiple directions.

Other Latinx theological institutions also contribute to the development of Latinx theologies. As mentioned previously, the Academy of Catholic Hispanic Theologians of the United States (ACHTUS) is one of the major ways Hispanic/Latin@ theology has become institutionalized. Although its regular membership comprises Roman Catholic scholars, ACHTUS is also an important contributor to the new Latinx theological *en conjunto* through the collaborative work of ACTHUS and its work in the *Journal of Hispanic/Latino Theology.*

Another organization that has played an important role within the Latino/a scholarly community is the Asociación para la Educación Teológica Hispana (AETH, Association of Hispanic Theological Education), which was launched in 1991. AETH works in the United States, Canada, Puerto Rico, and in Latin America and the Caribbean for the promotion and improvement of theological education and its impact on the lives of people, churches, and communities. More specifically, AETH describes itself as promoting and certifying "the quality of Hispanic theological education programs and contribut[ing] to the development of the leadership of women and men who strengthen our congregations and communities." AETH is involved in theological education in multiple settings, ranging from Bible institutes to regionally accredited graduate theological seminaries.[71] One of AETH's primary goals is to encourage and strengthen theological education for Latinxs. From its inception, AETH's membership has been open to all theological educators at all levels who are engaged in some way with Hispanic religious contexts, including historic mainline Protestants, Roman Catholics, and Pentecostals. However, the majority of its members are Protestant, and indeed AETH has been perceived by some as a Protestant equivalent of ACHTUS. AETH has established regional chapters and is a growing publisher of works on Hispanic theology, both in English and Spanish.

Finally, ad hoc consultations and meetings have figured prominently in the historical development of Latinx theologies. In the 1990s these included the October 1991 national ecumenical conference on Hispanic theology at Union Theological Seminary in New York City titled "La Fe Que Hace Justicia" ("Faith Doing Justice"). This conference prepared the ground for cooperative initiatives that were to follow, such as the interdenominational conference titled "Aliens in Jerusalem: The Emerging

---

[71] See the AETH website, https://www.aeth.org/?language=english. See also José Daniel Montañez, "AETH," in De La Torre, *Hispanic American Religious Culture,* 2:663: Martínez, *The Story of Latino Protestants in the United States,* 154–55.

Theological Voice of Hispanic Americans," at Drew University in Madison, New Jersey, in 1994. The Hispanic Churches in American Public Life program examined the impact of Catholic, pentecostal, historic mainline Protestant, and new religious communities on civic engagement in politics, education, business, social programs, and community activism in the Latino/a community. The two directors of this study were Pentecostal Jesse Miranda of the National Alliance of Evangelical Ministries (AMEN) and Roman Catholic Virgilio Elizondo of the Catholic Mexican American Cultural Center (MACC, since 2008 the Mexican American Catholic College), with historian and religious studies scholar Gastón Espinosa as project manager. One of the outcomes of that study project was the book *Latino Religions and Civic Activism in the United States.*[72] In addition to special conferences and meetings, Latinx theologians, biblical scholars, and others in religious studies have been increasingly active in a variety of professional meetings and societies, including the American Academy of Religion, American Historical Association, American Society of Church History, Association for the Sociology of Religion, American Studies Association, Latino Studies Association, Religious Education Association, Religious Research Association, Society of Biblical Literature, and Society for the Scientific Study of Religion.

Concluding Reflections on *Historia*

Latinx in the United States have a long-standing presence; it is not simply or solely the story of recent arrivals, although this too is part of Latinx *historias*. From one perspective we can speak of the origins of Latinx religious traditions and theologies by focusing on the understandings of a particular community, such as that which developed in San Antonio or among the Hispanos of New Mexico, or amid the rapidly developing Pentecostalism in the social borderlands in the early twentieth century. Latinx theologies include expressions both of an immigrant church and, in some areas, of deeply rooted faith communities that have had to contend with larger cultural, religious, social, and political entities and forces. Undoubtedly, local Latinx theologies existed before there was something more formally designated as "Latinx theology," but telling a strict chronological story is a difficult task. Like subterranean roots and shoots, Latinx theologies have multiple connections spreading in various directions, and occasionally it is difficult to follow the story line. And indeed, depending on where one starts the storytelling, there are now

[72] Gastón Espinosa, Virgilio Elizondo, and Jesse Miranda, eds., *Latino Religions and Civic Activism in the United States* (New York: Oxford University Press, 2005).

several generations of Latinx theological articulations. As noted at the beginning of this chapter, the *historias* of Latinx theologies is not solely about chronological genealogy but of all kinds of Latinx theological, religious, cultural, social, and political connections. But it is also something more: it is about Latinx telling their own stories, and what that means. Historian Daisy Machado expressed it in this way:

> What is at the core for Latinas and Latinos is the ability to free ourselves from the restrictions imposed by ideological imperatives of an idealized history that serves to exclude and marginalize. What I am referring to is the ability to redefine what has been called by the dominant society as the "norm" and acknowledge that Latinas/os are also "normative" because our ancestors have been permanent residents of this hemisphere for centuries. We are not the aliens. We are the heirs of a rich and diverse history that has been over five centuries in the making.[73]

---

[73] Daisy L. Machado, "Latina/o Church History: A Haunting Memory," in *Hispanic Christian Thought at the Dawn of the 21st Century: Apuntes in Honor Justo L. González*, ed. Alvin Padilla, Roberto Goizueta, and Eldin Villafañe (Nashville: Abingdon Press, 2005), 123.

5

The Everyday

Reflections on Context, Intersectionality, and Latinx Religions

All religious thought is contextual. The religious manifestations of any given community are a reflection of the experiences and actions of said community. Therefore, to better understand Latinx religious expressions of all types—spoken, written, and embodied—it is crucial to understand the everyday existential experiences of Latinx communities. To study the variety of Latinx religiosity and discourse is to discover a vibrant and fluid field. Religious perspectives of the last century, or even the last millennium, will forever be rooted in the prior commitments and thoughts of those undergoing the everyday experiences of that particular time. Religious perspectives and theologies of the past were not immune from the ideological tendencies of the era from which they had sprung, nor from the socioeconomic status of the one (usually male) writing the theology in those particular times. Because those theologians and religious scholars constructed their "studying of God" from within their own cultures, biases, customs, and traditions, they were more apt to provide us with information as to who they were than who God is (but perhaps that is an inherent aspect of the "study of God"—that it also is a study of humanity). While these past religious views may be informative, a connection with the present community may be lost due to the passage of time or demographic shifts in culture. A continuity cannot be assumed.

Contemporary, scholarly, Latinx-based religious and theological thought that developed several decades ago has been a liberative-driven conversation that was contextualized upon what it means to be part of a Latinx faith community. But contexts are always in flux. We are cognizant that while there may be some continuity, the world faced by Latinxs in the previous century is different in many respects from that of Latinx communities today. Of course, this assessment includes the theological and religious perspectives articulated in the first edition of this book (2001), which also have experienced some changes over the intervening years. While oppressive structures remain, however, they are manifested differently and are better masked in our environment, whether they wear a guise of political correctness, try to cloak entrenched misogyny as impartiality, or even drop the mask altogether and show blatant and vile white supremacy and nationalism. Every new generation of Latinx scholars of religion must recontextualize the interpretive framework in light of contemporary circumstances. If theology is indeed a grassroots process tied to local faith communities, as most Latinxs claim it to be, then it stands to reason that as the social, economic, political, and cultural situations of Latinx peoples change, new religious perspectives and interpretations need to develop, both to acknowledge and to give voice to those changes.

If theology is to remain an active, relevant component of the lives of Latinx peoples in the United States in order to illuminate how the Deity makes Godself known to a people, then religious views must be updated to include the changing ethos of Latinxs. If all religious perspectives and theologies serve a particular people for a specific moment in time, then religious perspectives and theologies must always be giving way to newer understandings that can help communities, specifically marginalized communities, to better understand the movement of God within their midst. To codify and institutionalize all Latinx religious perspectives of the past as timeless, unchanging truth does a disservice to today's Latinxs. While such religious perspectives may still provide insight, each new Latinx generation must wrestle with and define for themselves the complex intersectionality of their social location, their spirituality, and the overall society in which they find themselves.[1]

Certainly, if religious perspectives and theological concepts are not rooted in the Latinx community, then they are not Latinx-based.

---

[1] Patricia Hill Collins and Sirma Bilge define "intersectionality" as "a way of understanding and analyzing the complexity in the world, in people, and in human experiences. The events and conditions of social and political life and the self can seldom be understood as shaped by one factor. They are generally shaped by many factors in diverse and mutually influencing ways" (Patricia Hill Collins and Sirma Bilge, *Intersectionality* [Malden, MA: Polity Press, 2016], 2). See also Patricia Hill Collins, *Intersectionality as Critical Social Theory* (Durham, NC: Duke University Press, 2019); and Richard Delgado and Jean Stefancic, *Critical Race Theory: An Introduction* (New York: New York University Press, 2017), 10–11.

Being ethnically Hispanic or having a Latinx-sounding last name is not enough. The foundation for any religious perspective to be Latinx must be actual embodied Latinx communities, even though such community-based concepts are neither universal nor absolute. Care must be taken not to romanticize the Latinx community, lest we also develop romanticized Latinx religious thought. Particular Latinx religious assertions may not be the "truth," but still they remain unapologetically based on truth claims derived from disenfranchised and marginalized Latinx communities. Naturally these disenfranchised communities never remain constant, but rather they are always in flux. Therefore, we recognize that as Latinx contexts change, so must the methodology by which particular communities determine how to struggle for their dignity and how they name their resources for that struggle. In short, Latinx religious thought, including the various expressions of Latinx theology, must be changing constantly to reflect the changing communities from which it arises.

The religious contributions made by previous generations of Latinx scholars are crucial to present Latinx understandings of the religious discourse and any praxis that may flow from that. Yet, as Miguel De La Torre reminds us,

> As crucial as are concepts like *lo cotidiano, nepantla, la lucha, en conjunto,* and *acompañamiento,* they are several decades old. While it is true that the lack of academic excellence among many Euroamericans who have never heard of these terms, let alone understand them, is prevalent, Latina/os have been engaged in the same conversation occurring within the Hispanic community of yesteryear. The social location that produced these concepts has changed, and so must the Hispanic approach to these concepts.[2]

Our challenge in articulating Latinx religious discourse is not to dismiss concepts developed by previous generations of Latinx scholars. Without a doubt their works and contributions remain completely relevant. Nonetheless, if our hope is to make the Latinx religious discourse relevant to the present (and next?) generations of the Latinx disenfranchised communities, then these earlier concepts compel examination, expansion, and further development. Constructing Latinx theologies is an ongoing process that calls for discerning life-giving connections with the past, insightful flexibility in the present, and an openness to the future. Some concepts may no longer serve as useful in the new

---

[2] Miguel A. De La Torre, *Latina/o Social Ethics: Moving beyond Eurocentric Thinking* (Waco, TX: Baylor University Press, 2010), 87.

contexts; in other instances, newer paradigms based on the radical activism focused on the liberation of Latinx from the prevailing dominant social structures may be necessary. It is to this task that this chapter turns its attention. We endeavor to root ourselves in the everyday of Latinx practice and discourse as we peer into the immediate future, examining the changing ethos of today's Latinx community. We concede that the chapter does not list every conceivable challenge the Latinx community faces. Some readers will insist that certain items mentioned are not as important as others that were not included. This chapter is neither a book of prophecies, nor does it aspire to chart the course Latinx religious thought should take. Rather, based on the multiple and significant changes occurring within the Latinx community within the larger context of global challenges, we attempt to identify the emerging perspectives that are being constructed to meet these new challenges of the Latinx everyday.

Generational Considerations

As we have emphasized repeatedly, the U.S. Latinx population is not uniform, and one of the ways this manifests is in generational differences. An example of these differences is the group sometimes called Latinx Millennials. The term "Millennials" refers to those persons born between 1980 and 1996.[3] Sometimes this age cohort also is called Generation Y or Generation Next. They are described as "digital natives," the "net" generation, or the "digital" generation.[4] As other generations were marked by shared public happenings (as examples, members of certain generations can relate to these particular events in their lifetimes: the Great Depression; December 7, 1941; the launch of Sputnik; the assassinations of John F. Kennedy, Malcolm X, Martin Luther King Jr., and Robert F. Kennedy; the Vietnam War; Watergate, etc.), so it is, too, with Millennials/Generation Y or Generation Next. Millennials are the generation that

---

[3] Some researchers break this out more finely into two groups: Older Millennials, born 1980 to 1989; and Younger Millennials, born 1990 to 1996. Some researchers also shift the dates by one year, i.e., 1981 and 1995. See Michael Dimock, "Defining Generations: Where Millennials End and Generation Z Begins," Pew Research Center, January 17, 2019, https://www.pewresearch.org/fact-tank/2019/01/17/where-millennials-end-and-generation-z-begins/.

[4] "Generation Y, more commonly known as Millennials, falls between Generation X and Generation Z. Although the dates of their birth years range depending on what source is used, one could put it as encompassing the 1980s and early 1990s." Corey Seemiller and Meghan Grace, *Generation Z Goes to College* (San Francisco: Jossey-Bass, 2016), 4.

lived through September 11, 2001, school-church-campus shootings, the emergence of social media, the introduction of the widespread use of mobile devices, the Great Recession, and the elections of both Barack Obama and Donald Trump as president of the United States.[5]

Sociologist Nilda Flores-González contrasts Latino Millennials with the Latinx generations that preceded them. Flores-González describes Latinx baby boomers (1946–1964) as mainly Mexicans and Puerto Ricans, although a good number of Cubans were in that mix as well. Latinx boomers often were raised by parents who emphasized assimilation and accommodation as the pathway to economic and social upward mobility. Some of the Latinx boomers were radicalized when confronted with the reality of racism and the barriers to equality, prompting them to join the struggle for civil rights. The Latinx Generation X (1965–1980) benefited both from gains in civil rights and expanded economic opportunities for some. With the passage of the Civil Rights Act of 1965, Latinx Generation X also saw an infusion of new streams of immigration from the Caribbean, Central America, and South America, adding to the diversity of the U.S. Latinx population.[6] One of the direct results of the emergence of Latinx Generation X is that the next cohort, that is, Latinx Millennials, are an extremely diverse generational group when compared with Latinx Boomers.

Flores-González reports that "Latino millennials share many of traits that characterize the millennial generation more generally, but racialization processes shape their social, economic, and political experiences in particular ways. We need to consider these cohort-specific experiences to understand why Latino millennials see their position in the U.S. society as marginal."[7] That generational experience of marginalization is one of the characteristics to consider when seeking to understand Latinx Millennials. In comparison, during the 1990s, some Latinx members of the Generation X age cohort embraced the self-identification of Generation Ñ, a bicultural and bilingual identity that acknowledged their simultaneously living within two worlds, one Latinx and the other Euroamerican, without losing anything in the "translation."[8] Latinx Millennials, on the other hand, self-identify in a context of numerical growth with a simultaneous experience of marginalization.

[5] Nilda Flores-González, *Citizens but Not Americans: Race and Belonging among Latino Millennials* (New York: New York University Press, 2017).
[6] Ibid., 24–26.
[7] Ibid., 24.
[8] Bill Cruz, Bill Teck, and Editors of *Generation Ñ Magazine*, *The Official Spanglish Dictionary: Un User's Guía to More Than 200 Words and Phrases That Aren't Exactly Español or Inglés* (New York: Fireside, 1998).

To get a further sense of the growth and potential of the Latinx Millennials age cohort, in 2016, of all the potential eligible Latinx voters, 44 percent were Latinx Millennials. But even when considering one age cohort, another generation is always coming up behind them. An increasing percentage of Latinx people who identify as religiously unaffiliated are Latinx Millennials and Latinx Generation Z. As Corey Seemiller and Meghan Grace note,

> Generation Z refers to those born from 1995 through 2010. Having their world completely shaped by the Internet, they are often also aptly referred to as digital natives, the Net Generation, or iGeneration. They make up a quarter of the US population and will become a third of the population by 2020. They are the most racially diverse generation to date.[9]

The interests and concerns of these younger generations call out for Latinx theologies to interact with them to better understand their ways of meaning-making, methods of interpretation, and patterns of congregating/gathering.

Everyday Religion of the People

A major topic in the development of U.S. Latinx theologies is popular religion. Popular religion is not limited to Christianity but is a phenomenon that appears in many different religious traditions and contexts. Gilbert Cavazos-González lists some of the many other terms that are used to describe this rich phenomenon:

> Folk religion, family traditions, pious exercises, popular Catholicism, faith expressions, popular piety, popular devotion, *senus fidelium, or religiosidad popular* (popular religiosity). In the not-so-distant past it was seen as belonging to the uneducated masses and was juxtaposed to the true religion of an elitist Christianity. Popular religion, however, is an elusive categorization given to a changing reality that can no longer be ignored or snubbed as superstition, unorthodox, or antiquated.[10]

---

[9] Corey Seemiller and Meghan Grace, *Generation Z Goes to College* (San Francisco: Jossey-Bass, 2016), 6.

[10] Gilberto Cavazos-González, "Popular Religion," in *Hispanic American Religious Culture*, vol. 2, ed. Miguel A. De La Torre (Santa Barbara, CA: ABC-CLIO, 2009), 713.

While the term "popular religion" can be convenient, it also can be misleading and narrow if we are not clear about what we mean. Like others wanting clarification, Theresa Delgadillo makes a distinction between institutional and noninstitutional religion when she distinguishes "the term religion to refer to organized, institutionalized, traditional religions in Western thought and the term spirituality to refer to non-Western and non-institutional forms of relation to the sacred."[11] In Christian contexts, popular religion or spirituality is primarily those religious or spiritual expressions found outside the institutional church that address aspects— both affective and intellectual—of religious spirituality in a holistic way. An emphasis on popular religion as well as "official" or formal religion is a recognition that Christian faith, spirituality, and practices are formed, nourished, and sustained in multiple ways, including through everyday piety and expressions. Latinx popular religion is not a curious, exotic, theologically backward, or even inferior oddity of an eccentric, voiceless, uniform people. Rather, Latinx popular religion is a short-hand way to refer to a motherlode of vibrant, creative, and dynamic theological, cultural, and spiritual practices of diverse groups of peoples. Through popular religion, Latinx peoples voice and act out their own theological and spiritual understandings of the Divine, themselves, and the world. Orlando Espín states that without an honest appreciation of what he refers to as "the faith of the people," one has an impoverished understanding of the entire Latinx reality. Its importance is such that Espín sees at work

> an epistemology of suffering (and of living) for most Latinos. I am not blind to its numerous shortcomings. I do believe, however, that too much of the Latino universe is understood and shared through the popular religious network to have it easily dismissed (in Latino and Euro-American scholarship) as ultimately irrelevant.[12]

Other Latinx theologians also emphasize that the religion of the people ought to be taken seriously on its own terms and not be automatically devalued.[13] Popular religion as "the faith of the people" includes the

---

[11] Theresa Delgadillo, *Spiritual Mestizaje: Religion, Gender, and Nation in Contemporary Chicana Narrative* (Durham, NC: Duke University Press, 2011), 3.

[12] Orlando O. Espín, *The Faith of the People: Theological Reflections on Popular Catholicism* (Maryknoll, NY: Orbis Books, 1997), 169.

[13] See Edwin David Aponte, *¡Santo! Varieties of Latino/a Spirituality* (Maryknoll, NY: Orbis Books, 2012); Hector Avalos, ed., *Introduction to the*

religious and spiritual understandings and accompanying practices that flow from and form part of their everyday lives, whether they are sanctioned formally by institutional, academic, or ecclesiastical authorities or not. Popular religion has profound theological significance, pastoral importance, cultural relevance, and spiritual accessibility. Furthermore, the religion of the people is not necessarily always and everywhere at odds with "official religion" or institutional understandings of faith. Indeed, many times popular religion has such alluring force that institutional religion has adjusted itself by incorporating elements of popular religion into formal faith and practice.

When defining "popular religion," Espín emphasizes that the term "popular" refers to the people, many of whom are disenfranchised, and who are the ones generating a religion of the marginalized *pueblo* that becomes the expression of the creativity of the popular classes.[14] The majority of its practitioners are not religious professionals, but the laity in the true sense of the word *populus*, "the people, the whole people." More specifically, the reality of Latinx popular religion as the religion of the people contests any understanding of religion that sees a clear and neat division between what is sacred and profane, not that there is a confusion or even fusion between what is "holy" and what is not. Rather, it is to say that the holy (however understood) is present in the everyday, including aspects of popular culture, and is always accessible.[15]

Latinx popular religion also means that the boundaries of what is acceptable may be stretched, at the very least, as multiple sources

---

U.S. Latina and Latino Religious Experience (Boston: Brill Academic Publishers, 2004); Miguel A. De La Torre and Gastón Espinosa, eds., *Rethinking Latino Religions and Identity* (Cleveland: Pilgrim Press, 2006); Anita de Luna, *Faith Formation and Popular Religion: Lessons from the Tejano Experience* (Lanham, MD: Rowman and Littlefield, 2002); James Empereur and Eduardo C. Fernández, *La Vida Sacra: Contemporary Hispanic Sacramental Theology* (Lanham, MD: Rowman and Littlefield, 2006); Eduardo C. Fernández, *La Cosecha: Harvesting Contemporary United States Hispanic Theology (1972–1998)* (Collegeville, MN: Liturgical Press, 2000); Jeanette Rodriguez, *Our Lady of Guadalupe: Faith and Empowerment among Mexican-American Women* (Austin: University of Texas Press, 1994); Anthony M. Stevens-Arroyo and Ana María Díaz-Stevens, eds., *An Enduring Flame: Studies on Latino Popular Religiosity* (New York: Program for the Analysis of Religion among Latinos, 1994).

[14] Orlando O. Espín, "Popular Religion as an Epistemology of Suffering," *Journal of Hispanic/Latino Theology* 2, no. 2 (November 1994): 65–67.

[15] On religion and popular culture, see Terry Ray Clark and Dan W. Clanton Jr., eds., *Understanding Religion and Popular Culture* (New York: Routledge, 2012); and Bruce David Forbes and Jeffery H. Mahan, *Religion and Popular Culture in America*, 3rd ed. (Oakland: University of California Press, 2017).

and resources are drawn upon. Another feature is that Latinx popular religion relies heavily upon indigenous Indian and African beliefs and practices, depending on specific local contexts. Since popular religion is a dynamic reality, these various sources are worked and reworked within specific settings. Theologian C. Gilbert Romero described popular religion from within the Latinx Catholic context as "a form of popular devotion among Hispanics based more on indigenous cultural elements than on official Roman Catholic worship patterns."[16] Additionally, commenting from the perspective of a Chicano/a/x context, Gilbert R. Cadena and Lara Medina observe,

> While most Catholic theologians work primarily within the institutional framework of the Roman Catholic Church, it is important to recognize the non-Christian sources of religious expressions vital to the self-determination of Chicanas and Chicanos. . . . Many Chicanos, as mestizo peoples, often find their motivations and behavior come more from the ethics of indigenous ancestors than they do from Christian influence.[17]

It is both simple and profound to say that Latinx popular religion has always been there. Popular religion is not a new invention, fad, or concept. Latinx popular religion, religiosity, or spirituality (as it is sometimes referred to in Protestant contexts) incorporates discernible practices that may or may not use particular material objects for communicating with God and the spiritual realm. Also, popular religion assists in the Latinx understandings and interpretations of the joys and struggles in ordinary life. Through Latinx popular religions, the so-called natural and supernatural realms are recognized as closely intertwined.

A consideration of popular religion also includes what has been termed "material religion." Material religion simply is a focus on the physical objects and related themes associated with the practice of religion in particular communities. In living out religion and spirituality daily, people do so in an embodied way with concrete "stuff," much of it commonplace material but infused with deeper meaning. The material dimensions of religion include physical aids to religious practice such as candles, photographs and pictures, special mementos, printed

---

[16] C. Gilbert Romero, *Hispanic Devotional Piety: Tracing the Biblical Roots* (Maryknoll, NY: Orbis Books, 1991), 2.

[17] Gilbert R. Cadena and Lara Medina, "Liberation Theology and Social Change: Chicanas and Chicanos in the Catholic Church," in *Chicanas and Chicanos in Contemporary Society*, 2nd ed., ed. Roberto M. De Anda (Lanham, MD: Rowman and Littlefield, 2004), 168.

music, statues and statuettes, palm leaves, prayer handkerchiefs, church buildings and special locations, medals, funeral home fans, and prayer cards, all physical items that are used within religious/spiritual communities because they carry some sort of significance or meaning. Colleen McDannell asserts that, in the material dimension, religious communities might be overlooked:

> People build religion into the landscape, they make and buy pious images for their homes, and they wear special reminders of their faith next to their bodies. Religion is more than a type of knowledge learned through reading holy books and listening to holy men. The physical expressions of religion are not exotic or eccentric elements that can be relegated to a particular community or a specific period of time.[18]

Material dimensions of religion are part of a community's everyday life and knowledge. The material elements of religion are vehicles for the expression and transmission of the religion of the people, and through which we can better understand the popular religion of a group.

Jeanette Rodríguez, in her study of Mexican American women and their devotion to the Virgin of Guadalupe, defines "popular religiosity" as a complex folk faith system that consists of "spontaneous expressions of faith which have been celebrated by the people over a considerable period of time." People celebrate because they want to and not because they have been mandated by any official hierarchy. Additionally, Rodríguez views popular religiosity as a "source of power, dignity, and acceptance" for the "poor and marginalized." As such, popular religiosity developed as an encouragement for people to put their faith into practice and, in turn, narrate, act out, and represent "the people's own history."[19]

Latinx popular religion may be public or private, practiced by individuals, families, or whole communities. In many contexts, women—especially older women—are the de facto community elders serving as facilitators, leaders, innovators, educators, and keepers of the popular religion. These Latina women, in turn, pass on what is important to succeeding generations of women: mother to daughter, grandmother to

---

[18] Colleen McDannell, *Material Christianity: Religion and Popular Culture in America* (New Haven, CT: Yale University Press, 1995), 1; see also David Morgan, ed., *Religion and Material Culture: The Matter of Belief* (New York: Routledge, 2010).

[19] Jeanette Rodríguez, *Our Lady of Guadalupe: Faith and Empowerment among Mexican-American Women* (Austin: University of Texas Press, 1994), 143–44.

granddaughter, aunt to niece, or with *una hija de crianza* (a type of foster daughter treated as a blood relative). In such community settings, the *abuelitas* (grandmothers) become the wisdom figures for all, not just for the immediate family.

Since Latinx popular religiosity is not restricted to any particular economic class, it appears anywhere and everywhere. An important characteristic of Latinx popular religiosity is its grassroots practices, which inform and shape theology and in turn affect devotional and spiritual practices. Therefore, Latinx popular religion is found in homes, during corporate worship, or at makeshift sites, such as roadside memorials to those who have died in automobile accidents. Latinxs bring their important personal devotions and wisdom sayings into all circumstances of their lives. Examples of expressions of Latinx popular Catholicism include devotional practices such as the celebrations of feast days of patron saints, family devotions and the keeping of a home altar, pilgrimages, and special devotions to a particular saint.

María Pilar Aquino asserts that a purposeful communal decision is made in order for popular religion to be central in the daily life experiences of Latinxs. In an observation that is applicable to both popular Catholicism and popular Latinx Protestantism, Aquino argues that U.S. Latinx theology must honor the communal choice and

> take *this* faith and not another as the starting point for theological reflection and as the organizing principle of our theologizing. It could be argued that, as understandings of the faith, all theologies presuppose and imply faith. But what Latino/a theology emphasizes is that the faith of the people is the faith lived and expressed primarily and fundamentally within the concrete reality of popular Catholicism.[20]

Moreover, in considering this central function that popular religion plays in the historical, cultural, social, and congregational contexts of Latinx, Roberto Goizueta states,

> What remains unchallenged and often taken for granted is, first, the fundamentally sacramental character of the U.S. Hispanic way of life, wherein physical existence is seen as intrinsically related to the supernatural, transcendent realm of the sacred. Secondly, U.S.

---

[20] María Pilar Aquino, "Theological Method in U.S. Latino/a Theology: Toward an Intercultural Theology for the Third Millennium," in *From the Heart of Our People: Latino/a Explorations in Catholic Systematic Theology*, ed. Orlando O. Espín and Miguel H. Díaz (Maryknoll, NY: Orbis Books, 1999), 28.

Hispanic theologians assume the crucial significance of this sacramentality for the theological task, i.e., any theology done from the perspective of U.S. Hispanics cannot ignore this fact and still remain rooted in the experience of U.S. Hispanics.[21]

The focus on popular religion on the faith of the people challenges U.S. Latinx theologies to put its principles into practice by always going back to the community.

In the historical growth of Latinx theologies, Latinx Catholic explorations of popular religion or religiosity also influenced the formal study of Latinx Protestant popular religion. Some of the same key features also are present in Latinx Protestant popular religion, although the manifestation may be different. Among Latinx Protestants, especially in those communities influenced by Pentecostalism, there is a profound emphasis on the Holy Spirit and the believer's experience of the Spirit. That experience shapes the expressions and practices of the faith of the people in Latinx pentecostal and charismatic settings. Added to this mix is the historical aversion of many Latinx Protestants to overt elements of Latinx popular Catholicism, specifically praying to saints or lighting candles, and the results are different manifestations of Latinx Protestant popular spirituality. These factors combine to produce different expressions of popular religion, even while some underlying shared characteristics of Protestants and Catholics can be identified.

Elizabeth Conde-Frazier describes Latinx Protestant spirituality as showing four prominent characteristics that serve as both interrelated expressions and resources: doctrine, discipline, liturgy, and personal action.[22] Given that Latinx Protestant popular religiosity or spirituality reflects its Protestant context, alternative material symbols emerge that are deemed theologically acceptable. These might be a plain, empty cross in a church sanctuary or a verse from the Bible in a prominent place in a church building or, interestingly enough, the commonplace portrayal of a northern-European-looking Jesus.

Beyond these material expressions, Latinx Protestant popular religion is verbally expressed and acted on through *testimonios* (testimonies), daily devotions, Christian service, prayer vigils, *coritos* or *estribillos* (choruses), and community worship. Within all of these material and ver-

---

[21] Roberto S. Goizueta, *Caminemos con Jesús: Toward a Hispanic/Latino Theology of Accompaniment* (Maryknoll, NY: Orbis Books, 1995), 18–19.

[22] Elizabeth Conde-Frazier, "Hispanic Protestant Spirituality," in *Teología en Conjunto: A Collaborative Hispanic Protestant Theology*, ed. José David Rodríguez and Loida I. Martell-Otero (Louisville, KY: Westminster John Knox Press, 1997), 125.

bal dimensions, the study and exposition of the Bible plays an important role. Within Latinx Protestant contexts are several additional distinctive elements, including the heritage of the Protestant Reformation and the central role of the Word of God, both read in the Bible and spoken through sermons and testimonies. The almost sacramental emphasis on the Word strongly influences the nature of Latinx Protestant popular religion.

If U.S. Latinx theology indeed uses the lived faith of the people/ *pueblo* as a major starting point and resource, then it must be acknowledged that the faith of the U.S. Latinx peoples takes on a wide variety of forms and expressions. This includes the fact that not all U.S. Latinx people are Christians. Other Latinx institutional and grassroots religious practices and devotions do not fit under the rubrics of either Roman Catholicism or a particular expression of Protestantism. Some of these draw more heavily and directly upon indigenous Indian traditions or African sources. These alternatives are also manifestations and expressions of the grassroots faiths of Latinx peoples. Through these other ways, Latinxs find routes of knowledge, understanding, and meaning-making; pursue ways toward health and healing; and find accessible paths that furnish a sense of holistic balance in life.

Latinx popular religion also means beliefs and practices beyond some boundaries. Some of the better-known alternative expressions and practices include various types of *curanderismo* (a way of folk healing and medicine), different types of *espiritismo* (spiritism), and Cuban Santería. In addition to the above options, a growing number of Latinx people in the United States are affiliated with Judaism and Islam, joining the historically small number of U.S. communities in those traditions. Complicating the Latinx spiritual landscape further is that some Latinxs connect with several spiritual or religious traditions simultaneously and see no contradiction or mutual exclusion in their multiple allegiances, as noted in an article by Miguel A. De La Torre titled: "I'm a Southern Baptist, Roman Catholic Child of Elegguá—Deal with It."[23] Indeed, they view these hybrid multiple avenues as complementary and acceptable combinations for meaning-making and life. All of these expressions and practices have a direct impact on Latinx communities.

As a type of Latinx popular religion, Mexican American or Chicano/a/x *curanderismo* is a dynamic and fluid combination of indigenous

---

[23] Miguel A. De La Torre, "I'm a Southern Baptist, Roman Catholic, Child of Elegguá—Deal with It," *Cuba Counter Points: Public Scholarship about a Changing Cuba* (October 31, 2015), https://cubacounterpoints.com/archives/2633.

Mesoamerican and Spanish popular religious outlooks and orientations as a health-care system that assumes natural or supernatural causes of sickness and therefore offers natural or supernatural treatment.[24] Religion scholar Luis León defines *curanderismo* as

> a wide variety of community-based healing movements organized around somatic techniques of power; from home remedies such as herbal teas and ointments, to spiritual or symbolic open heart surgery, and other spiritual operations conducted to heal cancer for example. Social ills and family problems are also addressed in *curanderismo*.[25]

The practice of *curanderismo* is quite extensive within Mexican American and Chicano/a/x communities in the United States, whether they are in Los Angeles; South Texas or Dallas; St. Louis; Chicago or Aurora, Illinois; or New York City. Gastón Espinosa asserts that for many "Latin Americans, there are no such things as 'bad accidents' or 'good luck'; everything is shaped by the supernatural world, for good or ill. This conviction is prevalent throughout [. . .] *curanderismo* or folk healing."[26] In an example of the agency of those who chose to pursue *curanderismo*, Luis León quotes from an interview with a *curandera* from Southern California about someone who approached her: "'One twenty-six-year-old man [. . .] was a practicing Catholic [. . .] but, as he put it, 'The Catholic Church does not understand everything, and they are not always correct about everything.'"[27]

Another type of Latinx popular religion is *espiritismo*. Also known as Kardecism or spiritism, it was initially considered a scientific movement rather than a religious movement when it became the rage throughout Latin America during the nineteenth century. *Espiritismo* was a combination of scientism, progressivist ideology, Christian morality, and mysticism. As it spread through the Western Hemisphere, *espiritismo* generally

---

[24] For an overview of different types of spiritual healing in the United States, see Linda L. Barnes and Susan S. Sered, eds., *Religion and Healing in America* (New York: Oxford University Press, 2005).

[25] Luis D. León, "Religious Movement in the United States–Mexico Borderlands: Toward a Theory of Chicana/o Religious Poetics" (Ph.D. diss., University of California, Santa Barbara, 1997), 18.

[26] Gastón Espinosa, "'God Made a Miracle in My Life': Latino Pentecostal Healing in the Borderlands," in Barnes and Sered, *Religion and Healing in America*, 123.

[27] Luis D. Leon, "Borderlands Bodies and Souls," in *Mexican American Religions: Spirituality, Activism, and Culture*, ed. Gaston Espinosa (Durham, NC: Duke University Press, 2008), 307.

took the form of small groups of mediums assisting their clients in communicating with the spirits of the dead. People turned to *espiritismo* for help and guidance with the struggle of daily life.

Although often grouped together with *espiritismo* by outsiders, Santería is a distinct religious expression whose roots are African, the *regla de Ocha* of the Yoruba people of western Africa.[28] Santería, the "worship of saints," is of Cuban origin and is increasingly popular among U.S. Latinx.[29] Santería is also known as the *Lucumí* or *Lukimi*, and indeed some practitioners prefer that term and find "Santería" offensive.

Olodumare, the supreme being in Santería/*Lukumi*, provides *ashé*, the ancient and basic life force to everything that exists. This sacred energy becomes the power, grace, blood, and life force of Olodumare and nature, embracing all mystery, all secret power, and all divinity. *Ashé* is absolute, illimitable, pure power, which is nondefinite and not definable. *Ashé* is a nonanthropomorphic form of theism.[30] Religious traditions of enslaved Yoruba took root on Caribbean soil as they encountered beliefs and practices from Europeans and indigenous Tainos, resulting in unique hybrids. Even when Latinx reject Santería and insist solely on their Christianity, they still may observe the adage, "Tenemos que respetar los Santos" (We have to respect the Saints). Clearly, Santería can be classified as a popular religion and, as such, cannot be ignored.

The official Roman Catholic or Protestant Church places itself above the "unofficial" popular religion of the people and seeks to reduce *curanderismo, espiritismo*, and Santería to the sphere of ignorance and impurity. The official religion exercises power in the way it sees the unofficial religion from the margins. "We" (read official religion)

---

[28] For more on this Afro-Cuban religion, see David H. Brown, *Santería Enthroned: Art, Ritual, and Innovation in an Afro-Cuban Religion* (Chicago: University of Chicago Press, 2003); C. Lynn Carr, *A Year in White: Cultural Newcomers to Lukumi and Santería in the United States* (New Brunswick, NJ: Rutgers University Press, 2016); Miguel A. De La Torre, *Santería: The Beliefs and Rituals of a Growing Religion in America* (Grand Rapids: Eerdmans, 2004); Joseph M. Murphy, *Botánicas: Sacred Spaces of Healing and Devotion in Urban America* (Jackson: University Press of Mississippi, 2015); Joseph M. Murphy and Mei-Mei Sanford, ed., *Òsun across the Waters: A Yoruba Goddess in Africa and the Americas* (Bloomington: Indiana University Press, 2001); Solimar Otero and Toyin Falola, eds., *Yemoja: Gender, Sexuality, and Creativity in the Latina/o and Afro-Atlantic Diasporas* (Albany: State University of New York Press, 2013).

[29] Mary Ann Clark, *Santería: Correcting the Myths and Uncovering the Realities of a Growing Religion* (Westport, CT: Praeger Publishers, 2007).

[30] Pierre Verger, "The Yoruba High God: A Review of the Source," *Odu: Journal of Yoruba and Related Studies* 2, no. 2 (1966): 36–39.

operate from doctrinal knowledge; "they" (read unofficial religions) are confused. "Our" beliefs are pure; "theirs" are impure. "Our" task is to correct their confusion. Seeing the other as "confused" relegates them to an inferior social position while elevating official religion to an authoritative location from which paternal correcting can originate. Yet followers of these unorthodox religious traditions do not consider themselves "confused" in their beliefs. As they define their own sacred space, *curanderismo, espiritismo,* and *Lukumi*/Santería ought to be recognized as a unique phenomenon bound to Latinx cultural life and understood on their own terms.

Another group that needs to be considered when discussing Latinx religions are Latinx Jews. The impact of medieval and early modern Iberia (Spain and Portugal) upon the Americas is undisputed, including the contributions of Iberian Judaism. Consequently, any discussion of Latinx Jews in the United States must note the significance of the Iberian Jewish community, including those who became *conversos* (converts). During the Middle Ages, under Muslim (Moorish) rule, Al Andalus was the site of a thriving Jewish community known as *Sefarad*, as Zion Zohar summarizes: "Jews settled in Spain during Roman times and endured life there during Christian rule. . . . Sephardic culture reached its full flowering following the Muslim conquest in 711 and for the next several centuries, under Islam."[31] At one point the medieval Jewish community in Iberia was the largest Jewish community in the world.[32] As discussed in chapter 1, some U.S. Latinx are reconnecting with their Jewish heritage, or converting to Judaism. Many who are reconnecting have discerned a Jewish tie going back through the colonial period of New Spain back to *Serafad*, which is medieval Jewish Iberia.

The Christian kingdoms' *reconquista* (reconquest) of Iberia from the Moors brought an end to *Serafad*, and in 1492, Spanish Jews—those Jews who openly practiced their faith, those converts who continued to practice Judaism in secret (known as Marranos/crypto-Jews), and those *conversos* to Christianity—faced expulsion, conversion, or worse. In what became a Sephardic diaspora, some of the Spanish Jewish population went to Amsterdam in northern Europe, some went to the eastern Mediterranean, while others migrated to the very margins of the Spanish Empire in the Americas.[33] Nevertheless, the Spanish Inquisition still fol-

---

[31] Zion Zohar, ed., *Sephardic and Mizrahi Jewry: From the Golden Age of Spain to Modern Times* (New York: New York University Press, 2005), 6.

[32] Henry Kamen, *The Spanish Inquisition: A Historical Revision,* 4th ed. (New Haven, CT: Yale University Press, 2014), 13.

[33] Richard L. Kagan and Philip D. Morgan, eds., *Atlantic Diasporas: Jews, Conversos, and Crypto-Jews in the Age of Mercantilism, 1500–1800* (Baltimore:

lowed the Spanish Jews to New Spain (Mexico), Peru, and New Granada (Colombia, Venezuela, and Panama).[34] Of those who either survived or avoided the Inquisition, many settled in the remote areas of New Spain / Mexico, areas that are now parts of New Mexico and Arizona, where their descendants still live, some of whom continued their Jewish traditions and practices as crypto-Jews (secret Jews).[35] As mentioned in chapter 1, some Latinx believe they are of Jewish heritage and have chosen to embrace a Jewish identity. In addition to rediscovery of Jewish roots or conversion to Judaism, since 1965 there has been a migration of Latin American Jews to the United States. As with other Latinx communities, family rites, rituals, stories, and objects—all the elements of popular religiosity—are markers of Latinx Jewish tradition and spirituality. This is part of the larger U.S. Latinx religious context.

Yet another manifestation of the faith of the Latinx people is Islam, which includes both historical echoes and the more recent embracing of Islam by Latinxs in the United States. Like the Iberian Jewish community, Islam in Iberia was a Muslim presence that lasted nearly eight hundred years, leaving a profound but too often forgotten influence on Spanish and Portuguese cultures, and then Latin American cultures as well. This imprint was transferred to the Americas and is an element in the mestizaje/mulatez of Latin America and the United States. Spanish literature, music, and thought are filled with African and Islamic themes.

Just as some Latinxs are exploring the possibility of Jewish roots, others are finding a connection with their Muslim heritage from Spain. In recent years a small but growing number of Latinx are converting to Islam.[36] Some of these Latinxs describe this religious switching not as conversion, but as reversion, that is, a return to Muslim origins in medieval Iberia. In 2018, estimates of the number of Latinx Muslims ranged from 198,000 to 250,000, and if the higher figure is used, it represents a growth from 1 percent in 2009 to 7 percent in 2018 of

Johns Hopkins University Press, 2009).

[34] John F. Chuchiak IV, ed. and trans., *The Inquisition in New Spain, 1536–1820* (Baltimore, MD: Johns Hopkins University Press, 2012), 235–56.

[35] Yirmiyahu Yovel, *The Other Within: The Marranos, Split Identity, and Emerging Identity* (Princeton, NJ: Princeton University Press, 2009), 387; See also Stanley M. Hordes, *To the End of the Earth: A History of the Crypto-Jews of New Mexico* (New York: Columbia University Press, 2005); Cary Herz, Ori Z. Soltes, and Mona Hernandez, *New Mexico's Crypto-Jews: Image and Memory* (Albuquerque: University of New Mexico Press, 2007).

[36] See Valerie Russ, "More Latinos Are Becoming Muslims: 'Islam Is Not as Foreign as You Think,'" *Philadelphia Inquirer*, May 5, 2019.

Muslims who identified as Hispanic or Latinx. The Institute for Social Policy and Understanding reported that "Hispanic Muslims are the fastest-growing ethnic group in the Muslim community, which may present a natural bridge to the wider Hispanic community."[37] Sizable communities of Latinx Muslims exist in Chicago, Los Angeles, Miami, New York City, Houston, and Newark. In reflecting the realities of Latinx Muslims in the United States, Harold D. Morales states,

> When we recognize Latino Muslims as reciprocal participants in the constant inheriting and reworking of what it means to be a Latino, a Muslim, a Latino Muslim, and American, of what it means to be a convert or a revert, of what it means that Muslims left an indelible mark on the identity of Spain, Latin America, and the United States, and of what it means to have a racialized religion or race-religion at the dawn of the twenty-first century, then we avoid the pitfalls of a recognition politics that is based on static, subordinating, and propositional formulations of identity and we come to better recognize ourselves and others as interdependent subjects.[38]

Latinx Ecumenism and Theology *en Conjunto*

Using the word "ecumenism" can be risky in that, in some quarters, ecumenism is considered to be of little relevance, either limited to the theological hopes of a time past or in other quarters as an indicator of heretical theological liberalism. Among the simultaneously exciting, challenging, and sometimes frustrating features of Latinx theologies are the conversations and collaborations between Latinx Protestants and Roman Catholics. The very fact that any of this occurs at all is remarkable, given the checkered history of contacts between Protestants and Catholics in Latin America and the United States. This fluid reality is seen by some as an expression of a type of new ecumenism that is developing in U.S. Latinx communities.

---

[37] Dalia Mogahed and Azka Mahmood, "American Muslim Poll 2019: Predicting and Preventing Islamophobia," Institute for Social Policy and Understanding, May 2019, 25. See also Harold D. Morales, *Latino and Muslim: Race, Religion, and the Making of a New Minority* (New York: Oxford University Press, 2018), 7; Hjamil A. Martínez-Vázquez, "Islam," in *Hispanic American Religious Culture*, vol. 1, ed. Miguel A. De La Torre (St. Barbara, CA: ABC-CLIO, 2009), 306.

[38] Harold D. Morales, *Latino and Muslim in America: Race, Religion, and the Making of a New Minority* (New York: Oxford University Press, 2018), 210.

Initially, the relationships between Latinx Catholics and Protestants were in the form of formal dialogue on common matters of theology and pastoral concerns. In several conferences, Catholics and Protestants have sought together to further explicate and understand Latina/o theology. For example, in 1991 a symposium hosted by the Mexican American Program at the Perkins School of Theology in Dallas, Texas, focused on the five hundredth anniversary of the *encuentro* (encounter) of 1492 between Europeans and Indians. Catholic and Protestant theologians from the United States and Latin America presented papers on the subject. Another important interdenominational consultation was a conference titled "Aliens in Jerusalem: The Emerging Theological Voice of Hispanic Americans," which was held in 1994 at Drew University in Madison, New Jersey. This ecumenical gathering (the papers of which were revised and appear in the volume *Hispanic/Latino Theology: Challenge and Promise*) examined three broad areas of Latinx theology: sources (the Bible, history, cultural memory, literature, oral tradition, Pentecostalism); contexts (urban communities, the experience of exile, the complex case of Puerto Ricans, feminist perspectives); and examples (*mujerista* theology, popular religiosity). Since 1994 other important conversations, conferences, and gatherings in numerous settings have occurred, including, in 2010, the Spring Institute of Lived Theology: Theology, Migration, and the Borderlands in San Diego.

Other ecumenical/interdenominational collaborative efforts have resulted in written projects produced together by Latinx (and some non-Latinx) Roman Catholic, Protestant, Jewish, and atheist authors, including *Mestizo Christianity* (1995); *A Reader in Latina Feminist Theology* (2002); *New Horizons in Hispanic/Latino(a) Theology* (2003); *Handbook of Latina/o Theologies* (2006); *Rethinking Latino(a) Religion and Identity* (2006); *Jesus in the Hispanic Community* (2009); *Building Bridges, Doing Justice* (2009); *Hispanic American Religious Culture* (2009); *In Our Own Voices* (2010); *Religion and Politics in America's Borderlands* (2013); *Latino/a Biblical Hermeneutics* (2014); *The Wiley Blackwell Companion to Latino/a Theology* (2015); *Latinxs, the Bible, and Migration* (2018); and *Borderland Religion* (2018).[39]

---

[39] Arturo J. Bañuelas, ed., *Mestizo Christianity: Theology from the Latino Perspective* (Maryknoll, NY: Orbis Books, 1995); María Pilar Aquino, Daisy L. Machado, and Jeanette Rodríguez, eds., *A Reader in Latina Feminist Theology: Religion and Justice* (Austin: University of Texas Press, 2002); Benjamín Valentín, ed., *New Horizons in Hispanic/Latino(a) Theology* (Cleveland: Pilgrim Press, 2003); Edwin David Aponte and Miguel A. De La Torre, ed., *Handbook of Latino/a Theologies* (St. Louis: Chalice Press, 2006); Miguel A. De La Torre and Gastón Espinosa, ed., *Rethinking Latino(a) Religion and Identity* (Cleveland:

A great deal of theological discussion, influence, and cross-fertilization of ideas and perceptions has taken place. Examples of this cross-fertilization at an early stage of the development of Latinx theologies were individuals such as Roman Catholic Virgilio Elizondo as resources for Latinx Protestant theologians, while simultaneously, Protestant Methodist Justo González is a source for the theological work of Latinx Catholics. This commitment to interdenominational conversation and work *en conjunto* covers at least three to four generations of contemporary Latinx theological scholarship, and includes senior Latinx scholars mentoring early-career Latinx. This mentoring takes place across traditional denominational barriers as Catholics mentor Protestants and Protestants, Catholics.

One result and expression of this *en conjunto* Latinx theology is three collaborative institutions in which Latinx engage each other across denominational boundaries, which owe much to the vision and leadership of Methodist Justo González. As described in the previous chapter, the first Latinx institution is the Hispanic Summer Program (HSP), a collaborative consortium that provides graduate seminary programs in Latinx religion and theology taught by Latinx faculty drawn from across the United States, Canada, and Puerto Rico. The second is the Hispanic Theological Initiative (HTI), whose mission is "cultivating Latinx PhD students across the nation by uniting and leveraging institutional resources (human, financial, and infrastructural)."[40] Third is the Asociación para la Educación Teológica Hispana (AETH [Association for Hispanic Theological Education]), which seeks to "promote and certify the quality of Hispanic theological education programs and contribute

Pilgrim Press, 2006); Harold J. Recinos and Hugo Magallanes, eds., *Jesus in the Hispanic Community: Images of Christ from Theology to Popular Religion* (Louisville, KY: Westminster John Knox Press, 2009); Orlando O. Espín, ed., *Building Bridges, Doing Justice: Constructing a Latino/a Ecumenical Theology* (Maryknoll, NY: Orbis Books, 2009); Miguel A. De La Torre, ed., *Hispanic American Religious Cultures* (Santa Barbara, CA: ABC-CLIO, 2009); Benjamín Valentín, ed., *In Our Own Voices: Latino/a Renditions of Theology* (Maryknoll, NY: Orbis Books, 2010); Sarah Azaransky, ed., *Religion and Politics in America's Borderlands* (Lanham, MD: Lexington Books, 2013); Francisco Lozada Jr. and Fernando F. Segovia, eds., *Latino/a Biblical Hermeneutics: Problematics, Objectives, Strategies* (Atlanta, GA: SBL Press, 2014); Orlando O. Espín, ed., *The Wiley Blackwell Companion to Latino/a Theology* (Malden, MA: Wiley Blackwell, 2015); Efraín Agosto and Jacqueline Hidalgo, eds., *Latinxs, The Bible, and Migration* (New York: Palgrave Macmillan, 2018); Daisy L. Machado, Bryan S. Turner, and Trygve Wyller, eds., *Borderland Religion: Ambiguous Practices of Difference, Hope, and Beyond* (New York: Routledge, 2018).

40 HTI website, "Mission," http://hti.ptsem.edu/about/mission/.

to the development of the leadership of women and men who strengthen our congregations and communities."[41] AETH, the HSP, and the HTI all have continuing impact on the development and dissemination of Latinx theologies. Through these three institutions, one can see the broad vision that Justo González had for an overlapping and supportive matrix for Latinx theologies and ministries in the United States.

Another important, early collaborative effort was the groundbreaking work of the Program for the Analysis of Religion among Latinos (PARAL) at the City University of New York, under the leadership of Roman Catholic Anthony Stevens-Arroyo. Another place for dialogue with a broader scholarly scope takes place within the Latino/a Religion, Culture, and Society Group, a unit of the American Academy of Religion. Cooperative work also happens through the Wabash Center, the Louisville Institute, the Forum of Theological Exploration (FTE), and the Association of Theological Schools. These institutional expressions have proven to be highly successful and richly productive centers of new ecumenism between Protestants and Catholics. This ecumenism is broader than is usually realized, as scholars of religion with or without any particular religious commitment participate in exploring Latinx religion and culture.

Ecumenical work between Latinx Catholics and Protestants has not occurred without struggle, disappointments, and ongoing frustrations. They remain part of the present and future challenges of Latinx theologies. A common concern among both U.S. Latinx Catholics and Protestants is deeply held doctrinal differences. Nevertheless, many Protestants and Catholics share a desire for a greater and more effective Christian witness within U.S. Latinx communities.

One area of challenge is that collaborative conversations and relationships between Latinx Catholics and Protestants may be more common among theologians, scholars, and denominational officials than among Latinx people at the level of grassroots faith communities where mutual suspicion and old stereotypes persist and continue to wield power. Even with years of building trust, misunderstandings still occur.

An ongoing concern of many Latinx Catholics regarding Protestants falls under the label of "sheep stealing," that is, the proselytizing or conversion of Catholics to Protestantism. This practice reflects a lingering anti-Catholicism among some Protestants. Furthermore, it is related to real differences in an understanding of the nature of evangelization by Catholics and Protestants. How can these differences be resolved?

---

[41] AETH website, "Who We Are," https://www.aeth.org/quienes-somos?language=English.

Undoubtedly, this will take time and intentional effort. Different perspectives on evangelism and evangelization are among other issues that need extended discussion in ecumenical forums.

Intra-Latinx Oppression

During the early years of articulating Latinx Christian theology, it faced the constant threat of being torn apart by differences—cultural, racial, class—existing among distinct national and ethnic groups as well as other types of difference—theological, gender, sexual identity, and so on. There appears to have been a conscious decision made among early Latinx religious scholars to minimize those differences and, instead, concentrate on areas of commonality. Hispanic/Latinx pan-ethnic unity was pursued, but perhaps at the cost of masking those areas that threatened to tear Latinx communities apart or to weaken the resolve that comes with unity.

Different Spanish-speaking groups sneer at the way Spanish is spoken by members of another group. Stereotypes of national groups, which are not tolerated if spoken by the dominant Euroamerican culture, become acceptable ways by which one Latinx group refers to Latinx persons with different national origins. When there is a shared sense of Latinx identity, some groups are judged as being insufficiently Latinx. For example, tensions exist between recent arrivals from Mexico and "established" Mexican Americans who in the past may have supported the anti-immigration propositions in California.

The desire of Latinx religion scholars to evoke a pan-ethnic unity can diminish the reality of how sexism, racism, and classism are alive and well within the social space that Latinxs occupy. Furthermore, casting Latinx solely as victims obscures the dubious role they can also play as victimizers. As Latinx theology has developed, several Latinx theologians began to insist that some Latinxs are simultaneously the oppressed and the oppressors, a fact that is inconvenient and sometimes ignored by those who would lump them all together solely as victims of U.S. hegemony. Usually, traditionally disenfranchised groups construct well-defined categories as to who the perpetrators and who the victims of injustices are. All too often, Latinxs tend to identify the oppressive structures of the dominant Eurocentric culture while overlooking repression originating within their own communities. Within the marginalized space of the Latinx community, structures of oppression exist along gender, race, sexual identity, and class lines, creating the need for an initiative to move beyond the rhetoric of blame.

Another example of the emergence of intra-Latinx oppressive structures is witnessed in the rise of the exilic Cuban community in Miami.

During the early 1960s, the U.S. media broadcast numerous stories of penniless Cubans rising from adversity to success. These stories stereotyped Miami's Latinx community as "the Cuban success story."[42] By lumping exilic Cubans with Mexicans, Puerto Ricans, and other Latin Americans under the constructed term "Hispanic," Latino/as masked the power and privilege that come with lighter racial composition and upper- and middle-class status. The success Cubans found in Miami resulted from the demographics of those who immigrated, rather than any intrinsic Cuban characteristics.

The social background exilic Cubans brought to the United States affected the construction of Cuban ethnicity once in this country, setting them apart from the minority reality of other Latinx peoples. Suzanne Oboler's social-scientific research shows how middle- and upper-class, college-educated Latinx integrate into the dominant culture. Like previous southern and eastern European immigrants, these Latino/as are seen as "white," thus enabling their ability to reach "first-class" citizen status relatively quickly. Because the first two waves of Cubans (1959–1973) consisted mostly of white, middle-class Cubans with some level of education, they were able to define their ethnic identity along the predominant ethnic and racial classifications of the United States and enter into U.S. citizenship with relative ease when compared to the experience of other Latinx groups, while paradoxically still experiencing the racialized exclusion for being Latinx. Oboler observes that "as the lived experiences of Latino/as and African Americans increasingly attests, citizenship is meaningful only in the lives of those who continue to be excluded from the rights and benefits it guarantees."[43]

While discrimination against exilic Cubans is a reality and is reflected in the distribution of income, exilic Cubans, more than any other Hispanic group, still earn higher average incomes and more frequently occupy professional-level jobs. Within one generation, this group, unlike any other ethnic group arriving to U.S. shores, captured the political, economic, cultural, and social structures of a major U.S. city. Miguel De

---

[42] The titles of several press articles from that period indicate the construction of the Cuban success story: "Cuba's New Refugees Get Jobs Fast," *Business Week*, March 12, 1966, 69; Tom Alexander, "Those Amazing Cubans," *Fortune*, October 1966, 144–49; and "Cuban Success Story in the United States," *U.S. News and World Report*, March 20, 1967, 104–6.

[43] Suzanne Oboler, "Redefining Citizenship as Lived Experience," in *Latinos and Citizenship: The Dilemma of Belonging*, ed. Suzanne Oboler (New York: Palgrave Macmillan, 2006), 8; Suzanne Oboler, *Ethnic Labels, Latino Lives: Identity and the Politics of (Re)Presentation in the United States* (Minneapolis: University of Minnesota Press, 1995), 138–41, 162–63.

La Torre is the first religion scholar to address the exilic Cuban theological location within the context of political and economic power in the
Miami community, attempting to uncover the race, class, and gender
oppression existing within their own space. Latinx theologians are beginning to scrutinize these spaces where former oppressed Hispanics mount
social structures without dismantling inherent systems of oppression.[44]
What happened in Miami may serve as a paradigm of what to avoid for
other Latinx groups as they begin to gain some forms of economic and
political clout.

Latinization of the United States

Christopher Columbus's journey to the so-called New World included
a crusade to make the Americas Spanish and Christian. The first "thanks-
giving" in what was to be called the United States was not conducted
by Protestant pilgrims at Plymouth Rock but by Spanish Catholics in
1526 at a settlement named San Miguel, near the site where Jamestown
would be founded nearly a century later. What would become the southern United States originally fell under the jurisdiction of the bishop of
Santiago de Cuba. From the Chesapeake Bay to the San Francisco Bay,
colonies, cities, and missions dotted the landscape. The decline of the
Spanish Empire and the consequential rise of the U.S. Empire contributed to the expulsion, marginalization, and disenfranchisement of Latinx
residing within U.S. territories. The Spanish goal of making the Americas
Spanish and Catholic in the clash of empires gave way to Manifest Destiny by the United States and its particular understandings of Protestant
Christianity, which range from distinct types of evangelical Christianity
to the most amorphous type of civil religion or cultural religion that
employs Christian language and symbols.[45]

---

44 See Miguel A. De La Torre, *La Lucha for Cuba: Religion and Politics on the
Streets of Miami* (Berkeley: University of California Press, 2003); and Miguel A.
De La Torre, *The Quest for the Cuban Christ: A Historical Search* (Gainesville:
University Press of Florida, 2002).

45 Peter Gardella asserts that the concept of civil religion is "unified by four
values—personal freedom (often called liberty), political democracy, world peace,
and cultural (including religious, racial, ethnic) tolerance—that have come to
dominate American civil religion" (Peter Gordella *American Civil Religion: What
Americans Hold Sacred* [New York: Oxford University Press, 2014], 3); see also
Philip Gorski, *American Covenant: A History of Civil Religion from the Puritans
to the Present* (Princeton, NJ: Princeton University Press, 2017). On cultural religion see Catherine L. Albanese, *America: Religions and Religion*, 5th ed. (Boston:
Wadsworth, 2013), 290–98.

Yet the advances made by U.S. Manifest Destiny are being reversed, and some observers have named this reversal *la reconquista* (the reconquest), although that may not be the best image to describe what is happening. In the past, Latinx faced the danger of assimilation to the North American culture. Now, North America is in so-called peril of assimilating to Hispanic culture. The end of the twentieth century witnessed the creation of a new people through the Latinx mestizaje/mulatez in the United States, which seems to indicate a reversal and healing of the consequences of the Euroamerican venture of making the continent white and Protestant.

The rapid increase of the Latinx population within U.S. territory has set in motion a reversal of Manifest Destiny, a Latinization of the dominant Eurocentric culture's concept of expansion. As the fastest-growing ethnic group, Latinx's influence will be even greater in the twenty-first century. Contrary to general opinion, this growth is not due to "illegal" immigration; rather, it is fueled by natural causes—births outweighing deaths. This increase of a Latinx presence is leading to a defensive reaction among North American whites against the perceived danger of a Latinx *comunidad* struggling to become empowered. Hence, virulent immigration rhetoric demanding a more militarized border or xenophobic laws like voter ID regulations represent desperate attempts to stunt the growing Latinx influence.

Challenge of New "Undocumented" Immigrants

When the subject of Latin American immigration to the United States comes up in conversation, the image that often prevails in popular imagination is that of a flood of "illegal" Central Americans crossing the border at night, or that the United States is being "invaded" by caravans of immigrants. These inaccurate and discriminatory images are common in the rhetoric of some divisive politicians, particularly at election time, who seek to establish blame for a whole host of social ills, concerns, and anxieties. During the 2008 presidential campaign, Colorado representative Tom Tancredo led the anti-immigration charge, "Many who enter the country illegally are just looking for jobs, but others are coming to kill you, and you, and me, and my children and my grandchildren."[46] As bad as that was, Tancredo's racist rhetoric was exceeded by that of Donald Trump and many of his supporters from 2015 onward as they embraced white nationalist racist language. Blaming undocumented and alternatively documented immigrants provides easy answers to the economic hardships faced by many U.S. Americans, but the attitudes and

---

[46] Dan McLean, "Immigration's Tancredo's Top Topic," *New Hampshire Sunday News*, June 12, 2005.

language still became heated when the economy improved, indicating there was something more at play when undocumented immigrants are accused of being rapists and bringing crime to the United States. For some white Euroamericans, whether they are confronted with economic hardship or with cultural uneasiness as the shifts in demographic realities begin to sink in, it is reassuring to blame someone for their troubles and apprehension. Undocumented immigrants become the scapegoat that conveniently explains the effects of downsizing faced by "real" Americans. This rhetoric of fear and distortion is part of the impetus of a number of acts that restricted services to immigrants.

Also, this rhetoric of fear raises disturbing questions on how Latinx people are seen, whether they are recent arrivals or U.S. citizens who can trace their family back generations of citizens to 1848. If a white Euroamerican motorist was stopped and failed to be carrying a driver's license, would they also be arrested? Would they be taken back to the station to have their documentation checked? If not, why the different treatment between Latinx and non-Hispanics? Is it that Latinx-looking people are getting arrested on flimsy charges in order to verify documentation status? In other words, based on ethnic characteristics, are all Latinxs guilty of being undocumented until proven innocent? These questions are not hypothetical but reflect the daily experiences of Latinx persons of all classes.

The causes of the immigration quandary are complex and go beyond simplistic indignations expressed by politicians who use fear to solicit votes. The jingoist Eurocentric religious-based philosophy of Manifest Destiny suggested that God's kingdom would be realized through the United States fulfilling a divinely ordained, apocalyptic mission of occupying the new promised land (from the Arctic north to the isthmus south) given to them by God, and then Christ would return in all his glory.[47] Manifest Destiny provided part of the rationale for the international land grab of northern Mexico in order to create what became the U.S. Southwest,[48] accompanied by a century of gunboat diplomacy.[49] According to Miguel De La Torre,

---

[47] Amy S. Greenberg, *Manifest Destiny and American Territorial Expansion: A Brief History with Documents*, 2nd ed. (Boston: Bedford/St. Martin's Press, 2018); John D. Wilsey, *American Exception and Civil Religion: Reassessing the History of an Idea* (Downers Grove, IL: InterVarsity Press, 2015).

[48] The immediate consequences of the U.S. invasion of Mexico, known as the Mexican-American War, meant the United States acquisition of gold deposits in California, silver deposits in Nevada, copper deposits in Arizona, oil in Texas, and all of the natural harbors (except Veracruz) necessary for commerce. The United States obtained the natural resources embedded in the land and the cheap Mexican labor living on the land, required by the United States to create wealth. Hence the common saying, "We didn't cross the border, the borders crossed us."

[49] "Gunboat diplomacy" describes a foreign policy in which the full force of

For over a century, as we have seen, the U.S. military protected U.S. corporations as they built roads in developing countries throughout Latin America to extract, by brute force if necessary, their natural resources and make use of cheap labor. Some of the inhabitants of those countries, deprived of their livelihood, followed the same roads as their countries' resources. They are following what over time was stolen. They come to escape the violence and terrorism left behind. The ethical or moral question we should be asking about the undocumented is not *why* they come, but what responsibilities and obligations exist for the U.S. in causing the present immigration dilemma.[50]

There is no denying that immigrants crossing borders face death. But violence is not limited to those dying in the desert attempting hazardous crossings. It also includes rape of Latina women and girls; denial of basic medical services to detained immigrants, resulting in death; economic abuse of Latinx persons in the workplace, preventing the family from simply surviving; and separating husbands from their wives or Latinx parents from their children, and placing separated children in cages. Probably no greater human rights violation is occurring within the United States today than the institutionalized violence experienced by the undocumented. According to the Culture of Cruelty study conducted by the humanitarian organization No More Deaths, more than thirty thousand incidents of abuse and mistreatment of migrants at the hands of U.S. Border Patrol agents have been documented. The report states,

Individuals suffering severe dehydration are deprived of water; people with life-threatening medical conditions are denied treatment; children and adults are beaten during apprehensions and in custody; family members are separated, their belongings confiscated and not returned; many are crammed into cells and subjected to extreme temperatures, deprived of sleep, and threatened with death by Border Patrol agents.[51]

---

the U.S. military was at the disposal of U.S. corporations to protect their interest throughout Central America and the Caribbean. Throughout the twentieth century, eleven countries experienced twenty-one U.S. military invasions and twenty-six covert CIA operations, meaning significant interference in national self-determination. The consequences resulting from U.S.-installed "banana republics" are the creation of poverty, strife, transnational migration, and death.

[50] Miguel A. De La Torre, *Trails of Hope and Terror: Testimonies on Immigration* (Maryknoll, NY: Orbis Books, 2009), 16.

[51] No More Death, "Culture of Cruelty," https://nomoredeaths.org/abuse-documentation/a-culture-of-cruelty/.

Based on almost thirteen thousand interviews with migrants who were in Border Patrol custody, the study made the following discoveries:

- Only 20 percent of people in custody for more than two days received a meal.
- Children were more likely than adults to be denied water or given insufficient water.
- Many of those denied water by Border Patrol were already suffering from moderate to severe dehydration at the time they were apprehended.
- Physical abuse was reported by 10 percent of interviewees, including teens and children.
- Families were separated and expatriated at different times with women and children returned to dangerous border towns after dark.

The report concludes,

> It is clear that instances of mistreatment and abuse in Border Patrol custody are not aberrational. Rather, they reflect common practice for an agency that is part of the largest federal law enforcement body in the country. Many of them plainly meet the definition of torture under international law. No undocumented immigrant is safe when in the custody of U.S. enforcement agents.[52]

Although there is a continuing flow of Mexican immigrants, the last part of the twentieth century saw increasing numbers coming to the United States from other parts of Latin America. Many Central Americans, especially Salvadorans and Guatemalans, settled in urban areas of Los Angeles, Washington, DC, and New York City. Dominicans are a growing presence in the northeastern part of the United States. Nicaraguans began to arrive in large numbers to the United States as a result of the war in that country in which the United States funded rebel forces. As the war in Nicaragua dragged on, spilling over to neighboring countries, it generated a Honduran migration to the United States. Mayans from Chiapas, Mexico, and Guatemala can be found in Houston, Los Angeles, San Francisco, Florida, Texas, and Nebraska. The journeys of Mayans show the complexity of these recent migrations. Mayans have maintained their preconquest cultural identities and languages, and therefore if they speak Spanish at all, it is as a second language. Other newer Latin

---

[52] Ibid.

American immigrants settling in the United States were often political refugees from life-threatening situations in Central and South America, including Chileans, Colombians, Ecuadorians, Salvadorans, and Peruvians. Portuguese-speaking Brazilians have migrated to the United States in the last quarter of the twentieth century, pushing the limits of what it means to be Latinx. Additionally, an increasing number of Mexican and U.S.-born individuals with Mexican origins are migrating to nonmetropolitan and agricultural areas in the United States. Some researchers suggest various reasons for this settlement, including the desire to re-create traditional agricultural activities and economic patterns.

The growth of a varied Latin American presence throughout the United States is partly fueled by these new waves of immigrants and has produced scenes that some thought they would never see in their part of the country. Latinx day workers line up in places like the commuter town of Mamaroneck outside New York City, hoping to be hired for the day in gardening or small construction jobs. North Carolina has a growing Latinx population within its midst, as some cease being migratory agricultural workers on tobacco farms and become year-round residents working on dairy farms or at local restaurants.

All these diverse groups contribute in different ways to the constantly shifting U.S. Latinx shared identity, but these diverse Latinx groups also have been accompanied by increased reaction to the growth of the Latinx population. Daisy L. Machado, Bryan S. Turner, and Trygve Wyller summarized an aspect of the current challenge:

> The presidential elections in the US in 2016 demonstrated the strong attraction of populism and nativism and in particular the need to defend borders against unwanted "outsiders" such as Muslims and Mexicans. These developments only serve to reinforce the idea that borders and boundaries are unsurprisingly sites of contestation, ambiguity, and periodically violence.[53]

Mexicans, Chicanos/as, Chicanx, Xicana

Throughout the Southwest, South, and Midwest, tensions exists between the older and better-established Mexican American communities, which at times refer to themselves as Chicana/o/x or Mexican Americans, and the more recent arrivals. From the rural agricultural fields to

---

[53] Daisy L. Machado, Bryan S. Turner, and Trygve Wyller, "Traces of a Theo-Borderland," in Daisy L. Machado, Bryon S. Turner, and Trygve Wyller, eds., *Borderland Religion: Ambiguous Practices of Difference, Hope and Beyond* (New York: Routledge, 2018), 4.

the meatpacking plants to the sweatshops, incidences of Chicano/a/x persons taunting new arrivals with insults like "wetbacks" are common. Likewise, recent immigrants refer to the Chicana/o/x persons with the derogatory term "*pocho*." As children, Chicano/a/xs had to endure shame from a dominant culture that scorned them for not speaking English correctly. Now as adults, they are mocked by the newer arrivals for not speaking proper Spanish. They may be *la raza* (the race), but more recent arrivals question if they are *la gente* (the people).

These tensions mask questions concerning class, levels of U.S. acculturation, and generational differences marked by when entry into the United States took place. These tensions are not limited to those of Mexican descent. Similar manifestations occurred in Miami during the 1980s between the established Cuban community and the new arrivals who were pejoratively labeled *Marielitos*. These intranational tensions also exist among Puerto Ricans, between those who reside in the United States looking down at their cousins on the island, as well as among Dominicans in New York and the various Central American communities. As these tensions play out within local congregations, Latinx theologians must deal with the creation of intra-Latinx forms of prejudices and discrimination.

This is one of the points where intersectional realties come together. Jacqueline Hidalgo observes the generational changes in the Movimiento Estudiantil Chicanx de Aztlán (MEChA), writing that MEChA is

> a U.S. Latina/o/x organization present on many high school and college campuses across the country, voted to change their fifty-year old name. They decided that they had to drop two of the most mythically politicized facets: "Chicanx" and "Aztlán." Although they haven't decided on a final name, right now they have chosen an Espanglish acronym: Movimiento Estudiantil Progressive Action (MEPA).[54]

What is a Mexican American movement that chooses to stop using Chicano/a/x and Aztlán? The leadership that made this change has made clear that they are not abandoning their history, but that they want to be attentive to this present time and the diversifying Latinx population, and therefore are asking for deeper analysis of the concepts embedded in terms like Chicano/a/x and Aztlán.

---

[54] Jacqueline Hidalgo, "Beyond Aztlán: Latina/o/x Students Let Go of Their Mythic Homeland," Contending Modernities, Notre Dame University, April 11, 2019, https://contendingmodernities.nd.edu/global-currents/beyond-aztlan/.

Postmodern/Postcolonial Thought

Within academia, postmodern and postcolonial conversations impact every discipline of higher education. Briefly stated, "postmodernity" is a philosophical concept claiming that absolute truths are constructed by a given society within a particular time period. Therefore, assertions of objectivity in truth or knowledge are untenable. Any objective claims to universality are basically an exercise in power. In short, postmodernity is a skeptical inquiry into all claims of authority.[55] "Postcolonialism" can broadly be understood as a people's attempt to reclaim or construct an identity apart from the negative consequences of the colonial venture, which can best be understood as the "white man's burden" of bringing civilization and Christianity to the natives.

At the start of the century, some Latinx scholars of religion embraced postmodern and postcolonial analysis while others have responded to this dialogue with suspicion and skepticism. Among the first Latinx scholars to incorporate these forms of critical analysis was Fernando Segovia, who made use of a postmodern methodology in what he calls a "theology of the diaspora." Segovia envisions such a theology as deeply rooted in the theoretical contexts of postmodernism and liberation theology. "Diaspora theology" is defined as

> a postmodernist theology—theology that argues for a multitude of matrices and voices, not only outside itself but also within itself, and regards itself as a construct, with thorough commitment to self-analysis and self-criticism as a construct; a postcolonial theology—a theology that is grounded in the margins, speaks from the margins, and engages in decolonization both within and from the center; and a liberation theology—a theology that seeks to re-view, re-claim, and re-phrase its own matrix and voice in the midst of a dominant culture and theology. It is also a theology with exile, flesh-and-blood exile, at its heart and core.[56]

As a postmodern theology, Segovia's theology of the diaspora attempts to celebrate the radical diversity of the Latinx ethos, rather than a so-called objectivity of European theologies. More recent generations of

---

[55] See Jean-François Lyotard, *The Postmodern Condition: A Report on Knowledge*, trans. Geoff Bennington and Brian Massumi (Minneapolis: University of Minnesota Press, 1984), xxiv.

[56] Fernando F. Segovia, "In the World but Not of It: Exile as Locus for a Theology of the Diaspora," in *Hispanic/Latino Theology: Challenge and Promise*, ed. Ada María Isasi-Díaz and Fernando F. Segovia (Minneapolis: Fortress, 1996), 201.

Latinx religious scholars are using postmodern and postcolonial thought in their scholarship, thus moving away from the suspicion held by older Latinx religious scholars.

And yet, few seem to totally commit. Some of those who do use a postmodern analysis within their scholarship still hold on to a modernist (very Christian) understanding of liberation, refusing to reduce their religious convictions to an interesting perspective among the multitude of possible perspectives. Many Latinx engaged in the postmodern and postcolonial discourse claim Latinx liberative theology does contain universal truths that are not solely restricted to Latinx or other oppressed groups. Critical analysis often is used to understand oppressive social structures, not as a complete methodology. It remains to be seen if the religion of the colonizers will be jettisoned by newer generations of Latinx scholars fully committed to either postmodern or postcolonial thought.

Puerto Rico, a Colony in a Postcolonial World

Puerto Rico and Puerto Ricans provide a unique challenge for Latinx theologies and its future development in the life and ministry of the Christian church in North America. Since 1898, when it was acquired from Spain as booty in the Spanish-American War, Puerto Rico has been a colonial possession of the United States. Almost immediately, the United States embarked upon a process of Americanization of the people and culture. Under U.S. rule, the first few governors of Puerto Rico were appointed Euroamericans. Even the spelling of the island's name was briefly changed to "Porto Rico" in order to be friendlier to Euroamerican patterns of pronunciation. By 1911 English was made the official language, and U.S. patterns of government and education were imposed.

This radical shift in political sovereignty also affected the religious life of the island. Roman Catholicism had been formally established in Puerto Rico in 1511. Over the centuries the Puerto Rican Catholic Church diversified along urban and rural lines as it struggled with a scarcity of qualified ministers, an inadequate distribution of resources for ministry, and only sporadic interest from Spain. Reflecting its rich indigenous, African, and European heritage, popular religion included devotions to Our Lady of Monserrate, *La Virgen Negra* (the Black Virgin). The institutional church, which favored an urban elite, had an ambivalent relationship with rural society.

With the coming of U.S. rule, state sponsorship of the church ended, and many Spanish Catholic clergy and religious workers under the Spanish colonial authorities departed. Euroamerican religious workers and clergy arrived to "missionize" a land that had already had a Christian presence for four hundred years. During much of the early period of U.S. sovereignty, institutional Catholic efforts partook in the Americanization drive, and until the 1960s the Catholic bishops of Puerto Rico were Euroamericans.

Simultaneously, although there had been a small Protestant presence during the Spanish period, many Protestant denominations from the United States saw an opening for evangelism and sent missionaries to work in Puerto Rico. The North American Protestant mainline churches entered into a comity agreement, which recognized delineated areas of respective ministries so that they would not directly compete with one another (a process also implemented in Cuba). Many viewed this effort to Protestantize the island as the natural complement of Americanization. Meanwhile, initially undetected or disregarded by either Roman Catholics or mainline Protestants, pentecostal Protestant Christians began their work in Puerto Rico, an act particularly significant for the phenomenal growth of Pentecostalism on the island.

With the conquest of Puerto Rico by the United States in 1898, the migration of Puerto Ricans from the island to the U.S. mainland began. By 1917 the U.S. Congress had granted all Puerto Ricans U.S. citizenship. This new status allowed Puerto Ricans to be drafted into the armed forces for service in World War I. Although there had been a constant flow of Puerto Rican migrants to the mainland since 1898 (with an accompanying reverse migration), it was really after World War II that a combination of factors brought about the great migration of Puerto Ricans to the United States. Initially, the majority settled in the Northeast, with New York City a major point of entry.

As new Puerto Rican communities established themselves in the continental United States, the response of churches was inconsistent and sometimes tepid. In some locations, Puerto Rican migrants seized the initiative and leadership, replicating island traditions in new urban settings. Initially, many church leaders, both Catholic and Protestant, viewed Puerto Ricans as an alien and problematic people. Given the void resulting from institutional church neglect, many pentecostal and conservative Protestant ministries made their initial gains among newly arrived immigrants, some of whom carried their new faith back to Puerto Rico with them.

Since the 1960s, civil rights activism and new theological perspectives began to change institutional church perceptions and approaches to Puerto Ricans, both on the mainland and on the island. Latinx theology sees Puerto Ricans, whether on the island or the mainland, as U.S. citizens living in a society that treats them as illegal aliens. From one perspective all Puerto Ricans—Islanders and diaspora—are multicultural Latinx. There are Puerto Ricans in the United States whose primary language is not Spanish and who, if they visit the *isla* at all, do so only to see relatives. Their only experience of a Puerto Rican community is Humboldt Park in Chicago, La Park in Hartford, El Barrio in East Harlem, or El Bronx in New York. Attitudes of Puerto Ricans *de la isla*, who question the authenticity of Puerto Ricans from *afuera* (from "the outside," a common Puerto Rican island idiom for the mainland United States), create tensions and challenge Latino/a theology.

Despite its Commonwealth status and official name, Estado Libre Asociado de Puerto Rico (Free Associated State of Puerto Rico), and the fact that for more than a century Puerto Rico has been a U.S. colony, Puerto Rican culture and the Spanish language persist. This popular resistance is especially astonishing when one compares what happened with Hawaii, another island acquired by the United States in 1898.

In September 2017 Puerto Rico was hit by two massive category 5 hurricanes, Irma and Maria. The island was devastated, Puerto Rico was without power, and recovery responses were inadequate, including from the U.S. federal government, all of which contributed to a major humanitarian crisis with a hurricane-related death toll estimated at three thousand to forty-six hundred. Tens of thousands of Puerto Ricans left the Island and relocated to different parts of the United States, with a large contingent going to Florida.

The question for Latinx theology is how to think and act theologically in the face of this Puerto Rican reality. Theologian Teresa Delgado says it best regarding what the response should include:

> Unless Puerto Rican theologians reflect upon their experience of God within the context of Puerto Rican life, the reality of colonization for Puerto Ricans will be slow to emerge as a relevant theme for all US Latinxs. The devastating legacy of colonization—an aspect of present-day Puerto Rican experience that is a unique distinction among US Latinx—continues to plague the US Puerto Rican community.[57]

As noted earlier, the complicated and somewhat ambivalent attitude of Puerto Ricans toward the United States (in times of relative peace as well as crisis) presents another dimension of the challenge facing Latinx theology.

---

[57] Teresa Delgado, *A Puerto Rican Theology: Prophesy Freedom* (New York: Palgrave Macmillan, 2017), 8.

Social Locations and Latinx Religious Scholars

It is common for Latinx religious scholars to claim to be "organic intellectuals" emerging from and remaining connected to the people. Typically, when the phrase is evoked there is at least an echo of the concept of the organic intellectual as developed by philosopher Antonio Gramsci.[58] In other words, the assertion is that Latinx religious scholars as organic intellectuals operate within the social locations of the disenfranchised Latinx communities as agents acting to raise critical consciousness about oppression and joining in a praxis toward liberation.

At this point, critical self-awareness is appropriate. No doubt, many of these scholars were born into and arose from economically depressed social and cultural spaces. Yet with education comes privilege, including a type of "cultural capital."[59] A dilemma can arise between the organic intellectual grounded in the local communities of faith and the college-educated religion scholar who possesses unique types of cultural capital. Are the voices of Latinx religion scholars truly from the margins, even though their professor's salaries afford them the privilege of choosing not to live in the barrio? While several Latinx religious scholars chose to continue living among and with the poor, physically accompanying them in their struggle for existence, others have chosen otherwise, and there may be very good reasons for those choices. But is a Latinx scholar who no longer lives with the disenfranchised able to be a voice with them? Can there still be solidarity when a certain type of cultural capital is obtained and employed? Does the security of a job and the safety of a middle- or upper-class home disconnect a Latinx religious scholar who "escaped" from those still trapped in the economic oppression of the barrio?

Additionally, often (but not always), advanced higher education may yield theological graduates who are more to the religious left than their congregations. If many Latinx congregations express more socially,

---

[58] See these words from Antonio Gramsci's *Prison Notebooks*: "All men [*sic*] are intellectuals, but not all men have in society the function of intellectuals," and "One of the most important characteristics of any group that is developing toward dominance is its struggle to assimilate and to conquer 'ideologically' the traditional intellectuals, but this assimilation and conquest is made quicker and more efficacious the more the group in question succeeds in simultaneously elaborating its own organic intellectuals." Quoted in Roger S. Gottlieb, ed., *An Anthology of Western Marxism from Lukacs and Gramsci to Socialist-Feminism* (New York: Oxford University Press, 1989), 115, 116.

[59] See Pierre Bourdieu, *The Field of Cultural Production: Essays on Art and Literature* (New York: Columbia University Press, 1993); Terry Rey, *Bourdieu on Religion: Imposing Faith and Legitimacy* (New York: Routledge, 2007).

politically, and theologically conservative religious worldviews, to what degree does the scholarship written by Latinx religious scholars represent those perspectives? Are Latinx religious scholars voicing the theologies being created by Latinx faith communities, or are they imposing their own views, influenced by their university and theological education, upon Latinx faith communities? Can educated Latinx religious scholars be part of *la comunidad* when suspicions still exist within the faith community toward those with advanced academic degrees? As more Latinx obtain their doctorates in various fields and enter the ranks of the middle- and upper-class intelligentsia, questions like these will require greater deliberation, and ideally deliberation *en conjunto*.

Queering Latinx Religious Thought

When it comes to LGBTQ+ issues, no one position is held collectively by Latinx religion scholars. In some parts of the Latinx community there seems to be a Latinx LGBT bias that differs from the homophobia of the dominant U.S. culture. It can be argued that Latinxs do not fear the homosexual; rather, homosexuals are often held in contempt as men who choose not to prove their manhood. Unlike white Euroamericans, where two men engaged in a sexual act are both called homosexuals, among Latinx only the one who places himself in the "position" of a woman is gay. In fact, in several Latinx cultures, the man who is in the dominant position during the sex act, known as *bugarrón*, is able to retain, if not increase, his machismo. Also missing from most Hispanic theological analysis is the space occupied by lesbians. While gays constitute a "scandal" as men forsaking their manhood, lesbians are usually ignored due to the overall machismo of a society that grounds its sexuality on the *macho*'s desires, repressing feminine sexuality. In Latinx contexts, tolerance of lesbians is partly due to their unimportance to the *macho*'s construction of sexuality. They simply have no space in the dominant construction. Worse still is the overall limited conversation of Latinx academics concerning bisexuals and transgendered people.

Even though there are Latinx religious scholars who are gay, lesbian, bisexual, or transgendered, the adage "Se dice nada, se hace todo" (Say nothing, do everything) has remained the accepted norm of the Latinx theological community. A review of theological literature reveals limited discussions of Latinxs on this issue. For many Latinx religious scholars who are clergy associated with more theologically and sociologically conservative congregations and denominations that view homosexuality as a sin, or for those who teach at more conservative seminaries, coming out as gay can be a career-ending move.

Possibly the first time this issue has been raised in a Latinx-based academic book on Latinx religiosity was the small section that appeared in the first edition of this book, *Introducing Latino/a Theologies*, in 2001. Among the first scholars to publish on queer issues from a Latinx religious perspective were Luis León and Miguel De La Torre in the book *Out of the Shadows into the Light: Christianity and Homosexuality*.[60] The first book written by a Latinx religious scholar on this topic that was geared not to scholars but to the Latino/a church member for the purpose of raising consciousness was *A La Familia*.[61] Also among the first Latinx theologians to proactively deal with raising consciousness among Latinx churches is Orlando Espín, who has served as co-convener of the Latinx Roundtable of the Center for LGBTQ and Gender Studies in Religion (CLGS) at the Pacific School of Religion since 2010. The center has published in Spanish a number of brief booklets, all having to do with LGBT issues and religion intended for the Latinx context.

As a newer Latinx generation obtains PhDs in religion and enter the academy, many are more versed in queer theory. Among these newer Latinx scholars, many are openly identifying with their sexual identity, some because they see themselves as scholars rather than practitioners of a faith tradition, while others reject the dichotomy that one cannot be religious and openly gay, lesbian, bisexual, or transgendered. The degree to which this openness is a result of the generational shifts occurring among Latinx religious scholars awaits further study.

Pondering the Future of the New Everyday

All theologies remain a reflection of a certain people within a specific time period. One of the questions concerning the future of Latinx religious thought is if its dependence on the vitality of its grassroots foundation will remain a crucial characteristic. If being faithful to the preferential option of or for the Latinx community, especially those who are oppressed, remains a major concern of Latinx religion scholars, then Latinx religious thought can develop and mature along with the changing Latinx people and their shifting intersectional contexts. If instead the focus shifts from relationships with living communities to a more

---

[60] Luis Leon, "Cesar Chavez, Christian Love, and the Myth of (Anti) Machismo," and Miguel A. De La Torre, "Confession of a Latino Macho," both in *Out of the Shadow into the Light: Christianity and Homosexuality*, ed. Miguel A. De La Torre (St. Louis: Chalice Press, 2009), 59–75, 88–103, respectively.

[61] Miguel A. De La Torre, *A La Familia: A Conversation about Our Families, the Bible, Sexual Orientation, and Gender* (Washington, DC: Human Rights Campaign, 2011).

exclusively academic methodology of studying how people, in this case Latinx, construct religious beliefs, rituals, and practices, then this thing that we have been defining as Latinx religious discourse may lose its "organic intellectual" image.

An increasingly younger Latinx population as well as growing diversification of that population have positioned Latinx communities within reach of redefining what it means to be a citizen or resident of the United States. If future demographic forecasts are correct and Latinx peoples represent over a quarter of the U.S. population by 2040, their traditions and customs will move from the margins toward the mainstream. What we call Hispanic or Latinx religion, religiosity, and spirituality may cease to be an "interesting perspective" and become, instead, one of the central voices within North American civil and theological discourses. As Latinx peoples move from society's margins, their theologies—as a reflection of how they understand the Deity and identify meaning and purpose in life from their varied and intersectional spaces—can also be expected to change.

Select Bibliography

Throughout this book we have sought to provide an entry-level description of, and invite appreciation for, Hispanic-Latino/a-Latinx theologies, traditions, religiosity, spirituality, and practices. Of necessity we simplified complex concepts at the risk of misrepresenting people and thoughts. However, no one should draw the conclusion based on our theological sketch that theoretical concepts from Latinx perspectives lack depth, are not in conversation with other viewpoints, or that they do not engage in serious scholarship. Fortunately for anyone who desires to pursue Latinx theologies beyond this brief introduction, there is a growing collection of significant resources that reflect the creativity, diversity, complexity, and profundity of Latinx religious and theological perspectives from a variety of scholars and practitioners. When the first edition of this book was written, we included a short paragraph discussing the thesis of each listed book. The growth in scholarship since then prohibits us from creating such an annotated bibliography in this second edition.

Consequently, in order to encourage further exploration of Latinx theologies and in the spirit of *teología en conjunto* and with advice from many *colegas*, this section provides a select bibliography of books whose major focus is Latinx religious discourse and practice broadly understood. Latinx scholars have written books concerning non-Hispanic concepts that require our attention; nevertheless, they may not be listed here because our purpose in creating this list is to provide a Latinx-centric bibliography of theology and religion. We have further limited ourselves to works that have appeared as books, but of course exceedingly more can be found elsewhere as book chapters, journal articles, essays, podcasts, blogs, and other online resources.

We revised and expanded the bibliography from that which appeared in the 2001 edition, adding more recent works that have appeared since that time, while acknowledging that any bibliography only captures a moment in time. It should be noted that while we consulted with other

Latinx religious scholars and those studying U.S. Latinx religions, by definition any selected bibliography is incomplete, and there may be some disappointments about what was not included. Finally, some of the older works are kept in this bibliography because of their significance to the historical development of Latinx theologies in the United States.

These books were chosen because they specifically deal with the religious perspectives and practices of Latinx communities within the multiple intersectional realities of the United States. While obviously the list is not exhaustive, however, it includes works from within the Latinx *comunidad* and those persons allied with such communities that have made important contributions to theology done *latinamente* (in the best positive sense) and in expounding Latinx religiosity and spirituality that is done *en la lucha* (in the struggle) in the United States, and the related contexts of everyday religious and spiritual life. The purpose of this selected bibliography is to allow newcomers to Latinx religious thought to make informed decisions as to which other books they wish to read, study, or explore.

Abalos, David T. *Latinos in the United States: The Sacred and the Political.* 2nd ed. Notre Dame, IN: University of Notre Dame Press, 2007.

Agosto, Efraín. *Preaching in the Interim: Transitional Leadership in the Latino/a Church.* Valley Forge, PA: Judson Press, 2018.

———. *Servant Leadership: Jesus and Paul.* St. Louis: Chalice Press, 2005.

Agosto, Efraín, and Jacqueline Hidalgo, eds. *Latinxs, The Bible, and Migration.* New York: Palgrave Macmillan, 2018.

Alfaro, Sammy. *Divine Compañero: Toward a Hispanic Pentecostal Christology.* Eugene, OR: Pickwick, 2010.

Aponte, Edwin David. *¡Santo! Varieties of Latino/a Spirituality.* Maryknoll, NY: Orbis Books, 2012.

Aponte, Edwin David, and Miguel A. De La Torre, eds. *Handbook of Latina/o Theologies.* St. Louis: Chalice Press, 2006.

Aquino, María Pilar. *Our Cry for Life: A Feminist Theology from Latin America.* Maryknoll, NY: Orbis Books, 1993.

Aquino, María Pilar, Daisy L. Machado, and Jeanette Rodríguez-Holguín, eds. *A Reader in Latina Feminist Theology: Religion and Justice.* Austin: University of Texas Press, 2002.

Aquino, María Pilar, and Maria José Rosado-Nunes, eds. *Feminist Intercultural Theology: Latina Explorations for a Just World.* Maryknoll, NY: Orbis Books, 2007.

Atkins-Vasquez, Jane, ed. *Hispanic Presbyterians in Southern California: One Hundred Years of Ministry.* Los Angeles: Hispanic Commission, Synod of Southern California and Hawaii, 1988.

Avalos, Hector, ed. *Introduction to the U.S. Latina/o Experience*. Boston: Brill Academic Publishers, 2004.

———. *Strangers in Our Own Land: Religion in U.S. Latina/o Literature*. Nashville: Abingdon Press, 2005.

Azaransky, Sarah, ed. *Religion and Politics in America's Borderland*. Lanham, MD: Lexington Books, 2013.

Baldwin, Deborah J. *Protestants and the Mexican Revolution: Missionaries, Ministers, and Social Change*. Urbana: University of Illinois Press, 1990.

Barreto, Eric D. *Ethnic Negotiations: The Function of Race and Ethnicity in Acts 16*. Tübingen: Mohr Siebeck, 2010.

Barreto, Raimundo, and Roberto Sirvent, eds. *Decolonial Christianities: Latinx and Latin American Perspectives*. London, UK: Palgrave Macmillan, 2019.

Barton, Paul. *Hispanic Methodists, Presbyterians, and Baptists in Texas*. Austin: University of Texas Press, 2006.

Barton, Paul, and David Maldonaldo Jr., eds. *Hispanic Christianity within Mainline Protestant Traditions: A Bibliography*. Decatur, GA: Asociación para la Educación Teológica Hispana (AETH), 1998.

Bañuelas, Arturo J., ed. *Mestizo Christianity: Theology from the Latino Perspective*. Maryknoll, NY: Orbis Books, 1995.

Bettinger-Lopez, Caroline. *Cuban Jewish Journeys: Searching for Identity, Home, and History in Miami*. Knoxville: University of Tennessee Press, 2000.

Brading, D. A. *Mexican Phoenix: Our Lady of Guadalupe, Image, and Tradition across Five Centuries*. Cambridge: Cambridge University Press, 2001.

Branson, Mark Lau, and Juan F. Martínez. *Churches, Cultures, and Leadership: A Practical Theology of Congregations and Ethnicities*. Downers Grove, IL: InterVarsity Press, 2011.

Brackenridge, R. Douglas, and Francisco O. Treto-Garcia. *Iglesia Presbiteriana: A History of Presbyterians and Mexican Americans in the Southwest*. San Antonio, TX: Trinity University Press, 1974.

Busto, Rudy V. *King Tiger: The Religious Vision of Reies López Tijerina*. Albuquerque: University of New Mexico, 2005.

Cardoza-Orlandi, Carlos F. *Mission: An Essential Guide*. Nashville: Abingdon Press, 2002.

Cardoza-Orlandi, Carlos F., and Justo L González. *To All the Nations from All the Nations: A History of the Christian Missionary Movement*. Nashville: Abingdon Press, 2013.

Carroll R. M. Daniel. *Christians on the Border: Immigration, the Church, and the Bible*. Grand Rapids: Baker Academic, 2008.

Carroll, Michael P. *The Penitente Brotherhood: Patriarchy and Hispano-Catholicism in New Mexico*. Baltimore, MD: Johns Hopkins University Press, 2002.

Casarella, Peter, and Raul Gómez, eds. *El Cuerpo de Cristo: The Hispanic Presence in the U.S. Catholic Church*. Chestnut Ridge, NY: Crossroad, 1998.

Castañeda, Carlos Eduardo. *Our Catholic Heritage in Texas, 1519–1950*. 7 vols. Austin, TX: Von Boekmann-Jones, 1958.

Castañeda-Liles, María Del Socorro. *Our Lady of Everyday Life: La Virgen de Guadalupe and the Catholic Imagination of Mexican Women in America*. New York: Oxford University Press, 2018.

Cavazos-González, Gilberto. *Beyond Piety: The Christian Spiritual Life, Justice, and Liberation*. Eugene, OR: Wipf and Stock, 2010.

———. *Tradiciones of Our Faith: Sharing Faith Interculturally / Compartiendo la fe interculturalmente*. Franklin Park, IL: World Library Publications, 2012.

Chávez, Angélico. *The Old Faith and Old Glory: Story of the Church in New Mexico since the American Occupation, 1846–1946*. Santa Fe: privately printed, 1946.

———. *Our Lady of the Conquest*. Albuquerque: History Society of New Mexico, 1948.

Conde-Frazier, Elizabeth, *Hispanic Bible Institutes: A Community of Theological Construction*. Scranton, PA: University of Scranton Press, 2004.

———. *Listen to the Children: Conversations with Immigrant Families / Eschuchemos a los Niños: Conversaciones con familias inmigrantes*. Valley Forge, PA: Judson Press, 2011.

Conde-Frazier, Elizabeth, S. Steve King, and Gary A. Parrett, eds. *A Many-Colored Kingdom: Multicultural Dynamics for Spiritual Formation*. Grand Rapids: Baker Academic, 2004.

Costas, Orlando E. *Christ outside the Gate: Mission beyond Christendom*. Maryknoll, NY: Orbis Books, 1982.

———. *The Church and Its Mission: A Shattering Critique from the Third World*. Wheaton, IL: Tyndale House, 1974.

———. *Comunicación por medio de la predicación: Manual de Homilectica*. Miami, FL: Editorial Caribe, 1989.

Crane, Ken R. *Latino Churches: Faith, Family, and Ethnicity in the Second Generation*. New York: LFB Scholarly Publishing, 2003.

Crespo, Orlando. *Being Latino in Christ: Finding Wholeness in Your Ethnic Identity*. Downers Grove, IL: InterVarsity Press, 2003.

Cruz, Samuel, ed. *Christianity and Culture in the City: A Postcolonial Approach*. Lanham, MD: Lexington Books, 2013.

——. *Masked Africanism: Puerto Rican Pentecostalism.* Dubuque, IA: Kendall Hunt, 2005.

Dalton, Frederick John. *The Moral Vision of César Chávez.* Maryknoll, NY: Orbis Books, 2003.

Daniel, Ben. *Neighbor: Christian Encounters with "Legal" Immigration.* Louisville, KY: Westminster John Knox Press, 2010.

Davis, Kenneth G., ed. *Misa, Mesa y Musa: Liturgy in the U.S. Hispanic Church.* Shiller Park, IL: World Library Publications, 1997.

——, ed. *Misa, Mesa y Musa.* vol. 2 of *Liturgy in the U.S. Hispanic Church.* Shiller Park, IL: World Library Publications, 2008.

Davis, Kenneth G., and Edwin I. Hernandez, eds. *Reconstructing the Sacred Tower: Challenges and Promise of Latino/a Theological Education.* Scranton, PA: University of Scanton Press, 2003.

Deck, Allan Figueroa, ed. *Frontiers of Hispanic Theology in the United States.* Maryknoll, NY: Orbis Books, 1992.

——. *The Second Wave: Hispanic Ministry and the Evangelization of Cultures.* Mahwah, NJ: Paulist Press, 1989.

Deck, Allan Figueroa, and Jay P. Dolan, eds. *Hispanic Catholic Culture in the United States: Issues and Concerns.* Notre Dame, IN: University of Notre Dame Press, 1994.

De La Torre, Miguel A. *A La Familia: A Conversation about Our Families, the Bible, Sexual Orientation, and Gender.* Washington, DC: Human Rights Campaign, 2011.

——, ed. *Hispanic American Religious Culture.* vols. 1 and 2. Santa Barbara, CA: ABC-CLIO, 2009.

——. *La Lucha for Cuba: Religion and Politics on the Streets of Miami.* Berkeley: University of California Press, 2003.

——. *Latina/o Social Ethics: Moving beyond Eurocentric Moral Thinking.* Waco, TX: Baylor University Press, 2010.

——. *Leer la Biblia desde los Marginados.* Bilbao, Spain: Ediciones Mensajero, 2005.

——. *The Politics of Jesús: A Hispanic Political Theology.* Lanham, MD: Rowman and Littlefield, 2015.

——. *The Quest for the Cuban Christ: A Historical Search.* Gainesville: University Press of Florida, 2002.

——. *Santería: The Beliefs and Rituals of a Growing Religion in America.* Grand Rapids: Eerdmans, 2004.

——. *Trails of Hope and Terror: Testimonies on Immigration.* Maryknoll, NY: Orbis Books, 2009.

——. *The U.S. Immigration Crisis: Toward an Ethics of Place.* Eugene, OR: Cascade Books, 2016.

De La Torre, Miguel A., and Edwin David Aponte. *Introducing Latino/a Theologies*. Maryknoll, NY: Orbis Books, 2001.

De La Torre, Miguel A., and Gaston Espinosa, eds. *Rethinking Latino(a) Religion and Identity*. Cleveland: Pilgrim Press, 2006.

De Leon, Victor. *The Silent Pentecostals: A Biographical History of the Pentecostal Movement among Hispanics in the Twentieth Century*. Taylors, SC: Faith Printing Company, 1979.

Delgadillo, Theresa. *Latina Lives in Milwaukee*. Urbana: University of Illinois Press, 2015.

———. *Spiritual Mestizaje: Religion, Gender, Race, and Nation in Contemporary Chicana Narrative*. Durham, NC: Duke University Press, 2011.

Delgado, Teresa. *A Puerto Rican Decolonial Theology: Prophesy Freedom*. New York: Palgrave Macmillan, 2017.

de Luna, Anita. *Faith Formation and Popular Religion: Lessons from the Tejano Experience*. Lanham, MD: Rowman and Littlefield, 2002.

Díaz, Miguel H. *On Being Human: U.S. Hispanic and Rahnerian Perspectives*. Maryknoll, NY: Orbis Books, 2001.

Díaz-Stevens, Ana María. *Oxcart Catholicism on Fifth Avenue: The Impact of the Puerto Rican Migration upon the Archdiocese of New York*. Notre Dame, IN: University of Notre Dame Press, 1993.

Díaz-Stevens, Ana María, and Antonio M. Stevens-Arroyo. *Recognizing the Latino Resurgence in U.S. Religion: The Emmaus Paradigm*. Boulder, CO: Westview Press, 1998.

Dolan, Jay P., and Allan Figueroa Deck. *Hispanic Catholic Culture in the U.S.: Issues and Concerns*. Notre Dame, IN: University of Notre Dame Press, 1997.

———. *Mexican Americans and the Catholic Church, 1900–1965*. South Bend, IN: University of Notre Dame Press, 1994.

———. *Puerto Rican and Cuban Catholics in the U.S., 1900–1965*. South Bend, IN: University of Notre Dame Press, 1994.

Dolan, Jay, and Gilberto Miguel Hinojosa. *Mexican Americans and the Catholic Church, 1900–1965*. South Bend, IN: University of Notre Dame Press, 1994.

Durand, Jorge, and Douglas S. Massey. *Miracles on the Border: Retablos of Mexican Migrants to the United States*. Tucson: University of Arizona Press, 1995.

Elizondo, Virgilio. *Beyond Borders: Writings of Virgilio Elizondo and Friends*. Ed. Timothy Matovina. Maryknoll, NY: Orbis Books, 2000.

———. *The Future Is Mestizo: Life Where Cultures Meet*. Revised edition. Boulder, CO: University Press of Colorado, 2000.

———. *Galilean Journey: The Mexican-American Promise*. Revised and Expanded. Maryknoll, NY: Orbis Books, 2000.

————. *Guadalupe: Mother of the New Creation.* Maryknoll, NY: Orbis Books, 1997.

————, ed. *Way of the Cross: Passion of Christ in the Americas.* Maryknoll, NY: Orbis Books, 1992.

Elizondo, Virgilio P., Allan Figueroa Deck, and Timothy M. Matovina. *The Treasure of Guadalupe.* Lanham, MD: Rowman and Littlefield, 2006.

Elizondo, Virgilio P., and Timothy M. Matovina. *Mestizo Worship: A Pastoral Approach to Liturgical Ministry.* Collegeville, MN: Liturgical Press, 1998.

————. *San Fernando Cathedral: Soul of the City.* Maryknoll, NY: Orbis Books, 1998.

Embry, Jessie L. *In His Own Language: Mormon Spanish-Speaking Congregations in the United States.* Provo, UT: Brigham Young University, 1997.

Empereur, James, and Eduardo Fernández, *La Vida Sacra: Contemporary Hispanic Sacramental Theology.* Lanham, MD: Rowman and Littlefield, 2006.

Escobar, Samuel. *Christian Mission and Social Justice.* Harrisonburg, VA: Herald Press, 1978.

Espín, Orlando O., ed. *Building Bridges, Doing Justice: Constructing a Latino/a Ecumenical Theology.* Maryknoll, NY: Orbis Books, 2009.

————. *The Faith of the People: Theological Reflections on Popular Catholicism.* Maryknoll, NY: Orbis Books, 1997.

————. *Grace and Humanness: Theological Reflections Because of Culture.* Maryknoll, NY: Orbis Books, 2007.

————. *Idol and Grace: Traditioning and Subversive Hope.* Maryknoll, NY: Orbis Books, 2014.

————, ed. *The Wiley Blackwell Companion to Latino/a Theology.* Malden, MA: John Wiley and Sons, 2015.

Espín, Orlando O., and Miguel H. Díaz, eds. *From the Heart of Our People.* Maryknoll, NY: Orbis Books, 1999.

Espinosa, Gaston. *Latino Pentecostals in America: Faith and Politics in Action.* Cambridge, MA: Harvard University Press, 2014.

Espinosa, Gastón, Virgilio Elizondo, and Jesse Miranda, eds. *Hispanic Churches in American Public Life: Summary of Findings.* South Bend, IN: Institute for Latino Studies, University of Notre Dame, 2003.

————, eds. *Latino Religions and Civic Activism in the United States.* New York: Oxford University Press, 2005.

Espinosa, Gaston, and Mario T. García, eds. *Mexican American Religions: Spirituality, Activism, and Culture.* Durham, NC: Duke University Press, 2008.

Ferguson, Kathryn, Norma A. Price, and Ted Parks. *Crossing with the Virgin: Stories from the Migrant Trail.* Tucson: University of Arizona Press, 2010.

Fernández, Eduardo C. *La Cosecha: Harvesting Contemporary United States Hispanic Theology, 1972–1998.* Collegeville, MN: Liturgical Press, 2000.

———. *Mexican-American Catholics.* New York: Paulist Press, 2007.

Gálvez, Ayshia. *Guadalupe in New York: Devotion and Struggle for Citizenship Rights among Mexican Immigrants.* New York: New York University Press, 2010.

García, Ismael. *Dignidad: Ethics through Hispanic Eyes.* Nashville: Abingdon Press, 1997.

García, Mario T., ed., *The Gospel of César Chávez: My Faith in Action.* Lanham, MD: Sheed and Ward, 2007.

García-Johnson, Oscar. *The Mestizo/a Community of the Spirit: A Postmodern Latino/a Ecclesiology.* Eugene, OR: Pickwick, 2009.

———. *Spirit outside the Gate: Decolonial Pneumatologies of the American Global South.* Downers Grove, IL: IVP Academic, 2019.

García-Rivera, Alexandro. *The Community of the Beautiful: A Theological Aesthetics.* Collegeville, MN: Liturgical Press, 1999.

———. *St. Martín de Porres: The "Little Stories" and the Semiotics of Culture.* Maryknoll, NY: Orbis Books, 1995.

Goizueta, Roberto S. *Caminemos con Jesús: Toward a Hispanic/Latino Theology of Accompaniment.* Maryknoll, NY: Orbis Books, 1995.

———. *Christ Our Companion: Toward a Theological Aesthetics of Liberation.* Maryknoll, NY: Orbis Books, 2009.

———, ed. *We Are a People! Initiatives in Hispanic American Theology.* Minneapolis: Fortress Press, 1992.

Gómez, Raúl, ed. *The Languages of Liturgy / El Lenguaje de la Liturgia.* Chicago: Archdiocese of Chicago / Liturgy Training Publications, 2004.

Gómez-Ruiz, Raúl. *Mozarabs, Hispanics, and the Cross.* Maryknoll, NY: Orbis Books, 2007.

González-Andrieu, Cecilia. *Bridge to Wonder: Art as a Gospel of Beauty.* Waco, TX: Baylor University Press, 2012.

González, Justo L., ed. *¡Alabadle! Hispanic Christian Worship.* Nashville: Abingdon Press, 1996.

———. *Mañana: Christian Theology from a Hispanic Perspective.* Nashville: Abingdon Press, 1990.

———. *Mestizo Augustine: A Theologian between Two Cultures.* Downers Grove, IL: InterVarsity Academic, 2016.

———. *Santa Biblia: The Bible through Hispanic Eyes.* Nashville: Abingdon Press, 1996.

————, ed. *Voces: Voices from the Hispanic Church*. Nashville: Abingdon Press, 1996.

González, Justo L., and Pablo A. Jiménez. *Púlpito: An Introduction to Hispanic Preaching*. Nashville: Abingdon Press, 2005.

Gonzalez, Michelle A. *Afro-Cuban Theology: Religion, Race, Culture, and Identity*. Gainesville: University Press of Florida, 2006.

————. *Embracing Latina Spirituality: A Woman's Perspective*. Cincinnati: St. Anthony's Messenger Press, 2009.

————. *Sor Juana: Beauty and Justice in the Americas*. Maryknoll, NY: Orbis Books, 2003.

Groody, Daniel G. *Border of Death, Valley of Life: An Immigrant Journey of Heart and Spirit*. Lanham, MD: Rowan and Littlefield, 2002.

Guerrero, Andrés G. *A Chicano Theology*. Maryknoll, NY: Orbis Books, 1987.

Gutiérrez, Angel Luis, ed. *Voces del Púlpito Hispano*. Valley Forge, PA: Judson Press, 1989.

Hernández, Edwin I., Milagros Peña, Caroline Sotelo Viernes Turner, and Ariana Monique Salazar. *Spanning the Divide: Latinos/as in Theological Education*. Orlando, FL: Asociación para la Educación Teológica Hispana (AETH), 2016.

Hidalgo, Jacqueline M. *Revelation in Aztlán: Scriptures, Utopias, and the Chicano Movement*. New York: Palgrave Macmillan, 2016.

Guerrero, Andrés G. *A Chicano Theology*. Maryknoll, NY: Orbis Books, 1987.

Iber, Jorge. *Hispanics in the Mormon Zion, 1912–1999*. College Station: Texas A&M Press, 2000.

Imperatori-Lee, Natalia. *Cuéntame: Narrative in the Ecclesial Present*. Maryknoll, NY: Orbis Books, 2018.

Isasi-Díaz, Ada María. *En la Lucha: Elaborating a Mujerista Theology*. Rev. ed. Minneapolis: Fortress Press, 2004.

————. *La Lucha Continues: Mujerista Theology*. Maryknoll, NY: Orbis Books, 2004.

————. *Mujerista Theology: A Theology for the Twenty-First Century*. Maryknoll, NY: Orbis Books, 1996.

Isasi-Díaz, Ada María, and Eduardo Mendieta, eds. *Decolonizing Epistemologies: Latina/o Theology and Philosophy*. New York: Fordham University Press, 2012.

Isasi-Díaz, Ada María, and Fernando F. Segovia, eds. *Hispanic/Latino Theology: Challenge and Promise*. Minneapolis: Fortress Press, 1996.

Isasi-Díaz, Ada María, and Yolanda Tarango. *Hispanic Woman, Prophetic Voice in the Church: Toward a Hispanic Women's Liberation Theology*. New York: Harper and Row, 1988.

Jacobs, Janet Liebman. *Hidden Heritage: The Legacy of Crypto-Jews.* Berkeley: University of California Press, 2002.

Kiev, Ari. *Curanderismo: Mexican-American Folk Psychiatry.* New York: Free Press, 1968.

Kohn Rivera, Natalia, Neomi Vega Quiñones, and Kristy Garza Robinson. *Hermanas: Deepening Our Identity and Growing Our Influence.* Downers Grove, IL: InterVarsity Press, 2019.

León, Luis D. *La Llorona's Children: Religion, Life and Death in the U.S.-Mexican Borderlands.* Berkeley: University of California Press, 2004.

———. *The Gospel of César Chávez: My Faith in Action.* Berkeley: University of California Press, 2014.

López Pulido, Alberto. *The Sacred World of the Penitentes.* Washington, DC: Smithsonian Institution Press, 2000.

Lozado, Francisco, Jr. *Toward a Latino/a Biblical Interpretation.* Atlanta: SBL Press, 2017.

Lozado, Francisco, Jr., and Fernando F. Segovia, eds. *Latino/a Biblical Hermeneutics: Problematics, Objectives, Strategies.* Atlanta: SBL Press, 2014.

Lucas, Isidro. *The Browning of America: The Hispanic Revolution in the American Church.* Chicago: Fides/Claretian, 1981.

Machado, Daisy L. *Of Borders and Margins: Hispanic Disciples in Texas, 1888–1945.* New York: Oxford University Press, 2003.

Machado, Daisy L., Bryan S. Turner, and Trygve Wyller, eds. *Borderland Religion: Ambiguous Practices of Difference, Hope and Beyond.* New York: Routledge, 2018.

Madrid, Arturo. *In the Country of the Empty Crosses: The Story of a Hispano Protestant Family in Catholic New Mexico.* San Antonio, TX: Trinity University Press, 2012.

Maduro, Otto. *Maps for a Fiesta: A Latina/o Perspective on Knowledge and the Global Crisis.* Edited with an introduction by Eduardo Mendieta. New York: Fordham University Press, 2015.

———. *Religion and Social Conflicts.* Trans. Robert R. Barr. Maryknoll, NY: Orbis Books, 1982.

Maldonado, David. *Crossing Guadalupe Street: Growing Up Hispanic and Protestant.* Albuquerque: University of New Mexico Press, 2001.

———, ed. *Protestantes/Protestants: Hispanic Christianity within Mainline Traditions.* Nashville: Abingdon Press, 1999.

Martell-Otero, Loida I., Zaida Maldonado Perez, and Elizabeth Conde-Frazier. *Latina Evangélicas: A Theological Survey from the Margins.* Eugene, OR: Wipf and Stock, 2013.

Martínez, Juan Francisco. *Los Protestantes: An Introduction to Latino Protestantism in the United States.* Westport, CT: Praeger, 2011.

———. *Sea La Luz: The Making of Mexican Protestantism in the American Southwest, 1829–1900.* Denton: University of North Texas Press, 2006.

———. *The Story of Latino Protestants in the United States.* Grand Rapids: Eerdmans, 2018.

Martínez, Juan F., and Lindy Scott, eds. *Los Evangélicos: Portraits of Latino Protestantism in the United States.* Eugene, OR: Wipf and Stock, 2009.

Martínez-Vázquez, Hjamil A. *Latina/o y Musulman: The Construction of Latina/o Identity among Latina/o Muslims in the United States.* Eugene, OR: Wipf and Stock, 2010.

Martinez, Richard. *PADRES: The National Chicano Priest Movement.* Austin: University of Texas Press, 2005.

Matovina, Timothy. *Guadalupe and Her Faithful: Latino Catholics in San Antonio, from Colonial Origins to the Present.* Baltimore, MD: Johns Hopkins University Press, 2005.

———. *Latino Catholicism: Transformation in America's Largest Church.* Princeton, NJ: Princeton University Press, 2012.

Matovina, Timothy, and Gerald E. Poyo, eds. *¡Presente! U.S. Latino Catholics from Colonial Origins to the Present.* Maryknoll, NY: Orbis Books, 2000.

Matovina, Timothy, and Gary Riebe-Estrella, eds. *Horizons of the Sacred: Mexican Traditions in U.S. Catholicism.* Ithaca, NY: Cornell University Press, 2002.

Maynard-Reid, Pedrito U. *Diverse Worship: African-American, Caribbean, and Hispanic Perspectives.* Downers Grove, IL: InterVarsity Press, 2000.

Medina, Lara. *Las Hermanas: Chicana/Latina Religious-Political Activism in the U.S. Catholic Church.* Philadelphia: Temple University Press, 2004.

Medina, Lara, and Martha R. Gonzales, eds. *Voices from the Ancestors: Xicanx and Latinx Spiritual Expressions and Healing Practices.* Tucson: University of Arizona Press, 2019.

Medina, Néstor. *Christianity, Empire, and the Spirit: (Re)Configuring Faith and the Cultural.* Boston: Brill Academic Publishers, 2018.

———. *Mestizaje: (Re)Mapping Race, Culture, and Faith in Latina/o Catholicism.* Maryknoll, NY: Orbis Books, 2009.

Medina, Néstor, and Sammy Alfaro, eds. *Pentecostals and Charismatics in Latin American and Latino Communities.* New York: Palgrave Macmillan, 2015.

Morales, Harold D. *Latino and Muslim in America: Race, Religion, and the Making of a New Minority.* New York: Oxford University Press, 2018.

Mulder, Mark T., Aida I. Ramos, and Gerardo Martí. *Latino Protestants in America: Growing and Diverse*. Lanham, MD: Rowman and Littlefield, 2017.

Nabhan-Warren, Kristy. *The Cursillo Movement in America: Catholics, Protestants, and Fourth-Day Spirituality*. Chapel Hill: University of North Carolina Press, 2013.

———. *The Virgin of El Barrio: Marian Apparitions, Catholic Evangelizing, and Mexican American Activism*. New York: New York University Press, 2005.

Nanko-Fernández, Carmen. *Theologizing en Espanglish: Context, Community, and Ministry*. Maryknoll, NY: Orbis Books, 2010.

Ortiz, Manuel. *The Hispanic Challenge: Opportunities Confronting the Church*. Downers Grove, IL: InterVarsity Press, 1993.

———. *One New People: Models for Developing a Multiethnic Church*. Downers Grove, IL.: InterVarsity Press, 1996.

Ospino, Hosffman. *Hispanic Ministry in Catholic Parishes: A Summary Report of Findings from the National Study of Catholic Parishes with Hispanic Ministry (2011–2013)*. Boston: Boston College School of Theology and Ministry, 2014.

———. *Our Catholic Children: Ministry with Hispanic Youth and Young Adults / Nuestros jóvenes católicos: Pastoral Juvenil Hispana en los Estados Unidos*. Huntington, IN: Our Sunday Visitor Institute, 2018.

Padilla, Alvin, Roberto Goizueta, and Eldin Villafañe, eds. *Hispanic Christian Thought at the Dawn of the 21st Century: Apuntes in Honor of Justo L. González*. Nashville: Abingdon Press, 2005.

Paredes, Mario J. *The History of the National Encuentros: Hispanic Americans in the One Catholic Church*. Mahwah, NJ: Paulist Press, 2014.

Pazmiño, Robert W. *A Boy Grows in Brooklyn: An Educational and Spiritual Memoir*. Eugene, OR: Wipf and Stock, 2014.

Pedraja, Luis G. *Jesus Is My Uncle: Christology from a Hispanic Perspective*. Nashville: Abingdon Press, 1999.

———. *Mas Voces de la Iglesia Hispana*. Nashville: Abingdon Press, 2001

———. *Teología: An Introduction to Hispanic Theology*. Nashville: Abingdon Press, 2004.

Pérez, Laura E. *Chicana Art: The Politics of Spiritual and Aesthetic Altarities*. Durham, NC: Duke University Press, 2007.

Perez y Mena, Andrés Isidoro. *Speaking with the Dead: Development of Afro-Latin Religion among Puerto Ricans in the United States*. New York: AMS Press, 1991.

Perez y Mena, Andrés Isidoro, and Anthony M. Stevens-Arroyo. *Enigmatic Powers: Syncretism with African and Indigenous Peoples Religions among Latinos*. New York: Bildner Center Books, 1995.

Pineda, Ana María. *Romero and Grande: Companions on the Journey*. Hobe Sound, FL: Lectio Publishing, 2006.

Pineda, Ana María, and Robert Schreiter, eds. *Dialogue Rejoined: Theology and Ministry in the United States Hispanic Reality*. Collegeville, MN: Liturgical Press, 1995.

Pineda-Madrid, Nancy. *Suffering and Salvation in Ciudad Juárez*. Minneapolis: Fortress Press, 2011.

Pinn, Anthony B., and Benjamín Valentín, eds. *The Ties That Bind: African American and Hispanic American/Latino/a Theologies in Dialogue*. New York: Continuum, 2001.

——, eds. *Creating Ourselves: African Americans and Hispanic Americans on Popular Culture and Religious Expressions*. Durham, NC: Duke University Press, 2009.

Presmanes, Jorge L. *Preaching and Culture in Latino Congregations*. Chicago: Liturgy Training Publications, 2000.

Ramírez, Daniel. *Migrating Faith: Pentecostalism in the United States and Mexico in the Twentieth Century*. Chapel Hill: University of North Carolina Press, 2015.

Ramirez, Ricardo. *Fiesta, Worship, and Family: Essays on Mexican-American Perception of Liturgy and Family Life*. San Antonio, TX: Mexican-American Cultural Center, 1981.

Recinos, Harold J. *Good News from the Barrio: Prophetic Witness for the Church*. Louisville, KY: Westminster John Knox Press, 2006.

——. *Jesus Weeps: Global Encounters on Our Doorsteps*. Nashville: Abingdon Press, 1992.

——. *Voices on the Corner*. Eugene, OR: Resource Publications, 2015.

——. *Who Comes in the Name of the Lord? Jesus at the Margins*. Nashville: Abingdon Press, 1997.

——, ed., *Wading through Many Voices: Toward a Theology of Public Conversation*. Lanham, MD: Rowman and Littlefield, 2011.

Recinos, Harold J., and Hugo Magallanes, eds. *Jesus in the Hispanic Community*. Louisville, KY: Westminster John Knox Press, 2010.

Reyes, Patrick B. *Nobody Cries When We Die: God, Community, and Surviving to Adulthood*. Cleveland: Chalice Press, 2016.

Rieger, Joerg, ed. *Across Borders: Latin Perspectives in the Americas Reshaping Religion, Theology, and Life*. Lanham, MD: Lexington Books, 2013.

Rivera, Mayra. *The Touch of Transcendence: A Postcolonial Theology of God*. Louisville, KY: Westminster John Knox Press, 2007.

Rivera Pagán, Luis N. *Essays from the Margins*. Eugene, OR: Wipf and Stock, 2014.

———, ed., *Fe Cristiana y descolonización de Puerto Rico*. Cayey, PR: Mariana Editores, 2013.

———. *A Violent Evangelism: The Political and Religious Conquest of the Americas*. Louisville, KY: Westminster/John Knox Press, 1992.

Rodríguez, Daniel A. *A Future for the Latino Church: A Model for Multilingual, Multicultural, Multigenerational Hispanic Congregations*. Downers Grove, IL: InterVarsity Press, 2011.

Rodríguez, Jeanette. *Cultural Memory: Resistance, Faith, and Identity*. Austin: University of Texas Press, 2007.

———. *Our Lady of Guadalupe: Faith and Empowerment among Mexican-American Woman*. Austin: University of Texas Press, 1993.

———. *Stories We Live / Cuentos Que Vivimos: Hispanic Women's Spirituality*. Mahwah, NJ: Paulist Press, 1996.

Rodríguez, José David, and Loida I. Martell-Otero, eds. *Teología en Conjunto: A Collaborative Hispanic Protestant Theology*. Louisville, KY: Westminster John Knox Press, 1997.

Rodríguez-Díaz, Daniel R., and David Cortés-Fuentes, *Hidden Stories: Unveiling the History of the Latino Church*. Decatur, GA: AETH, 1994.

Romero, C. Gilbert. *Hispanic Devotional Piety: Tracing the Biblical Roots*. Maryknoll, NY: Orbis Books, 1991.

Rosario Rodríguez, Rubén. *Racism and God-Talk: A Latino/a Perspective*. New York: New York University Press, 2008.

Ruiz, Jean-Pierre. *Reading from the Edges: The Bible on the Move*. Maryknoll, NY: Orbis Books, 2011.

Sánchez, David A. *From Patmos to the Barrio: Subverting Imperial Myths from the Book of Revelation to Today*. Minneapolis: Fortress Press, 2008.

Sánchez-Walsh, Arlene. *Latino Pentecostal Identity: Evangelical Faith, Self, and Identity*. New York: Columbia University Press, 2003.

———. *Pentecostalism in America*. New York: Columbia University Press, 2018.

Sandoval, Moises. *Fronteras: A History of the Latin American Church in the USA since 1513*. San Antonio, TX: Mexican American Cultural Center, 1983.

———, ed. *On the Move: A History of the Hispanic Church in the United States*. 2nd ed. Maryknoll, NY: Orbis Books, 2006.

Segovia, Fernando F. *Decolonizing Biblical Studies: A View from the Margins*. Maryknoll, NY: Orbis Books, 2000.

———, ed. *Interpreting beyond Borders*. Sheffield, UK: Sheffield Academic Press, 2000.

Slobodsky, Santiago. *Decolonial Judaism: Triumphal Failures of Barbaric Thinking.* New York: Palgrave Macmillan, 2014.

Solivan, Samuel. *The Spirit, Pathos, and Liberation: Toward an Hispanic Pentecostal Theology.* Sheffield, UK: Sheffield Academic Press, 1998.

Stevens-Arroyo, Antonio M., ed. *Papal Overtures in a Cuban Key: The Pope's Visit and Civic Space for Cuban Religion.* Scranton, PA: University of Scranton Press, 2002.

Stevens-Arroyo, Antonio M., and Gilbert Cadena, eds. *Old Masks, New Faces: Religion and Latino Identities.* New York: City University of New York, Bildner Center, 1994.

Stevens-Arroyo, Antonio M., and Ana María Díaz-Stevens, eds. *Enduring Flame: Studies on Latino Popular Religiosity.* New York: City University of New York, Bildner Center, 1994.

Stevens-Arroyo, Antonio M., and Andrés Isidoro Pérez y Mena, eds. *Enigmatic Powers: Syncretism with African and Indigenous People's Religions among Latinos.* New York: City University of New York, Bildner Center, 1995.

Traverzo Galarza, David. *Orlando E. Costas: Un Hombre en el Camino, Vision y Esperanza Ante lo Eterno.* Rio Piedras: Editorial CENE-TEPA, 1995.

Tweed, Thomas A. *Our Lady of the Exile: Diasporic Religion at a Cuban Catholic Shrine in Miami.* New York: Oxford University Press, 1997.

Valentín, Benjamín, ed. *In Our Own Voices: Latino/a Renditions of Theology.* Maryknoll, NY: Orbis Books, 2010.

———. *Mapping Public Theology: Beyond Culture, Identity, and Difference.* Harrisburg, PA: Trinity Press International, 2002.

———, ed. *New Horizons in Hispanic/Latino(a) Theology.* Cleveland: Pilgrim Press, 2003.

———. *Theological Cartographies: Mapping the Encounter with God, Humanity, and Christ.* Louisville, KY: Westminster John Knox Press, 2015.

Vásquez, Manuel A. *More Than Belief: A Materialist Theory of Religion.* New York: Oxford University Press, 2011.

Vásquez, Manuel, and Marie Marquardt. *Globalizing the Sacred: Religion across the Americas.* New Brunswick, NJ: Rutgers University Press, 2003.

Vásquez, Manuel, Anna Peterson, and Philip Williams. *Building Self, Community, and Nation: Religion and Globalization in the Americas.* New Brunswick, NJ: Rutgers Press, 2001.

Villafañe, Eldin. *The Liberating Spirit: Towards an Hispanic American Pentecostal Social Ethic.* Grand Rapids: Eerdmans, 1993.

Villafañe, Eldín, et al. *Seek the Peace of the City: Reflections on Urban*

Ministries. Grand Rapids: Eerdmans, 1995.

Walker, Randi Jones. *Protestantism in the Sangre de Cristo, 1850–1920*. Albuquerque: University of New Mexico Press, 1991.

Wingeier-Rayo, Philip. *Cuban Methodism: The Untold Story of Survival and Revival*. Lawrenceville, GA: Dolphins and Orchids, 2004.

Index

1.5 generation, 49, 51, 52
18th Street Gang (Barrio 18), 49
2008 Great Recession, 63

A La Familia (De La Torre), 185
Academy of Catholic Hispanic
    Theologians of the United States
    (ACHTUS), 133–34, 145
acompañamiento as praxis-centered
    theology, 81–82, 151
Adams, John Quincy, 55
Agosto, Efraín, 86–87
Alfaro, Sammy, 107
Alicea-Lugo, Benjamin, xxv
aliens, Latinx branded as, 49, 53–56,
    57, 60, 181
Aliens in Jerusalem (conference),
    145–46, 167
Aponte, Edwin David, 70, 81
Apuntes Reflexiones Teológicas
    (journal), 135
Aquino, Jorge, 65
Aquino, María Pilar, 133, 140–41,
    159
Argentina, 18, 30, 35, 36
Arnaz, Desi, 8
Asociación para la Educación
    Teológica Hispana (AETH),
    144, 145, 168, 169
Assemblies of God, 23, 119–20, 127
atheists/agnostics, Latinx
    identifying as, 34
Aztlán (Aztec homeland), 14, 178

Baby Boomers, 153
Ball, Lucille, 8
Bañuelas, Arturo, 133
barrio theology, 62–63
Batista, Fulgencio, 46
Benavides, Luis, 111
Berrú-Davis, Rebecca, 70
Beyond Wages (report), 64
Bible, Latinx readings of, 83–90
Bonhoeffer, Dietrich, xix
Bonilla, Yarimar, 59
Border Patrol, 6–7, 175–76
Boza-Masvidal, Eduardo, xxxv
Brazil, 10, 33, 36, 47, 177
Buddhism, Latinx turning to, 35

Cadena, Gilbert, 157
Candomblé tradition, 33, 70
Cardoza-Orlandi, Carlos, 28
Casal, Lourdes, 10
Cascante-Gómez, Fernando, 82
Castro, Fidel, 50–51
Castro, Julián, 60
Catholicism
    Americanist impulse of U.S.
        Catholic Church, 124–25, 181
    conversions away from, 24–26
    cultural influence of, 68–69
    curanderismo, attitudes
        towards, 29, 162
    ecclesiology of, 101–102
    epistemology based on, 79–80
    Latinx Roman Catholics,
        22–23, 75

203